STRATUM SERIES

Government in Reformation Europe
1520–1560

STRATUM SERIES

*A series of fundamental reprints
from scholarly journals and specialised works
in European History*

GENERAL EDITOR: J. R. HALE

Published

FRENCH HUMANISM 1470–1600
Werner L. Gundersheimer

THE LATE ITALIAN RENAISSANCE 1525–1630
Eric Cochrane

In preparation

THE RECOVERY OF FRANCE IN THE FIFTEENTH
CENTURY
P. S. Lewis

PRE-REFORMATION GERMANY
Gerald Strauss

SPAIN IN THE FIFTEENTH CENTURY 1369–1516
Roger Highfield

Government in Reformation Europe
1520–1560

EDITED BY
Henry J. Cohn

Harper & Row, Publishers
New York, Evanston, San Francisco, London

GOVERNMENT IN REFORMATION EUROPE 1520-1560

First HARPER TORCHBOOK edition published 1972.

STANDARD BOOK NUMBER: 06-138418-6

Contents

Acknowledgements   7

Introduction   HENRY J. COHN   9

PART I: *The Problems and Institutions of Government*

1   The French Renaissance Monarchy as seen through the
    Estates General   J. RUSSELL MAJOR   43

2   The Administrative Structure of the State in the Six-
    teenth and Seventeenth Centuries   J. VICENS VIVES   58

PART II: *The Impact of the Reformation*

3   The Concordat of 1516: A Reassessment   R. J. KNECHT   91

4   The Role of Parliament in the Henrician Reformation
    G. W. O. WOODWARD   113

5   King or Minister? The Man behind the Henrician
    Reformation   G. R. ELTON   126

6   The Peace of Augsburg: New Order or Lull in the
    Fighting   HERMANN TÜCHLE   145

PART III: *Government in Action*

7   Albert of Brandenburg-Ansbach, Grand Master of the
    Order of Teutonic Knights and Duke in Prussia,
    1490–1568   WALTHER HUBATSCH   169

8   Financial Policy and the Evolution of the Demesne in
    the Netherlands under Charles V and Philip II
    (1530–60)   MICHEL BAELDE   203

6 CONTENTS

9 Royal Administration before the Intendants: *Parlements* and Governors GASTON ZELLER 225

10 The Provincial Governors of the Netherlands from the Minority of Charles V to the Revolt PAUL ROSENFELD 257

11 The Codification of Customary Law in France in the Fifteenth and Sixteenth Centuries RENÉ FILHOL 265

12 The 1550 *Sudebnik* as an Instrument of Reform HORACE W. DEWEY 284

Suggestions for Further Reading 310

Index 315

Acknowledgements

J. RUSSELL MAJOR, "The French Renaissance Monarchy as seen through the Estates General," from *Studies in the Renaissance*, IX (1962), 113–25. Reprinted by permission of The Renaissance Society of America, Inc.

J. VICENS VIVES, "Estructura administrativa estatal en los siglos XVI y XVII," from *XIe Congrès international des sciences historiques, rapports*, IV (1960), 1–24, translated by Frances M. Lopez-Morillas. Reprinted by permission of Princeton University Press.

R. J. KNECHT, "The Concordat of 1516: A Reassessment," from *Birmingham Historical Journal*, IX (1963), 16–32. Reprinted by permission of the publisher.

G. W. O. WOODWARD, "The Role of Parliament in the Henrician Reformation," from *Studies presented to the Historical Commission for the History of Representative and Parliamentary Institutions*, XX (1959), 15–24. Reprinted by permission.

G. R. ELTON, "King or Minister? The Man Behind the Henrician Reformation," from *History*, XXXIX (1954), 216–32. Reprinted by permission of the author.

HERMANN TÜCHLE, "Der Augsburger Religionsfriede. Neue Ordnung oder Kampfpause," from *Zeitschrift des Historischen Vereins für Schwaben*, LXI (1955), 323–40, translated by Michael Barry. Reprinted by permission.

WALTHER HUBATSCH, '*Albrecht von Brandenburg-Ansbach. Deutschordens-Hochmeister und Herzog in Preussen, 1490–1568*,' (Cologne and Berlin, 1960), excerpts from pp. 139–208, translated by Michael Barry. Reprinted by permission.

MICHEL BAELDE, "Financiële politiek en domaniale evolutie in de Nederlanden onder Karel V en Filips II (1530–1560)," from *Tijdschrift voor Geschiedenis*, LXXVI (1963), 14–30, translated by Chaninah Maschler and Henry J. Cohn. Reprinted by permission of the publisher.

GASTON ZELLER, "L'Administration monarchique avant les intendants: parlements et gouverneurs," from *Revue Historique*, CXCVIII (1947), 180–215, translated by Isabelle Cazeaux. Reprinted by permission of Presses Universitaires de France.

PAUL ROSENFELD, "The Provincial Governors of the Netherlands from the Minority of Charles V to the Revolt," from *Anciens Pays et Assemblées d'États*, XVII (1959), excerpts from pp. 1–63. Reprinted by permission.

RENÉ FILHOL, "La rédaction des coutumes en France aux XVe et XVIe siècles," in *La rédaction des coutumes dans le passé et dans le present*, ed. J. Gilissen (Brussels, 1962), pp. 63–78, translated by Isabelle Cazeaux. Reprinted by permission.

H. W. DEWEY, "The 1550 *Sudebnik* as an Instrument of Reform," from *Jahrbücher für Geschichte Osteuropas*, X (1962), 161–80. Reprinted by permission of Otto Harrassowitz Verlag.

Introduction

DURING the period of the Reformation, from about 1520 until
1560, the rulers of Europe grappled with an increasing burden of
problems in the day by day government of their countries. Existing tasks of government multiplied and some entirely new ones
were created as a result of the Reformation itself, of extensive
wars between the dynastic houses of Europe, and of the beginnings
of the price revolution of the sixteenth century. The methods of
government developed to meet these new commitments went
hand in hand with that heightened sense of royal authority and
that greater energy devoted by monarchs to curbing the political
influence of their nobles and other subjects which are perhaps
more familiar to students of the Reformation era.[1] There are
many disputed questions fundamental to an understanding of the
origins of the modern state: did "new monarchies" set a pattern
of ruling that marked a breach with medieval traditions? was
absolutist political theory becoming more influential? did representative institutions serve to buttress or to curb royal power? Yet
at least as important for the normal relations between the state
and society were those mundane problems of governing which
did not cease when political crises subsided or parliaments dispersed after their often brief and infrequent sessions.

The history of government in this sense is something other
than constitutional and political history, which rightly concentrate
on the fundamental institutional and political relationships between ruler and ruled and on the conflicts which altered that

[1] See especially A. J. Slavin (ed.), *The "New Monarchies" and Representative
Assemblies. Medieval Constitutionalism or Modern Absolutism?* (Boston, 1964) and
the general works in the Suggestions for Further Reading, pp. 310 ff. below.

balance. However, the developments in government considered in this volume affected not only the institutions and mechanics of administration, but the policies that were executed and the personnel who implemented them. Nor were they confined to the three great monarchies of England, France and Spain, but were to a greater or lesser degree important also for the Netherlands, the principalities of Germany and Italy, and Sweden, Russia and other countries. The similarities and differences between countries in this sphere were only in part determined by whether they were Catholic or Protestant, large or small states. Catholic rulers like the kings of Spain or the dukes of Bavaria were sometimes just as inclined as their Protestant fellows to seize the wealth of the church and control its administration, while small or hitherto relatively backward states like Sweden and the duchy of Prussia occasionally set the pace in some aspects of government.

It is true that the mid-sixteenth century was not exceptional in experiencing considerable transformations in government. From about 1450 onwards the activities of central administrative institutions had been expanded in France as a consequence of the gradual extension of control by the crown over provinces formerly ruled by royal dukes, in Spain after the unification of the kingdoms in 1479, and in the German principalities and the duchy of Moscow as their territories were enlarged and unified. Administrative reforms during the Reformation hardly ever made a radical break with the past and often remained incomplete; especially in the financial sphere, awareness of new problems was far greater than success in dealing with them. Nevertheless, from the 1520's to the 1540's the power of the state was more pervasive in most European countries than it had ever been before, and in many cases than it would be for centuries to come. The Reformation had a major part in this intensification of governmental activity.

Politically, if not doctrinally, the English Reformation made the cleanest break with the papacy, establishing a national, sovereign church which greatly enhanced the status and prestige of the monarch as its supreme head. Gustavus Vasa of Sweden, while avoiding for decades any direct breach with Rome, in practice established a Protestant church similar to that of England.[2] The Catholic rulers of France, Spain and Spanish Italy in large measure excluded the papacy from intervening in the government of their churches. By the middle of the century "the domination of the Church by the Crown was probably more complete in Spain . . . than in any other part of Europe."[3] German princes before the Reformation had been accustomed to play the major role in the administration and jurisdiction of the church and the control of its ceremonies and discipline. To extend these powers and to add to them the regulation of religious beliefs and education proved easiest in principalities like Prussia where the ruler had previously been a prelate enjoying both secular and ecclesiastical power,[4] but once the Diet of Speyer in 1526 had conceded to the princes the right to govern the religion of their subjects, Hesse, Saxony and other states quickly followed suit. For many of them, like the territories of the Albertine branch of the Wettin family in Saxony, the consequent sequestration of ecclesiastical property and increase in the tasks of central and local administration allowed the dukes to make their principalities for the first time into properly united lands.[5] Among the many new functions assumed by states throughout Europe were the dissolution of monasteries and other ecclesiastical foundations; the making of provision for unemployed priests, dispossessed monks, and the educational and welfare services which these foundations had helped to maintain; the seizure of other church property and the rearrangement or replacement of episcopal organization; appointments to a much larger number of benefices than before; all forms of religious discipline and the persecution of heretics; promulgation of ecclesiastical visitations, commissions and ordinances; and the creation of new councils, courts and officials for ecclesiastical matters.

[2] For all aspects of Swedish history, see M. Roberts, *The Early Vasas: A History of Sweden, 1523–1611* (Cambridge, 1968).

[3] J. Lynch, *Spain under the Habsburgs*, Vol. 1 (Oxford, 1964), p. 257.

[4] J. Lortz, *The Reformation in Germany* (London, 1968), Vol. 11, p. 23.

[5] H.-M. Kühn, *Die Einziehung des geistlichen Gutes im albertinischen Sachsen, 1539–1553* (Cologne, 1966), pp. 1–2, 97–98.

Secularization of church lands was carried out at different speeds and with varying thoroughness in Protestant countries. In Prussia it was achieved at one stroke in 1525, in Hesse within a year from 1526, in the electorate of (Ernestine) Saxony over a period of twelve years from 1531. The Pilgrimage of Grace (1536/7) in England enabled the government to begin bullying the larger monasteries which had been implicated in the rising into yielding themselves up to the crown, although the statute of 1536 had only dissolved monasteries of an annual value below £200; further acts of parliament initiated the dissolution of chantries, free chapels and similar institutions in the 1540's. The monasteries in Sweden were not dissolved by legislation or a single stroke, but by a gradual process of taking over their administration and forcing the monks out; Gustavus Vasa was unique in that nearly half his gains of church land came—after 1545—from the endowments of parish churches. Everywhere this large-scale transfer of property and social responsibilities thrust new administrative burdens onto the state. Arrangements had to be made for dissolving monastic communities, administering their lands and revenues, seeing to their leases, debts and lawsuits, and providing alternative occupations, residences or pensions for the displaced men and women.[6] The provision made for ex-monks and nuns was rarely generous, but even those who received small pensions or none created work for the royal officials. Although in Sweden education languished during the Reformation, in England and Germany the state as well as private benefactors used some of their gains from monastic lands to endow universities and schools. Henry VIII founded Trinity College, Cambridge, refounded Christ Church, Oxford, and endowed or re-endowed many schools, a work which was continued in his son's reign. In Hesse, both Saxonies and some of the other German principalities generous provision was made for new universities and schools or for reforming old ones; the content of religious teaching underwent searching revision and some monastic buildings became schools and colleges, others hospitals and almshouses. The

[6] G. R. Elton, *The Tudor Revolution in Government* (Cambridge, 1953), p. 203.

dissolution of the monasteries may not have been to any great extent responsible for the burgeoning problems of poverty, vagrancy, and beggary, but it fostered the growing realization throughout Europe that relief of these ills was the duty of the central government as well as of parish and urban authorities.

Bishoprics no less than monasteries experienced reorganization and loss of their lands in both Protestant and Catholic countries. The prince-bishoprics of Utrecht and Brixen were incorporated into the territories of the Habsburg brothers Charles V and Ferdinand I. From 1536 until the end of the century the arch-bishops of Canterbury and other English prelates were forced, to their own disadvantage, to exchange many of their lands with those of the crown. However, Henry VIII also established six new bishoprics and reorganized seven other cathedral churches with the personnel of their former monastic chapters. Charles V and Philip II created seven new dioceses in Spain;[7] it was on Philip's insistence, not that of the papacy, that between 1559 and 1561 the four existing sees in the Netherlands were supplemented by fourteen new ones, partly financed by the incorporation of rich abbacies, and regrouped under three archbishoprics. Already before the Reformation the French and Spanish crowns had acquired the exclusive patronage to all the highest ecclesiastical offices. In the Protestant principalities of Germany and in Sweden the rulers gained control of all lesser appointments in the church as well. At the dissolution of the monasteries Henry VIII acquired the right of presentation to some 40 per cent of English parochial benefices. Privileges previously enjoyed by the church, such as sanctuary and benefit of clergy in England and tax exemptions in most countries, were swept away.

In a century of deep religious divisions the upholding of religious uniformity became even more than before the preroga-tive of the secular authorities. Parliamentary Acts of Uniformity in the reigns of Edward VI and Elizabeth I established Prayer Books and norms of creed for clergy and laity alike. Whether lax

[7] J. Beneyto Perez, *Historia de la administración española e hispanoamericana* (Madrid, 1958), p. 407.

or stringent, enforcement of such measures was shared between the justices of the peace or other local agents of the crown and special ecclesiastical bodies under royal control such as the Elizabethan Courts of High Commission. Like Henry VIII and Queen Mary in England, Francis I of France, Charles V, and Philip II determined the pace at which the persecution of heretics went forward; the chief instruments of these policies, apart from royal edicts and lay officials, were the *parlement* of Paris and the Inquisitions of Spain, the Netherlands and Spanish Italy, all royal institutions. The decrees of the Council of Trent in 1563 were implemented in Catholic countries only to the extent that they were accepted by rulers, which in the case of Philip II, the most powerful of them, was hardly at all except in the Netherlands. Every aspect of religious discipline and marital and sumptuary regulation passed into the jurisdiction of the state. In Sweden the king in person disciplined the clergy and decided divorce cases.[8] When the compilation of parish registers was prescribed for the whole of England in 1538 and registers of births and deaths for France in 1539, it was a sign that the entire lives of subjects were deemed to fall within the purview of royal supervision, even though implementation of this legislation fell short of its intention. In Sicily, too, it was the viceroy whose regulations exhorted priests to behave with decorum and citizens to hear Mass regularly, observe the sabbath, and make confession.[9]

Such was the state of the church that the first priority was usually to send out visitation commissions to assess what was wrong and initiate reforms. Whether in Protestant England (1535), Sweden (1540) and electoral Saxony (1525–38), or in the Catholic duchies of Saxony (1535) and Bavaria (1541 and 1558),[10]

[8] Roberts, *op. cit.*, p. 168.

[9] D. Mack Smith, *A History of Sicily*, Vol. 1, *Medieval Sicily, 800–1713* (London, 1968), p. 161.

[10] I. Höss and T. Klein, *Das Zeitalter des Humanismus und die Reformation* (*Geschichte Thüringens*, ed. H. Patze and W. Schlesinger, Vol. III, Cologne, 1967), pp. 8–9; Kühn, *op. cit.*, pp. 10–12; S. Riezler, *Geschichte Baierns*, Vol. IV (Gotha, 1899), pp. 408, 508–10. Protestant Hesse had a whole series of visitations and ordinances for different ecclesiastical purposes from 1527 until the 1540's:

the visitors were for the most part not clergy, but lawyers and other officials. The purpose of these investigations might be as comprehensive a survey as in Bavaria or as limited as the reform of the monasteries undertaken in the duchy of Saxony. In the electorate of Saxony the secular clergy were reminded of their duties and an attempt was made to recover ecclesiastical property which the laity had expropriated in the confused early years of the Reformation. The condition of the clergy was examined in Sweden and a register of all church revenues compiled along the lines of the English *Valor Ecclesiasticus*. Special sequestration officials in the two Saxonies made similar inventories after the confiscation of monastic and other ecclesiastical lands. Government commissions sent out into the provinces for ecclesiastical and other purposes multiplied rapidly. In electoral Saxony there was a conflict of interest between the visitation commissioners, who wanted to maintain the parishes partly out of monastic revenues, and the sequestration commissioners, whose duty it was to preserve the monastic lands intact. In the autumn of 1536 three separate commissions—for dissolving the smaller monasteries, enquiring into the fitness of the clergy, and assessing and collecting a subsidy—were at work in Lincolnshire on the eve of the Pilgrimage of Grace. From 1536 until 1547 every English county also underwent the simultaneous ministrations of up to six different royal receivers collecting landed revenues and taxes. Additional general commissions to enquire into heresy and enforce religious policy were introduced under Edward VI and regularly renewed during the reigns of Catholic Mary and Protestant Elizabeth.[11] One frequent byproduct of visitations were church ordinances which regulated the behaviour of clergy and religious observance; these were comprehensive single legislative acts in Prussia and other German principalities, more piecemeal measures in England.

W. Sohm, *Territorium und Reformation in der hessischen Geschichte* (Marburg, 1915), pp. 34–35, 44–50, 65–66, 71–72, 95–101, 147–50.

[11] A. Fletcher, *Tudor Rebellions* (London, 1968), p. 21; Elton, *op. cit.*, pp. 206–7; G. Scott Thomson, *Lords Lieutenant in the Sixteenth Century* (London, 1923), pp. 129–31.

Among the more remarkable of the new kinds of official to emerge in the 1530's were the laymen appointed to exercise royal supremacy over all prelates, Thomas Cromwell as vicar-general in England and Conrad Pyhy as "superattendent" in Sweden. Superattendents in Denmark, on the other hand, like the super-intendents in Sweden and several German principalities, were clerics appointed by the ruler to replace the discredited bishops. Because the frontiers of bishoprics in Germany ran across those of the lay territories, the new superintendencies of Albertine Saxony comprised the same areas as the *Ämter*, the local secular ad-ministrative units, thus reinforcing the laicization of church administration.[12] Above the superintendents were placed con-sistories, collegially organized boards which were but one of the plethora of new councils and courts created when the church was reorganized as a department of state in most European countries. Similar to the consistories in competence, lay membership, and dependence on other state councils was the Ecclesiastical Council established in Catholic Bavaria in 1557 and renewed in 1570.[13] Perhaps the most influential of such institutions was the English Court of Augmentations. Set up in 1536 primarily to administer the lands of dissolved monasteries, it was soon given control of many other categories of crown lands. For a few years before its dissolution in 1554, it became the largest and most efficient independent revenue court of the kingdom, with a small council in London and a large staff of auditors and receivers throughout the country. Ecclesiastical appeals in Spain were routed to the Council of Castile rather than the Curia, the Inquisition was effectively a department of state, and in Sicily the church hierarchy was subordinate in all things to a prelate nominated by the king and sometimes called the vice-pope.[14]

The most readily quantifiable shift in the balance between church and state was caused by the taxation and confiscation of

[12] K. Blaschke, "Die Ausbreitung des Staates in Sachsen und der Ausbau seiner räumlichen Verwaltungsbezirke," *Blätter für deutsche Landesgeschichte*, XCI (1954), 92–3.

[13] H. Holborn, *A History of Modern Germany. The Reformation* (New York, 1961), pp. 281–2.   [14] Mack Smith, *op. cit.*, p. 161.

church property. The proportion of farms in Sweden owned by the crown increased at the expense of the church from 5 per cent. in 1523 to 28 per cent. in 1560. However much the rulers of England and some, though not all, German Protestant princes were later compelled by dire necessity to sell confiscated lands, they had meanwhile enjoyed an appreciable financial windfall. In addition, the sale of plate, lead and other moveables taken from churches and monasteries realized about £1½ million in England[15] and similar large amounts in other Protestant countries. Between 1485 and 1534 the English church had paid an annual average of about £5,000 to the papacy and £12,300 to the crown, but after 1534 Henry VIII increased the clerical subsidy, although church lands were fewer, and replaced annates to Rome by higher clerical First Fruits, so that for the rest of his reign annual taxes from the church averaged some £47,000, or about the same as royal revenues from the monastic lands immediately after their confiscation.[16] Increasingly frequent decimations on the revenue of the French clergy under Francis I eventually became an annual tax of several "tenths" (really a 5 per cent. tax), which was usually levied without papal consent; between 1563 and 1589 the church could only meet these obligations by selling half of its lands ·in France, a transfer of property into lay hands comparable to that in England.[17] The Spanish kings seized no lands of the church except the Military Orders, but in the long run they probably derived greater benefit from taxing the clergy than did Protestant rulers who had to sell church lands. They enjoyed revenues from the crusade tax levied on clergy and laity alike, the subsidy on ecclesiastical revenues, the royal one-third share of all tithes, a tax on parish property introduced in 1567, and the income of vacant

[15] W. C. Richardson, "Some Financial Expedients of Henry VIII," *Economic History Review*, 2nd Series, VII (1954), 48.

[16] J. J. Scarisbrick, "Clerical Taxation in England, 1485–1547," *Journal of Ecclesiastical History*, XII (1961), 41–54; A. G. Dickens, *The English Reformation* (London, 1964), pp. 41, 121.

[17] R. Doucet, *Les Institutions de la France au XVIe siècle* (Paris, 1948), Vol. II, pp. 834–5, 840–1; R. J. Knecht, *Francis I and Absolute Monarchy* (London, 1969), p. 11; G. Livet, *Les Guerres de Religion (1559–1598)* (Paris, 1962), p. 91.

bishoprics and the Military Orders, which by the end of the century together totalled perhaps half of the church's income and 20 per cent. of the state's revenues, about as much as it derived from the treasures of the Indies.[18] Among the several concessions for control over the church in Bavaria won from the papacy in 1523 was the right to collect a 20 per cent. crusade subsidy from the clergy; by 1547 the duke was receiving $33\frac{1}{3}$ per cent. and using some of the proceeds for the ordinary purposes of the state.[19]

Massive contributions from the church only went a small way towards relieving the financial needs of European rulers. By far the greatest drain on resources were wars like Charles V's campaigns in Italy and the other interminable conflicts which brought the Habsburg and Valois dynasties, the most powerful in Europe, to bankruptcy in the 1550's. Long-established state revenues from land and taxes failed to keep pace with the spiralling cost of mercenaries, armaments, fortifications, navies, diplomacy, royal building and magnificence, and an expanding administration. All was compounded by serious inadequacies in revenue collection and accounting procedures. The article by Dr. Baelde included in this collection reveals, in both great things and small, weaknesses which could be paralleled (in many cases even after the extensive reforms of the period) for all European countries: the absence of reliable advance budgets, confusing distinctions between ordinary and extraordinary revenues and expenditure, the problem of making funds available when and where they were required, the continued use of antiquated Roman numerals, and growing deficits the size of which could not even be properly estimated. Only Gustavus Vasa of Sweden was able for the last fifteen years of his reign to "live of his own," as medieval kings had been supposed to.

Not all rulers were as fortunate as the kings of France, two-

[18] Lynch, op. cit., Vol. i, pp. 129–30; J. H. Elliott, *Imperial Spain, 1469–1716* (London, 1963), pp. 192–3.

[19] Riezler, op. cit., Vol. iv, pp. 95–100, 412–13; F. L. Carsten, *Princes and Parliaments in Germany* (Oxford, 1959), p. 365.

thirds of whose taxation throughout the century came from the *taille*, a property tax which they increased at will from $1\frac{1}{2}$ million *livres* in 1507 to 4 millions in 1542, 6 millions in 1552 and $12\frac{1}{2}$ millions in 1585.[20] A similar function was fulfilled in many German principalities by the excise on beer and wine, levied with or without the consent of the Estates; in the decade after 1533 the excise in electoral Saxony yielded four times as much as did sequestered church lands.[21] Property taxes dependent on parliamentary consent could also appreciate considerably over the years—and produce exceptionally large sums in times of crisis—in countries where parliaments were subject to royal persuasion as in England or entirely subservient to the monarchy as were the Castilian Cortes. The English subsidy yielded an annual average of just under £12,000 between 1485 and 1509, £17,000 from 1509 until 1540, and £94,000 between 1541 and 1547;[22] in Castile the *servicio* nearly quadrupled in Charles V's reign, but this was also a period when prices doubled and receipts from the sales tax declined. Royal demesne revenues produced a declining proportion of total income because they tended to be static in a time of inflation, which in turn encouraged the sale of crown lands to meet pressing needs. Only in Sweden did augmented demesne lands administered by loyal officials make a sizeable contribution to the budget. Despite confiscation of the extensive lands of the duke of Bourbon in the 1520's, the proportion of the ordinary income of the French crown which was derived from the demesne declined steadily from its peak of 20 per cent.; however, growing sales of timber and other products of royal forests did overtake receipts from the rest of the demesne by mid-century. Similar growth in the yield from forests in Hesse and other parts of Germany (but not in England) indicates that among demesne revenues probably only timber prices rose rapidly enough during

[20] Doucet, *op. cit.*, Vol. II, pp. 576–7; G. Zeller, *Les Institutions de la France au XVIe siècle* (Paris, 1948), p. 259.

[21] Höss and Klein, *op. cit.*, p. 165.

[22] Calculated from Fletcher, *op. cit.*, p. 20; for Spain, Elliott, *op. cit.*, pp. 193–195.

the century to warrant such reforms as those undertaken in forest administration.[23]

Where increased taxation, ordinary revenues and confiscations of land could not meet growing deficits, recourse was had to expedients which raised money quickly but permanently harmed the administration, finances and economy of the state. Apart from the fiscal exploitation of debasing the currency and (in England) reviving antiquated feudal relationships, these consisted principally of the sale of anything which rulers had to sell: their lands, revenues, patents of nobility (especially in France and Spain), and administrative offices. Currencies may have been debased in part because there was a shortage of gold, and certainly once one government had reduced the precious metal content of its coins others had to follow, but the main reason for the heavy debasements in England, France and Sweden in the 1540's was to pay for wars. Manipulation of bullion prices through the Royal Mint in England yielded £1,270,000 between 1544 and 1551, compared with £976,000 received in the same period from taxation of the laity and clergy and £1,050,000 from the rent and sale of crown lands between 1544 and 1554.[24] By 1547 two-thirds of the lands confiscated from English monasteries had been sold off, and the alienation of these and other crown lands continued until little was left by the accession of James I. In much of Germany the rulers were forced by financial dependence on their Estates either to sell the monastic lands to the nobles or to use their revenues for education, charity and other public purposes. Despite the supposed fundamental law of the inalienability of French royal lands, they were sold or at least temporarily pledged in moments of crisis by

[23] H. Lapeyre, Les Monarchies européennes du XVIᵉ siècle (Paris, 1967), p. 69; M. Devèze, La Vie de la forêt française au XVIᵉ siècle (Paris, 1961), Vol. II, pp. 24, 170, 256; L. Zimmermann, Der ökonomische Staat Landgraf Wilhelms IV. (Marburg, 1933), Vol. I, pp. 268–83.

[24] C. E. Challis, "The Debasement of the Coinage, 1542–1551," Economic History Review, 2nd Series, xx (1967), 443, 446, 454. The estimate for profits from debasement may be slightly on the high side, see J. D. Gould, The Great Debasement: Currency and the Economy in Mid-Tudor England (Oxford, 1970), pp. 33, 187–98.

Francis I and in the normal course of affairs by his successors, so that revenues from this source were negligible by 1560.[25] Charles V's sales of demesne lands and rights of local jurisdiction in Spain far outweighed his remittances from the Indies; in Milan and Naples lands and all forms of treasury revenues were sold off precipitously from the late 1520's onwards, when such sales already formed the major part of the state's receipts in Naples.[26] The sale of offices by governments rather than by the office-holders themselves was less heavily concentrated in the first half of the sixteenth century, since it had begun earlier and was to climb to its peak in Europe in the seventeenth century and later. Nevertheless, the point at which such policies became systematic and open, often leading to the creation of offices specifically for the purpose of selling them and to the sale even of judicial offices, was reached in France in 1522 (when merchants were engaged to sell offices for the crown), in Naples under Charles V, and in Castile during the late 1550's.[27] The immediate effects were a phenomenal rise in expenditure on salaries and inefficiency in the courts and administration.

Deprived by their own expedients of existing sources of revenue, rulers found that their annual deficits increased steadily and total indebtedness by leaps and bounds. They could either raise short-term loans from bankers at international centres like Antwerp and Lyons, which often involved additional charges for foreign exchange transactions, or else sell redeemable annuities or bonds which were funded on government revenues or guaranteed by individual provinces and cities. Annuities had been common

[25] Devèze, op. cit., Vol. II, pp. 162–3.

[26] A. M. Guilarte, El régimen señorial en siglo XVI (Madrid, 1962), p. 303; F. Chabod, Storia di Milano, Vol. IX (Milan, 1961), pp. 302, 322, 325, 337–8; G. Coniglio, Il Regno di Napoli al tempo di Carlo V (Naples, 1951), pp. 208–9, 223, 253.

[27] The papacy had established this practice much earlier: K. W. Swart, Sale of Offices in the Seventeenth Century (The Hague, 1949), pp. 22–5, 84, 86; B. Guenée, Tribunaux et gens de justice dans le bailliage de Senlis à la fin du Moyen Âge (vers 1380–vers 1550) (Paris, 1963), pp. 99, 174–5, 533; R. Mousnier, La Venalité des offices sous Henri IV et Louis XIII (Rouen, 1945), pp. 24–5, 50, and passim; Coniglio, op. cit., pp. 12–13, 209.

in medieval cities and in the Netherlands, the German principalities, Aragon and Castile during the fifteenth century, but only
later were they adopted on a grand scale by the larger states, by
France from 1522, the papacy from 1526, and Spain under
Charles V. In France the *rentes* were at first guaranteed only on
taxes other than the *taille* at Paris, but from the 1550's they were
extended to other cities and from 1566 to the *taille* and demesne
revenues as well; thereafter, because interest was paid irregularly,
they were sold at a discount and fewer were issued.[28] Heavy
borrowing by the Spanish crown at Antwerp and Castile of short-
term loans at higher rates of interest than the annuities coincided
with periods of war, especially from the 1540's onwards. Annual
interest on short-term loans raised by the Netherlands government
increased from just under £(Artois)7,000 before 1514 to £112,195
in 1522, £217,385 in 1544, £424,765 in 1555, and £1,357,288 in
1556.[29] Henry II of France found it impossible to fulfil his commitments to bankers grouped in the *Grand Parti* of Lyons (1555),
while royal revenues in Castile and Milan were spent or pledged
several years in advance. The ensuing "bankruptcies" by the
monarchies of Spain (1557), France (1558), and Portugal (1560)[30]
were really attempts to decree the conversion of their floating
debts into consolidated debts, which had lower rates of interest
and were not subject to recall at short notice by the creditors.
Public finances had become closely linked with commerce and
the interests of merchants; bankers and governments now stood
or fell together.

Not surprisingly, the financial reforms undertaken in all major
states had little success. The only one among them to have a
slightly less burdensome expenditure on war and a more thorough-

[28] Lapeyre, *op. cit.*, pp. 301–6; F. Mauro, *Le XVI*e *siècle européen. Aspects
économiques* (Paris, 1966), p. 233; cf J. Bouvier and H. Germain–Martin,
Finances et financiers de l'Ancien Régime (Paris, 1964), pp.59–60, 79–81, 88–93.

[29] F. Braudel, "Les Emprunts de Charles-Quint sur la place d'Anvers,"
Charles-Quint et son temps (Paris, 1959), pp. 194, 201; H. van der Wee, *The
Growth of the Antwerp Money Market and the European Economy* (The Hague,
1963), Vol. II, pp. 199 n. 315, 203, 214.

[30] V. M. Godinho, "Les Finances publiques et la structure de l'état portugais
au XVIème siècle," *Revista de Economia* (Lisbon), XIV (1962), 114.

going financial reform, England, managed to avoid both state bankruptcy and heavy dependence on the Antwerp money market in the 1550's. For six years after the establishment of the Court of Augmentations in 1536, Thomas Cromwell and officials trained by him reorganized the financial administration into six independent "courts," or bureaucratic departments (including the diminished royal Exchequer), under the close supervision of the Privy Council; each court specialized in different categories of revenue and had its own receivers in the counties and head officers and auditors in a central office. These measures were, however, neither entirely new nor final, but part of a continuous process of experimentation in the financial administration of England during the fifteenth and sixteenth centuries. Cromwell himself occupied many minor financial offices and kept personal control of a substantial share of the revenues required for the exceptional expenses of government policy. In 1547 two of the revenue courts were amalgamated and in 1554 all but two of them became subdepartments of the renovated Exchequer; this compromise brought about an uneasy marriage between the new accounting procedures of the revenue courts and the old practices of the Exchequer, so that the objectives of economy and increased efficiency were but imperfectly realized.[31] Less far-reaching were the earlier French and Spanish reforms of 1523. In France accounting and auditing methods were improved and the administrative system temporarily purged of the influence of financiers, but the intention to channel all revenues through the reconstituted central treasury was scarcely observed. The supervisory Council of Finance set up in Spain in 1523, and copied in the Netherlands (1531) and Naples (1536), gave a better oversight of financial procedures without substantially altering them. The hand-to-mouth nature of French and Spanish financial policies hampered their revenue-collecting agencies and prompted bureaucratic incompetence in the central financial institutions. Yet conditions

[31] G. R. Elton, *The Tudor Constitution* (Cambridge, 1960), pp. 131–3; *idem*, *Tudor Revolution in Government*, pp. 151–2, 229–30, 241–3; G. L. Harriss and P. Williams, "A Revolution in Tudor History?," *Past and Present*, xxv (1963), 45–8.

would probably have been even worse but for the attempts that were made to set the financial administration right.

Financial reforms were only part of more extensive changes in the entire conciliar system of governments. Historians disagree as to whether these reforms were revolutionary. Professor Elton has suggested that they marked a change from medieval "household" to "national" bureaucratic methods, in which the initiative passed from royal administration to public administration. Thomas Cromwell's creation of the revenue courts, taken together with the new stature which he gave to his own office of secretary of state and his introduction of the Privy Council and reform of other councils in the 1530's, amounted in Professor Elton's view to a revolution in government. The new working Privy Council of nineteen members no longer contained noblemen who were in effect honorary councillors, it conducted and minuted its proceedings with greater regularity, and it retained a close supervision over all aspects of government; judicial hearings now came before the separate court of Star Chamber, even though the membership of the two bodies was largely the same. Critics have argued that the formal council was not radically different in its membership, functions and routine from some earlier royal councils, or from the informal inner ring of councillors who had usually conducted the business of government. The Privy Council was also an ineffective body between 1540 and 1558. Therefore, just as in the case of the financial institutions, the permanent council-board which finally became established in the reign of Elizabeth was the product not of an administrative revolution in the 1530's, but of successive attempts at reform in the fifteenth and sixteenth centuries. This controversy, too complex to summarize adequately here,[32] must remain undecided until further research on the Tudor council has been undertaken. In part it turns upon the meaning of

[32] See Elton, *Tudor Constitution*, pp. 87–93, 101–4; *idem*, *Tudor Revolution in Government*, *passim*; Harriss and Williams, *Past and Present*, xxv (1963), 24–35, 45–56; *ibid.*, xxxi (1965), 90–6; G. R. Elton, "The Tudor Revolution: A Reply," *ibid.*, xxix (1964), 42–9; *idem*, "Why the history of the Early-Tudor Council remains unwritten," *Annali della Fondazione italiana per la storia amministrativa*, I (1964), 268–96.

the word "revolution"; none of the protagonists would deny that the nine years of Cromwell's ascendancy saw vital administrative changes.

The fuller information available about the development of councils in other countries does suggest the need to reconsider some assumptions that have been made about sixteenth-century English administrative history. In the Netherlands, for instance, specialized councils were introduced over a period of time, supposed reforms effected little immediate change, and administrative practice did not always correspond to institutional demarcations. The judicial functions of the council were exercised by a separate court from 1504, and in 1531 there was a further threefold division into a Council of State, consisting mainly of magnates, for questions of high policy, a Privy Council of jurists to supervise legislation, administration and justice, and a Council of Finance. Yet many matters were submitted to two or three of these councils. Although the Council of State was the chief advisory body to the regents of the Habsburg rulers, the main business was decided as before on the advice of an inner body of no more than six members of the Council of State, who from 1535 included two jurists who had also been appointed to the Privy Council. The majority of the nobles were excluded from government even though Charles V had apparently made their Council of State the cornerstone of the administration.[33] In the Austrian lands of the Habsburgs and other German principalities the growth of bureaucratic methods and the emergence of specialized councils and courts under the oversight of a Princely Council (Hofrat) or, later, a Privy Council, was a gradual process beginning in the middle of the fifteenth century, often accelerating in the Reformation era, but nonetheless extending into the seventeenth century. Political needs of the moment or clashes of personality among councillors were as often the occasion for founding privy councils as was the conscious intention to promote administrative efficiency.

[33] M. Baelde, De Collaterale Raden onder Karel V en Filips II (1531–1578) (Brussels, 1965), pp. 23–5, 101–2, 155–8, 331–4; idem, "Les Conseils Collatéraux des anciens Pays-Bas (1531–1794)," Revue du Nord, L (1968), 203–7.

There were consequently many setbacks when periods of crisis passed or the personalities of dominant rulers or ministers asserted themselves; in all this the confidential secretaries and leading ministers of the princes played a more important role than the formal council-boards in which they and other councillors sat.[34]

The creation of a specialized hierarchy of councils reached its most developed form in Spain, but here too the reform of the Council of Castile and the setting up of the Councils of Finance and the Indies in the 1520's were only one stage in a process (described below by Professor Vives) lasting a century or more. At the same time, Charles V, who for several years had had an "informal" privy council, sought in 1522/3 to make his Spanish Council of State a privy council for all the affairs of his many lands, but this experiment was abandoned once Gattinara who had introduced it was no longer the emperor's principal minister, and after Charles himself had left Spain in 1529.[35] The similar Privy Council for the complex of lands in eastern Europe ruled by Charles's brother enjoyed only a precarious existence for at least a decade after its foundation in 1527, because its president and Ferdinand's chief adviser, the cardinal of Trent, was more often than not absent from the royal court on his master's business or his own private affairs, and therefore unable to take part in sessions of the Council; instead his advice was sought by means of lengthy correspondence.[36] On the European continent, at any rate, the reform of the highest conciliar institutions was not so much a purposeful revolution as a hesitant evolution.

As administrative tasks multiplied, the increased adoption of bureaucratic methods caused delays in the taking of decisions, but these were partly offset by the reliance which rulers placed on an

[34] There is a large specialist literature in German on this subject; for brief accounts, see F. Hartung, *Deutsche Verfassungsgeschichte vom 15. Jahrhundert bis zur Gegenwart* (8th edn., Stuttgart, 1964), pp. 77–9; H. J. Cohn, *The Government of the Rhine Palatinate in the Fifteenth Century* (Oxford, 1965), pp. 215–18, 249–50.

[35] F. Walser, *Die spanischen Zentralbehörden und der Staatsrat Karls V.*, ed. R. Wohlfeil (Göttingen, 1959), pp. 144, 157–60, 201, 232–3, 235–42, 262–3.

[36] Preserved in Archivio di Stato, Trent, Archivio Principesco Vescovile, Correspondenza Clesiana.

informal inner ring of councillors and on individual powerful ministers. Francis I regularly consulted a small number of councillors in the *conseil des affaires* (also called *conseil étroit*), which had no fixed membership, procedure or formal resolutions, but prepared all essential decisions of royal policy.[37] A small cabinet within the Council of Castile advised Charles V on those Castilian affairs on which he had to make decisions himself. Another group of about four councillors performed the same duty for the affairs of his wider empire. The regents of the Netherlands had their inner Council of State. English monarchs from the middle of the century relied on between four and six Privy Councillors to bear the brunt of the Council's regular work as well as to advise the sovereign on high policy.

Another means of communication between the ruler and the numerous councils he could not attend in person was through one or more secretaries of state. The advantages of this office included proximity to the king, whose correspondence the secretary wrote, and the lack of burdensome departmental responsibilities like those of the chancellor, the rival minister whom the secretary usually supplanted. The German princes had *Kammersekretäre* or *Kammerräte* who filled the same role. The gradual advance of the secretaries to the effective rank of leading ministers was given considerable momentum by the outstanding abilities of individual secretaries: Florimond Robertet in France, Francisco de los Cobos in Spain, Nicolas Perrenot de Granvelle in the Netherlands, and Thomas Cromwell in England. Cobos, for instance, was in effective control of Spanish affairs for over twenty years, mainly because he was trusted to manage Charles V's financial affairs; he also trained a professional staff for the royal secretariat, sat on almost every important council, and dealt with the correspondence relating to Castile, Italy and the Indies, so that the emperor was dependent on his memoranda for reaching decisions in these fields. The reorganization of the French royal council and secretaryships in 1547 provided for all four secretaries to attend the enlarged and now more formal *conseil des affaires*;

[37] Doucet, *op. cit.*, Vol. I, pp. 141–4.

their influence continued to grow until they replaced the great officers of state as chief advisers to the crown from the 1560's.[38]

The secretaries, like the chancellors Wolsey and Gattinara before them, assumed personal control of many administrative and financial tasks which properly belonged to the councils, and they profoundly influenced the policies of the rulers. The extent of such influence is difficult to gauge, as may be seen from Professor Elton's discussion below of the contributions of Henry VIII and Thomas Cromwell to the English secession from obedience to Rome. His view that the Henrician Reformation represents Cromwell's ideas and planning has not gone uncontested. Professor Scarisbrick argues cogently in favour of a more gradual development towards the notion of royal supremacy, the origins of which in Henry's thinking he places a year before Cromwell entered the circle of his leading ministers: "The late summer of 1530 . . . was probably the crucial moment in the story of Henry's jurisdictional struggle with universal papalism—indeed, perhaps the crucial moment of his reign. It saw him launch the claim to a national immunity against Rome's sovereignty; it saw him announce a personal claim to imperial status which could neither acknowledge nor allow any superior on earth."[39] Apart from such doubts about where initiative lay for policy on individual issues, it is also the case that throughout the sixteenth century single ministers in all countries did not for long dominate affairs of state, since political rivals soon arrived to threaten and usually to destroy their position. It was more common for monarchs to retain a measure of independence by balancing two existing factions within their court and council against one another, as Henry VIII did already during Cromwell's ascendancy and until the end of the reign.[40]

[38] Elliott, op. cit., pp. 155–6, 168–9; R. H. Keniston, Francisco de los Cobos: Secretary of the Emperor Charles V (Pittsburgh, 1960), pp. 81–2, 101–3, 257–60, 341–3; N. M. Sutherland, The French Secretaries of State in the Age of Catherine de Medici (London, 1962), pp. 11–12, 29–31, 39, 41–3, 51–2.

[39] J. J. Scarisbrick, Henry VIII (London, 1968), p. 273; see the whole section pp. 241–316; also Harriss and Williams, Past and Present, xxv (1963), 18–20.

[40] The role of the lesser personnel of the bureaucracy is described below at pp. 47–8, 78–87.

For local administration governments still had to rely heavily on nobles, gentry and others who had authority and standing in the provinces, counties and parishes. The provincial governors of France and the Netherlands, whose role is outlined in the contributions by Professors Zeller and Rosenfeld, had their counterparts in several countries, although the pattern was not a uniform one. The Swedish nobles did not become real provincial governors until the reign of Gustavus Adolphus in the seventeenth century. The Spanish viceroys, who were responsible to Madrid as deputies of the king in countries which were themselves kingdoms, were more like the heads of central governments than of provincial administrations. Like the provincial governors, the German *Amtleute* were noblemen by whose side financial officials and other specialists took on greater and greater responsibilities. The *Ämter* were agencies of the princely patrimony administering the demesne lands, but as taxation and control of church affairs loomed larger in the sixteenth century, so they developed into organs of state. Whereas the *Ämter* were smaller than governorships elsewhere, in Bavaria, Prussia and Albertine Saxony they came to be grouped into larger administrative units variously called *Rentämter*, *Hauptämter* or circles.[41] The office of lord lieutenant, created by the Tudors, had mainly military functions in the reign of Henry VIII, became general throughout England during the conflict between Somerset and Northumberland under Edward VI, and acquired the major part of its non-military tasks under Elizabeth.

The sheer quantity of new work in local administration, more than any real change in its character, led to the creation of new officials and made greater demands on existing ones; even the parish clergy were called upon to take a small part in secular administration in England and Sweden. The English justices of the peace shared in this development, but were unique as unpaid part-time officials who were not specialists but expected to implement the commissions and statutes of the government in any sphere. The amount and variety of their administrative duties increased rapidly throughout the century, as did their own numbers. The

[41] Hartung, *op. cit.*, pp. 79–80.

threat of removal from the commission, coupled with Privy Council and judicial control, served to make them if anything more efficient and less disloyal than the paid officers of the crown in other countries, who as often as not bought and inherited their posts.[42] In France supervision of local officials was exercised by several kinds of commissioners invested by the royal council or courts with judicial authority and powers to inspect the financial administration of the provinces and cities. Chief of these were the masters of requests, officers of ancient standing who were given virtually unlimited powers of intervention in both central and local government by two edicts of 1493 and 1553; their numbers grew from eight in 1493 to about a hundred in 1600. From such beginnings the later office of intendant was to emerge.[43]

In the tradition of medieval kings sixteenth-century rulers saw the administration of justice as their primary task, but they now made greater efforts to give royal jurisdiction effective supremacy over lesser jurisdictions and to secure uniformity in both judicial procedure and the substance of the law. Only in England was it possible to make the whole country a single unit for jurisdiction by the legislation of 1536 which subordinated to the royal courts all liberties and franchises like those in the counties palatine of Lancaster and Durham. In Spain royal officials called *corregidores* were introduced to replace the nobles who dominated municipal administration and courts, but in the countryside seigneurial jurisdiction even grew at the expense of the crown because the kings were forced to sell seigneuries or make grants of them to keep the nobles loyal. French royal courts encroached in a small way on seigneurial jurisdiction, especially for such crimes as false coining, but recent research has suggested that in both France and Spain there were no more conflicts over jurisdiction between royal and private courts than between different royal courts, since the normal practice was for the two kinds of court to co-operate.[44] Similar conditions may have prevailed in Germany, where the

---

[42] For details of English local administration, see Elton, *Tudor Constitution*, pp. 451–6.   [43] Doucet, *op. cit.*, Vol. I, pp. 154–9, 429.
[44] Guenée, *op. cit.*, pp. 529–30; Lapeyre, *op. cit.*, pp. 296–8.

advance of princely jurisdiction at the expense of the nobles was arrested or even reversed by the middle of the century, but in Spanish Italy wholesale royal alienations of lesser jurisdictions undoubtedly contributed to the notorious maladministration of the baronial courts.

Other countries also lagged behind England in not having a common law for the whole kingdom, but judicial procedure required improvement in England as much as elsewhere. The antiquated procedure of the three common law courts prevented the law from keeping pace with new developments, favoured the guilty in criminal cases, and often left plaintiffs in civil cases without a remedy. The alternative of speedier and more equitable justice was provided in the newer royal courts of Chancery, Star Chamber and Requests, which from earlier beginnings developed into busy and more formal courts in the 1520's and 1530's. Their procedure borrowed much, and the law of equity which they administered something, from Roman law, but it was not adopted when in conflict with statutes and the common law. These courts and the Councils of the North and the Welsh Marches, which exercised similar jurisdiction, assisted the crown to uphold law and order. Through their popularity with litigants in civil cases they reinforced respect for the uniform law of England.[45] Even more of an instrument of royal centralization was the French *Grand Conseil*, an offshoot of the royal council. From the 1520's onwards Francis I reserved more and more categories of causes for its exclusive jurisdiction. Cases in which the legal issues were obscure could also be, and were, "evoked" to the *Grand Conseil* from any of the numerous courts of the realm; its new powers were fully fashioned by 1552.[46] Less amenable to royal control but equally valuable for achieving more uniform administration of the law were the *parlement* of Paris, whose jurisdiction covered half the kingdom, and the other *parlements* with their travelling assize

[45] G. R. Elton, "Constitutional Development and Political Thought in Western Europe," *The New Cambridge Modern History*, Vol. II (Cambridge, 1958), p. 450; *idem, Tudor Constitution*, pp. 147–52.
[46] Doucet, *op. cit.*, Vol. I, pp. 202–6.

courts comparable to the English justices of assize. The separate supreme courts for each of the Spanish kingdoms, the Netherlands provinces, and the German principalities were similarly improved to ensure a proper system of appeals and legal uniformity, but like courts elsewhere they suffered from the delays of a litigious century.

An interesting but too often neglected feature of government policies were the attempts to codify and reduce the variety of laws and customs within countries on the European continent. Germany had both the largest number of divergent legal customs and—at least in its penal code—the greatest measure of success in synchronizing them. This was all the more remarkable because imperial legislation suffered from the handicap that, although it was usually drafted on the basis of those customs and statutes of the local rulers which had proved to be the best, it lacked binding force in the Empire. Its influence was entirely dependent upon further promulgation by the princes and cities. Thus Charles V's penal code of 1532, the *Constitutio Criminalis Carolina*, took three decades to prepare and was derived from similar legislation for the bishopric of Bamberg in 1507. Both codes were mainly the work of Johann Freiherr von Schwarzenberg, a noble lay judge and minister of the bishop. They combined the best German judicial practice of the late fifteenth century with the principles of Roman law as modified through the centuries and interpreted by North Italian jurists. Although the *Carolina* was mainly concerned with criminal procedure, reducing the use of torture and replacing the German trial with the fairer Roman law inquisition procedure, it also refined the substance of the law by introducing subtler Roman law definitions of crimes and the notion that the intent of the criminal and the circumstances of his crime should influence his punishment. However, several of the greater princes of the Empire insisted on a clause that the new code should not abrogate the established customs of the territories. Thus the *Carolina* and later minor additions only influenced territorial legislation over the course of subsequent decades, as the majority of rulers realized its great superiority and adopted most of its provisions. Even so, its limitations on torture were rarely observed, and Bavaria and the Austrian lands of the Habsburgs were among several principalities which issued criminal legislation throughout the sixteenth century without paying regard to the *Carolina*. Apart from these exceptions, however, the *Carolina*, just because it allowed regional variations, helped to create in a politically divided Germany a single penal code with minor variations which lasted until the eighteenth century.[47] In the field of civil procedure, by contrast, the legislation of 1495, 1521 and 1555, which consolidated the reception of Roman law procedure in the Imperial Supreme Court, was adopted in several of the codes by which the princes unified their legal systems, but not in Saxony or most of north Germany.[48]

In France, on the other hand, while procedure in criminal cases became more arbitrary, the civil law was codified for the whole kingdom. Especially during and after the reign of Francis I, judges were given greater powers to interrogate suspected criminals, the use of torture was intensified and severer penalties imposed, and there was rapid growth in the provinces of sharp, summary jurisdiction by provost-marshals and other royal officials.[49] The article by Professor Filhol reprinted below shows how slow was the process of first codifying and then reforming the innumerable customs of France, and how opposition by native jurists to Roman law impeded the full reception of its unifying principles. By the second half of the century, however, the painstaking work of the royal commissioners was producing considerable uniformity by introducing identical dispositions into the customs of many bailiwicks and encouraging the widespread adoption of the customs

[47] H. Conrad, *Deutsche Rechtsgeschichte*, Vol. II (Karlsruhe, 1966), pp. 407–15; E. Schmidt, *Einführung in die Geschichte der deutschen Strafrechtspflege* (3rd edn., Göttingen, 1965), pp. 142–3; H. von Weber, "Die peinliche Halsgerichtsordnung Kaiser Karls V.," *Zeitschrift der Savigny Stiftung für Rechtsgeschichte. Germanistische Abteilung*, LXXVII (1960), 289, 302–5, 310; G. Schmidt, "Sinn und Bedeutung der *Constitutio Criminalis Carolina* als Ordnung des materiellen und prozessualen Rechts," *ibid.*, LXXXIII (1966), 239–57.

[48] Conrad, *op. cit.*, Vol. II, pp. 365–7, 456–8.

[49] Doucet, *op. cit.*, Vol. I, pp. 117–19, 275–7; Zeller, *op. cit.*, pp. 196–9, 205–6; Guenée, *op. cit.*, p. 308.

of the *parlement* of Paris.[50] A codification of the laws of Castile in 1484 was followed by the "New Compilation" of 1567 which contained some 4,000 articles; similar codes were issued for the other Iberian kingdoms. In 1531 Charles V initiated in the Netherlands a programme of codification similar to that in France, but the work proceeded more slowly and was less complete; it was abandoned after 1581 in the United Provinces and reached its high point in the Spanish Netherlands from the late sixteenth century onwards. The number of different custumaries was reduced but remained large. Nevertheless, as in France and elsewhere, considerable progress had been made towards unifying civil procedure and the substantive laws relating to the family, property, succession, contracts and other issues.[51] In promoting the cumbersome task of codification rulers had shown a heightened awareness of the need for unity in the state; the limitations on their success revealed how imperfect was that unity.

One feature of the sixteenth-century state which is often and rightly given prominence is the extent of regionalism which limited the central government. Not only did each of the so-called "nation states" contain within its frontiers one or more minority nations like the Welsh or Basques, but "particularist" loyalties to provinces, cities, smaller territorial units, or the individual orders within society (clergy, nobles, officials, universities, guilds, etc.) were often stronger than obedience to central authority. Governments had to take account of local interests in making policy and use local men to carry it out. Professor Major takes the argument a stage further in suggesting that Renaissance monarchs by deliberately decentralizing their administration were simply recognizing the weaknesses of their power and not seeking to make it absolute. The role of governors and *parlements* in France

---

[50] Cf. also R. Filhol, *Le Premier Président Christofle de Thou et la réformation des coutumes* (Paris, 1937), pp. 187, 209.

[51] Lapeyre, *op. cit.*, p. 295; J. Gilissen, "La rédaction des coutumes en Belgique aux XVIᵉ et XVIIᵉ siècles," in *La rédaction des coutumes dans le passé et dans le présent*, ed. J. Gilissen (Brussels, 1962), pp. 87–92, 97–8; *idem*, "La rédaction des coutumes dans le passé et dans le présent. Essai de synthèse," *ibid.*, pp. 57–60.

and the codification of the differing customs of the realm are seen as part of this process; many provinces also retained their separate Estates, legislation, taxation, mints, and systems of weights and measures, and even different dates for the beginning of the year.[52] Yet this interpretation confuses two meanings of the word "centralization," and equates the geographical decentralization of institutions with a weakening of royal power. "Centralization" is historians' shorthand for the growth of central councils and financial, judicial, military and representative institutions which concentrated government in the hands of the state, but it also implies a geographical concentration in a capital city and in institutions responsible for the whole country. The two kinds of centralization need not coincide for efficient rule. Where long distances made communications poor, royal power was better served by provincial institutions and provincial officials who regarded themselves as the king's loyal government, but would not readily accept subordination to institutions and ministers in Paris. The provinces were even prepared to pay for their own *parlements*; their growing number was a sign of strength, not weakness, in the conflict of the crown with nobles and other particularist forces in newly acquired provinces. From the fifteenth century onwards French kings and their advisers pursued the strong combination of institutional centralization and, where necessary, geographical decentralization.[53]

Similar conditions prevailed in Spain and the Netherlands, while even in England, where alone geographical centralization on the capital was largely achieved, the government found separate councils useful for ruling Wales and the North. Such decentralization was firmly built into the constitution of Germany,

[52] See below, pp. 43–57; P. S. Lewis, *Later Medieval France: The Polity* (London, 1968), pp. 139–40; R. Mousnier, *Les XVIe et XVIIe siècles* (5th edn., Paris, 1967), p. 115; F. C. Spooner, *L'Économie mondiale et les frappes monétaires en France (1493–1680)* (Paris, 1956), p. 278.

[53] B. Guenée, "Espace et État dans la France du Bas Moyen Âge," *Annales. Économies. Sociétés. Civilisations*, XXIII (1968), 744–58; S. Mastellone, "Osservazioni sulla 'Renaissance monarchy' in Francia," *Annali della Fondazione italiana per la storia amministrativa*, I (1964), 426; Doucet, *op. cit.*, Vol. I, p. 37.

a vast country where the main initiative lay not with the central authorities, but with the large number of princes and imperial cities. Just as we have seen that imperial legislation negotiated by the virtually independent Estates could influence many of them, so Professors Tüchle and Hubatsch show later in this volume how control of religion (as of all matters of internal government) was exercised by individual rulers who then, under the loose reins of Habsburg presidency, made interim arrangements for the whole Empire in the Peace of Augsburg. The balance between national and provincial government in Germany was totally different from that in other countries, but it can be argued that only such a system could have achieved any measure of successful government in the special circumstances of the Empire.

It has been said of the kings of England and France in the early sixteenth century that they governed under the law and sought to establish the rule of law, not that of despots.[54] These views have not gone unchallenged. Professor Major's argument that French monarchs sought legal justification and the consent of their subjects for all their actions begs several questions about the nature of the law and representative institutions in this period. Reliance on legal claims was mainly a propaganda device when legal justification could usually be found for both points of view in any dispute. The consent of the small ruling elite in the French Estates and *parlements* should not be confused with popular support. When towns refused to pay taxes, this was no claim to exercise a right of consent, but a statement of inability to pay.[55] Rulers rarely became despots, but what they set out to achieve sometimes looked suspiciously like despotism; certainly some measure of absolute rule was enforced. It does not follow from their un-doubted lack of powerful standing armies or adequate revenues and administrative institutions that they could only rule on the basis of popular consent. When Tudor monarchs could not

---

[54] Below, p. 44; G. R. Elton, "The Law of Treason in the Early Reformation," *Historical Journal*, XI (1968), 236: ". . . Henry VIII's councillors [were] labouring to bring all England and all matters under the rule of law, and that law the common law of the realm."   [55] Mastellone, *loc. cit.*, pp. 424-5.

persuade parliament to act as they wished, they were quite prepared to bend the law to their interests. The judges were browbeaten and parliament outmanoeuvred to secure enactment of a statute in 1536 against the uses by which vassals of the crown had evaded payments arising from feudal incidents; uses were held by the judges to be illegal at common law after the king in person had harangued them and the judges of the royal courts had outvoted those of the common law courts, so that the House of Commons was presented with a *fait accompli*. The measure was largely nullified a few years later by the Statute of Wills, but it is the intention of the government that is significant, just as in the Statute of Proclamations of 1539, which was finally passed in an innocuous form after parliamentary opposition, the original draft had been designed to give the king sweeping legislative powers without recourse to parliament.[56]

Parliaments could occasionally resist the introduction of legislation or taxation which harmed the interests of the propertied classes or threatened tyranny, but theirs was essentially a rearguard action. For the most part they filled a subordinate role as the instruments of governments, not for obtaining popular consent, but as a means of propaganda to influence public opinion into accepting such policies as the royal supremacy in England and to obtain additional revenues and effective sanctions for the enforcement of government measures. Parliaments enjoyed "participation in government at the sovereign's command";[57] only later were they able to take more of the initiative by exploiting the precedents thus established. Except for a few parliaments in some German principalities, the provinces of the Netherlands and the kingdoms of Aragon, they could all be subverted or overcome in one way or

[56] J. W. M. Bean, *The Decline of English Feudalism, 1215–1540* (Manchester, 1968), pp. 258, 272–6, 282–5; E. W. Ives, "The Common Lawyers in Pre-Reformation England," *Transactions of the Royal Historical Society*, 5th Series, XVIII (1968), 163–4; J. Hurstfield, "Was there a Tudor Despotism after all?," *ibid.*, XVII (1967), 93–8.

[57] J. S. Roskell, "Perspectives in English Parliamentary History," *Bulletin of the John Rylands Library*, XLVI (1964), 474; Hurstfield, *loc. cit.*, pp. 98–107; see Professor Woodward's discussion below, pp. 113–25.

another. The rulers of the early sixteenth century eliminated political and religious dissent, often using emergency measures such as the English treason legislation, and raised up their own position as heads of state to even higher pinnacles. They were restrained less by the rule of law or the need for consent than by the inadequacy and opposition of their own officials; thus the *parlement* of Paris was becoming less the king's instrument than a barrier to royal authoritarianism.[58]

The role of parliaments is but one among several important topics which have received scant or no attention in this introduction and the selected articles. Constitutional history, political thought, and the somewhat barren exercise of classifying different types of governments have been eschewed. Nor is there much mention of the relations between rulers and their nobles, cities, and other subjects, the organization of war and diplomacy, the special problems of ruling subject provinces like Ireland and Spanish Italy, the suppression of rebellions, and the novel task of censoring printed books. Above all, the economic policies of governments, the large-scale active participation in industry and commerce of rulers in Germany, Portugal, Sweden, and Venice, and the beginning of the process by which governments slowly took over from municipal and parish authorities the ultimate responsibility for administering poor relief and other forms of welfare—all these have been omitted. Some selectivity was necessary within a vast field, articles or chapters in books were not available for certain subjects, and the editor's preferences have played a part. In general, emphasis has fallen on the day to day running of government rather than on abstract theorizing or such exceptional circumstances as rebellions. Some of the more original articles were chosen just because they have provoked controversy and even though they may have been faulted on matters of detail.

Professor Dewey's contribution on Russia stands a little apart. It shows how Russia since the end of the fifteenth century and

[58] See pp. 255-6, below; J. H. Shennan, *The Parlement of Paris* (London, 1968). p. 190; B. Guenée, "L'histoire de l'état en France à la fin du Moyen Âge," *Revue Historique*, CCXXXII (1964), 360.

especially in the reign of Ivan IV was acquiring many of the problems and institutions of European countries. Territorial unity was slowly built up, central departments of state run by a new class of secretaries were established, local government and military administration were reformed, parliamentary institutions began to meet from the middle of the sixteenth century, and the newly assumed title of tsar was buttressed by notions of Divine Right. Nevertheless, "the striking fact that Russia laid the foundations of absolute monarchy almost simultaneously with Valois France and Tudor England did not mean that she had found a short cut to overtake the rest of Europe."[59] She had not reached the same stage of economic development, the proposals of Ivan IV's ministers to secularize some of the extensive lands of the church could not be realized, and the nobles remained so powerful that at the end of his reign the tsar virtually destroyed the state he had so painstakingly erected, by establishing within it a large *opričnina*, or private demesne, where only nobles and others absolutely loyal to him implemented his tyrannical rule. Russia had to wait until Peter the Great before government on recognizably western lines could develop any further. The Russian example is a salutary reminder that in pursuing the similarities in the government of states one should not ignore the wide differences between them, and that reforms initiated in the era of the Reformation were by no means always completed in the same century.

[59] J. D. Clarkson, *A History of Russia* (Longmans, 1962), p. 140.

PART ONE

The Problems and Institutions of Government

1 The French Renaissance Monarchy as Seen through the Estates General[1]

J. RUSSELL MAJOR

THE Estates General played but a small role in the development of the French monarchy. So little did it accomplish that at first glance a serious study of its history hardly seems necessary except to explain why it failed. This negative approach may be justified, but I think the greatest value to be achieved by the study of the French Estates General and other representative institutions during the Renaissance lies in the insight it gives into the nature of the monarchy of that great age. Just as Neale has used the English parliament as a vehicle for studying Elizabethan government and society and Namier that of Georgian England, so the Estates General provides an opportunity to interpret the government of Renaissance France.

The conclusions that one reaches from such a study run counter to most existing interpretations.[2] It is the purpose of this paper to suggest (1) that the French Renaissance monarchs ruled according to law, not in defiance of it; (2) that they accepted the decentralization

[1] This paper was read before a meeting of the Society for French Historical Studies at Princeton on April 14, 1961. I am indebted to my colleague Dr. Douglas A. Unfug and to Professor Herbert H. Rowen of the University of Wisconsin-Milwaukee for reading and criticizing the manuscript.

[2] These conclusions are based largely on J. Russell Major, *The Deputies to the Estates General of Renaissance France* (Wisconsin, 1960); and *Representative Institutions in Renaissance France, 1421–1559* (Wisconsin, 1960). They differ to a considerable degree from even the most recent studies on the Renaissance monarchy. See F. Chabod, "Y a-t-il un état de la Renaissance," *Actes du colloque sur la Renaissance organisé par la société d'histoire moderne, 30 juin-juillet 1956* (Paris, 1958), pp. 55–78; H. R. Trevor-Roper, "The General Crisis of the 17th Century," *Past and Present*, XVI (1959), 31–64; and J. V. Vives, "Estructura administrativa estatal en los siglos XVI y XVII," *XIe Congrès international des sciences historiques, rapports, IV, histoire moderne* (Uppsala, 1960), pp. 1–24 [and below, pp. 58–87].

of the state, and made little effort to centralize it; (3) that they were inherently weak, not strong; (4) that the dynamic elements in society were the nobility and the bureaucracy, not the bourgeoisie; and (5) that the basis of a king's power lay in the support he could win from the people, not in a standing army or a bureaucracy. Most of these characteristics differ in some respects from those of the medieval monarchy which preceded it and from the monarchy of the old regime that followed. The Renaissance monarchy, then, marked a period in history that was born about the middle of the reign of Charles VII after a century of war and economic contraction, and died during the middle third of the seventeenth century in another period of foreign wars and economic crisis.[3]

The first characteristic of the Renaissance monarchs in France was that they ruled according to law, not in defiance of it. Much has been written about the arbitrary and despotic nature of these kings, but such statements are not well grounded in fact. The French kings were above all legitimate kings. Their claim to the crown was based on law, not force. When they fought a foreign

[3] Most historians have seen a difference between the medieval and the Renaissance monarchy, but few have drawn a dividing line between the Renaissance monarchy and that of the *ancien régime*. See F. Hartung and R. Mousnier, "Quelques problèmes concernant la monarchie absolue," *Relazioni del X congresso internazionale di scienze storiche, IV, storia moderna* (Florence, 1955), pp. 1–55. Recent research, however, supports the interpretation that the seventeenth century was one of crisis and produced many changes. E. J. Hobsbawm has shown that there was a general economic crisis in the seventeenth century. See his "The General Crisis of the European Economy in the 17th Century," *Past and Present*, v (1954), 33–53; and vi (1954), 44–65. In his *Histoire générale des civilisations*, ed. Maurice Crouzet (Paris, 1954), Vol. iv, Mousnier himself accepted the idea that there was a crisis and in his "État et commissaire. Recherches sur la création des intendants de province (1634–1648)," *Forschungen zur Staat und Verfassung. Festgabe für Fritz Hartung* (Berlin, 1958), pp. 325–44, he showed how the Thirty Years' War affected the development of the bureaucracy. It is my belief that the economic crisis and the Thirty Years' War brought the French Renaissance monarchy to an end and led to changes as important as those brought on by the Hundred Years' War and the economic crisis of 1330–1450. The Wars of Religion may have led to significant changes in political thought, but this should not blind us to the fact that few important changes in the army or in other institutions resulted, and that the bureaucracy was altered only by the establishment of the *droit annuel* [in 1604, which firmly established hereditary succession to most offices].

THE FRENCH RENAISSANCE MONARCHY

war, it was to win a territory, such as Naples or Milan, to which they had a dynastic claim, not lands nearer home to which they had no legal right. When the crown expanded internally, it was through the process of escheatment, not force; always legal means were preferred to illegal.

Since the king's present position and future prospects depended upon the law, he, in turn, had to respect the rights of his subjects. It was the Renaissance monarchs who convoked the three estates to codify the laws of the various provinces, bailiwicks, and other territories, and it was the Renaissance monarchs who finally recognized the right of the *parlement* of Paris to debate royal ordinances and make remonstrances. Judges in *parlement* served for life, and there is little evidence to suggest that they were intimidated into rendering judicial decisions favorable to the crown. The great were rarely punished and then only after a judicial trial. In England, in contrast, most judges served at the king's pleasure; and when this fact did not intimidate them enough, there was always parliament to pass a bill of attainder to dispose of some noble suspected of rebellious intentions, a disgraced minister, or an unwanted wife. Small wonder Machiavelli felt sure that the French kings were bound by law, more so than their fellow monarchs, and that the *parlements* would deliver judgments against them.[4]

This emphasis on law and justice is best illustrated by the decisions rendered in the king's council in disputed elections to the Estates General. Time and again during the Wars of Religion pro-royalist and pro-League candidates competed for seats and the disputes that resulted were appealed to the king in council. Here decisions were rendered, more often than not, in favor of the League candidate, in spite of the precarious position of the crown. Always, law and justice were the determining factors.[5]

A second characteristic of the Renaissance monarchy was its

[4] Major, *Representative Institutions* . . ., pp. 3–13.

[5] Major, *The Deputies.* . . . For decisions by the king in council against royal officials or for pro-League candidates, see especially pp. 21, 25–6, 30–3, 49, 50–1, 62, 82–3, 85–6, 111–12.

decentralization. Too often we have assumed that as the great feudal dynasties died out and their lands escheated to the crown, the monarchy became more centralized. But in fact the French kings always permitted the inhabitants of such newly acquired territories to keep their institutions and laws. They also appointed governors over these provinces who usurped as many regal powers as they could, so that the Burgundian governor during the Wars of Religion behaved as independently of the crown as the great dukes had a century or more before. The late Valois kings granted even greater authority to members of their family in the form of appanages. France was indeed fortunate that few royal princes reached middle age or left heirs.

The medieval monarchs had tried to keep the royal judicial and administrative institutions centralized, and when Charles VII began the long process of restoring the position of the monarchy after its virtual collapse during the reign of his insane father, he sought to continue this policy. When he came to the throne there were two *parlements*, or sovereign judicial courts, in unoccupied France. The one at Poitiers served the northern part of the realm while the other had been established in 1420 at Toulouse for the benefit of the southern region. By 1428 communication between Poitou and Languedoc had improved sufficiently to make possible the reunion of the two *parlements* at Poitiers. With the recapture of Paris in 1436 the now united *parlement* returned to the capital. In a similar manner, during the first third of his reign, Charles convoked the Estates General and the estates of Languedoïl instead of relying exclusively on the provincial estates as his predecessors had normally done.

Then, about 1440, for reasons that are not fully known, Charles abandoned the medieval preference for centralized royal institutions. Sovereign local *parlements* began to be established at Toulouse, Bordeaux, and other cities as provinces were reunited or annexed to the crown. The *Chambre des Comptes*, the *Cour des Aides*, and other financial institutions were treated in a similar manner. The Estates General was no longer convoked except in rare emergencies, but provincial estates continued to flourish in most of France. It was with this decision by Charles VII to decentralize royal institutions that the Renaissance monarchy was born, for in this act, more than in the demise of the great feudal dynasties, we find the real distinction between the medieval and the Renaissance.

Charles accepted decentralization in another way. In 1454 he ordered that local assemblies of the three estates be held to codify the customs of the various provinces, bailiwicks, and other localities. Once these local customs were definitely established and put into writing, it became virtually impossible to develop a common law for the entire kingdom by any means other than revolution. Thus private law and many aspects of public law escaped the hands of the king and remained decentralized like the judicial and financial courts and the representative assemblies.[6]

A third characteristic of the Renaissance monarchy was that it was inherently weak, not strong, because it had neither an adequate bureaucracy nor an adequate army. Around 1505 there were approximately 12,000 royal officials in France, or one official for each 1,250 inhabitants and one for each forty square kilometers. The number of royal officials increased during the course of the century, but at no time could they have interfered with the actions of the people to the degree found in a modern democracy. France in 1934 had one official for each seventy inhabitants and fifty-six for each forty square kilometers.[7]

[6] Major, *Representative Institutions* . . ., pp. 4–7, 21–32. The acceptance of decentralization was a characteristic of nearly all the Renaissance monarchies and was undoubtedly made advisable by the size of the states and the provincialism of the people, but as these conditions also existed in the previous period it is possible that the aesthetic outlook of the age was a factor. In his *Waning of the Middle Ages* (New York, 1949), J. Huizinga has shown that the love of detail and the acceptance of infinite variations at the cost of the unity of the whole characterized the work of the artist and the writer of the fifteenth century. May not the king in council have been likewise affected? In a similar manner the triumph of science and rationalism in the seventeenth century may be related to the desire for uniformity and order that characterized the monarchy of Louis XIV. For a pioneering work in this field, see J. E. King, *Science and Rationalism in the Government of Louis XIV, 1661–1683* (Baltimore, 1949).

[7] Mousnier, *Histoire générale des civilisations*, Vol. IV, p. 99. The central theme

To make matters worse the king could not control the few royal officials he had. In the first place, it was virtually impossible to remove an official because his office was generally a purchased property right. The English Tudors may actually have had a better bureaucracy because the justices of the peace, though unpaid, could be fired, while the French officials, though paid, could not easily be removed. In the second place, the royal chancery consisted of only 120 scribes, secretaries, and other officials in 1500 and only 200 by 1587, a pitifully small number to administer the central organs of a large and populous state.[8] If there were today only 1,800 bureaucrats in Washington, D.C., Mr. Kennedy would have a staff of about the same size in proportion to the population of the United States as Henry III of France had in 1587. Furthermore, Henry III's bureaucrats had no telephones, typewriters, or mimeograph machines. Technological as well as bureaucratic limitations prevented the government from issuing minute regulations or checking on enforcement. Only broad statements of general policy could be decreed, leaving local officials a wide latitude of interpretation and enforcement.

It is true that edicts and *ordonnances* were sometimes printed, but apparently this was done primarily to inform lawyers and other interested persons. Local government officials still expected to receive handwritten orders properly sealed by the chancery. As late as 1649 the mayor of Troyes refused to take any action when he received only printed instructions from a local official concerning the bailiwick assembly to elect deputies to the Estates General.[9]

The inadequate bureaucratic and technological development of the Renaissance monarchy is clearly revealed by the preliminaries to holding a meeting of the Estates General. To one who remembers the great efforts that were made to decide on the

_____

of Trevor-Roper's, Chabod's, and to a lesser extent Vives's interpretation of the Renaissance monarchy is the growth of the bureaucracy (see note 2 above). The bureaucracy did grow during the Renaissance, but not to the extent that it could have become as important a bulwark of the monarchy as we have been led to believe.

[8] R. Doucet, *Les Institutions de la France au XVIe siècle* (Paris, 1948), Vol. I, p. 109.   [9] Major, *The Deputies . . .*, p. 42.

procedure to be used in electing deputies to the Estates General of 1789, the vast number of documents that were published to serve as guides, and the twenty-three pages of minute regulations that were issued, it comes as a surprise to learn of the cavalier way in which the crown summoned the Estates General during the Renaissance. Although the Estates General of 1484 marked the first time that the bailiwick estates had ever been asked to serve as electoral assemblies, and the Estates General of 1560 marked a revival of bailiwick elections after three generations of disuse, there is no evidence that the royal council concerned itself with procedural problems, and we can categorically state that there was no assembly of notables to decide how the elections should be held and that no detailed instructions were sent to the bailiffs. It was enough to tell them to summon the three estates to meet in the principal seat of their jurisdiction to elect deputies. No instructions were given telling exactly who could vote, or on any of those other matters that so concerned the men of 1788. The Renaissance bailiff was left to his own devices and the fact that no two of the hundred-odd electoral jurisdictions proceeded in an identical manner caused no official concern. In 1614 the bailiwicks were told to elect one deputy from each estate, but when only one fourth of the electoral jurisdictions specifically obeyed this order the crown raised no objections.[10]

The royal army was as inadequate as the royal bureaucracy. The much-vaunted military force created by Charles VII had a paper strength of only 12,000 cavalrymen and 16,000 infantry militiamen. Even if these units had been kept up to strength, and they certainly were not, the new army would have been only about the size of two modern divisions. Even with the rapid transportation and communication of today and the immense superiority of the arms and training of the modern soldier over the civilian population, such a force could hardly subject a population of 15,000,000. Thus the armies of the Renaissance were too small to permit a king to hold his subjects in subjection against their will, and this was doubly true because the subjects themselves were well armed.

[10] *Ibid.*, esp. pp. 4–6, 119–31.

Anne de Montmorency is reported to have brought a retinue of 800 horsemen when he came to court in 1560 to attend the council of Fontainebleau, and he certainly could have mustered a much larger force had there been any need. Troyes marched 3,875 men before the duke of Orléans in 1544, Amiens had 3,000 men in 1597, and many other walled towns had comparable forces equipped with artillery and munitions. Though a king could have taken the fortified castles of Montmorency and captured any single town in his kingdom, it was cheaper and easier to avoid offending subjects, and any sort of attack on a large number of nobles or towns was clearly impossible.

Besides the smallness of the royal army and the presence of armed nobles and towns, there was a third check to limit the king's capacity to make war on his subjects: he could not count on the obedience and loyalty of his own troops. The cavalry was composed almost entirely of the local nobility and captained by members of the leading families of the provinces. The infantry militia was composed of bourgeois and peasants subject to call in case of war. Such an army was but a small step forward from the feudal levies of the Middle Ages. The mercenaries so numerous in time of war were no more trustworthy. These troops obeyed the orders of the officers who paid them, not those of the king. The Thirty Years' War produced many examples of this phenomenon; and the Fronde, which saw armies change sides at the bidding of a Condé or a Turenne, proved all too clearly that France was no exception to the rule. Louis XIV was the first French king to establish effective control over a large military force. Earlier, troops and civilians alike obeyed their monarch if they saw fit, but not otherwise. The army had been created to deal with foreign invaders and bandits. It was also capable of handling one or two rebellious magnates or several disobedient towns, but it could not cope with a large and unwilling population composed of the relatives and neighbors of its members. In the final analysis, the Valois, like the Tudors, had to rely on the support of their more powerful subjects.[11]

[11] Major, *Representative Institutions . . .*, pp. 9–10. The organization of the

A fourth characteristic of the Renaissance monarchy was that the dynamic elements of society were the nobility and the bureaucracy, not the bourgeoisie.[12] Historians of France have almost invariably believed that the Renaissance monarchs were opposed to the nobility and successfully destroyed its influence. To prove their point they have cited the extinction of the great feudal houses and the increased use of the lesser nobility and men of bourgeois extraction in the government. This is a highly questionable approach. The great feudal houses died out primarily because of a failure to produce male heirs and not because of royal policy. It would be as logical to interpret the assumption of the crown of France in 1498 by the duke of Orléans, in the person of Louis XII, or in 1515 by the count of Angoulême, in the person of Francis I, as victories of the great nobles over the crown as to interpret the reunion of Anjou and Provence to the crown under Louis XI as a victory of the king over the great nobility. The Renaissance monarchs sought to suppress rebellious nobles, yes,

---

French army changed during the course of the sixteenth century, but the generalizations cited above continued to hold true. See Doucet, op. cit., Vol. II, pp. 608–51. There is also evidence that by the close of the fifteenth century improved fortifications had mitigated the earlier advantage artillery had given to the offense: J. R. Hale, "International Relations in the West: Diplomacy and War," The New Cambridge Modern History (Cambridge, 1957), Vol. I, pp. 281–2; and "Armies, Navies, and the Art of War," ibid., Vol. II, pp. 491–4. This development favored the nobility and towns at the expense of the king.

[12] The revival of the aristocracy now seems to have been a general phenomenon during the sixteenth century. It has long been recognized that the nobility strengthened its position in Prussia, Poland, and most of eastern Europe during the Renaissance. In his "Rise of the Gentry, 1558–1640," Economic History Review, XI (1941), 1–38, R. H. Tawney has argued that the English gentry— the economic and social counterpart of the lower nobility on the Continent— improved its position. H. R. Trevor-Roper has recently challenged this interpretation, but with only partial success. See especially his "The Gentry, 1540–1640," Economic History Review, Supplement, 1954. Fernand Braudel finds a "seigneurial reaction" in the Mediterranean world between 1450 and 1550 in his La Méditerranée et le monde méditerranéen à l'époque de Philippe II (Paris, 1949), pp. 624–37. Some Italian cities fell into the hands of the aristocracy and the aristocratic revival found its expression in literature: P. Coles, "The Crisis of Renaissance Society: Genoa, 1488–1507," Past and Present, XI (1957), 17–47; and A. Hauser, The Social History of Art (New York, 1957), Vol. II, pp. 144–72.

but they did not make war on the nobility as a class. The nobles were their friends and companions at court, at the chase, and on the battlefield. It was upon the support of this dynamic class that much of their power depended.

That the nobility was dynamic may be demonstrated by the concessions it won from the crown. On this class the kings found it advisable to shower title after title. At the beginning of the sixteenth century there were only five lay peers in France, but between 1515 and 1600 twenty-eight new peerages were created. Lesser titles were handed out with even greater generosity. Henry III alone created fifty-five counties, marquisates, duchies, and principalities. These titles were not empty dignities; they gave their holders special privileges and their feudal courts greater importance. Gifts in money and in land were as profuse as gifts in titles, and nearly all the great ecclesiastical benefices went to the nobility. Even Louis XI, so often interpreted as an enemy of the nobility, was in reality one of its most generous benefactors. The holdings of the count of Armagnac were granted to over two dozen persons, nearly all of whom were nobles of the sword in his service. What happened to the rest of the lands that escheated to the crown during his reign is not known, but it is significant that at his death less than three per cent. of his income came from the royal domain. The Estates General of 1484 saw a popular reaction against the pensions he had granted, and the powerful position the house of Foix-Navarre won for itself in southern France was due largely to his support.[13]

Whether the energy of the nobility resulted from its improving economic status, as Tawney has suggested in the case of the English gentry, or whether it resulted from its increasingly desperate financial position, as Trevor-Roper insists, is difficult to say. The traditional interpretation advocated by Marc Bloch was that the French nobility was declining economically because its

[13] Major, *Representative Institutions* . . ., pp. 10–12, 51–2; Doucet, *op. cit.*, Vol. II, pp. 462–3; Jehan Masselin, *Journal des états généraux de France tenus à Tours en 1484*, ed. A. Bernier (Paris, 1835), pp. 348–9; C. Petit-Dutaillis, *Histoire de France*, ed. Lavisse (Paris, 1911), Vol. IV, Pt. II, p. 406.

income was fixed and prices were rising.[14] Recent research suggests, however, that many nobles found ways to increase both their revenue per acre and the number of acres they owned. In this they were greatly aided by the enforced sale of a large part of the lands of the church during the reigns of Charles IX and Henry III, a little-known event that may have been nearly as significant as the sale of monastic lands in England. Of importance also was their purchase of many peasant holdings.[15]

The nobility was as aggressive politically as it may have been economically. This fact is evidenced by the increased attendance in the electoral assemblies to the Estates General and the growing willingness of members of the great "county" families to serve. Even more marked was the nobles' increased participation in the provincial estates during the late sixteenth and seventeenth centuries.[16]

The growing percentage of men of minor noble or bourgeois extraction in the royal bureaucracy has led many persons to assume that this demonstrated the decline of the nobility. This is a very questionable generalization. The great nobles in France developed a relationship with the lesser nobility and many legally trained members of the middle class comparable to livery and maintenance in England, although it is doubtful whether this

[14] This interpretation is based primarily on P. Raveau, *L'Agriculture et les classes paysannes dans le Haut-Poitou au XVIe siècle* (Paris, 1926). It was accepted by M. Bloch, *Les caractères originaux de l'histoire rurale française* (Paris, 1955), Vol. I, pp. 126-31; and H. Sée, *Histoire économique de la France* (Paris, 1948), Vol. I, pp. 125-34.

[15] Braudel, *op. cit.*, pp. 624-37; L. Merle, *Le Métaire et l'évolution agraire de la Gâtine poitevine de la fin du moyen âge à la révolution* (Paris, 1958), esp. pp. 1-95; I. Cloulas, "Les Aliénations du temporel ecclésiastique sous Charles XI et Henri III (1563-1587)," *Revue d'histoire de l'église de France*, XLIV (1958), 5-56; V. Carrière, *Introduction aux études d'histoire ecclésiastique locale* (Paris, 1936), Vol. III, pp. 423-6. Even if the nobility as a class improved its financial status, many individual nobles must have suffered because the absence of primogeniture often led estates to be divided among many heirs (Bloch, *Supplement* by R. Auvergne, Vol. II, pp. 159-60). For the attempt by some noble families to avoid this fate, see R. Boutruche, *La Crise d'une société: seigneurs et paysans du Bordelais pendant la guerre de cent ans* (Paris, 1947), pp. 285-94, 386-95.

[16] Major, *The Deputies . . .*, esp. pp. 137-8.

relationship was formalized by indentures. These people, called *clients* by the French historians, were often placed by their influential patrons in key royal administrative and judicial posts where they were expected to exhibit a higher loyalty to their patron than to their king. Much of the duke of Guise's power during the Wars of Religion came from his *clients* who held royal offices, and the duke of Sully later informed Cardinal Richelieu that the reason Henry IV made office-holding hereditary was to weaken the influence of the great nobles in the bureaucracy.[17]

Not all royal officials were *clients* of the great nobles, however. Many behaved in a very aggressive manner, showing little respect for the other privileged classes or the orders of the king. They were the second dynamic element in Renaissance society and what little progress was made towards centralization resulted largely from their efforts. Some members of this class on their own initiative tried to usurp seigneurial jurisdiction in the countryside.[18] The duke of Nevers found his right to convoke his duchy to elect deputies to the Estates General challenged on every occasion by the royal officials of the neighboring bailiwick of Saint-Pierre-le-Moutier. Happily for the duke, the king in council invariably sided with him against the royal officials.[19] The local royal officials also tried to wrest control of the towns from the bourgeoisie in spite of all the king in council could do to restrain them. This struggle fills the electoral history of the Estates General because in the Renaissance even noble royal officials sat with the third

[17] E. Perroy comments on the efforts of the great nobles to place their supporters in the royal bureaucracy and on their relations with the lesser nobility in "Feudalism or Principalities in Fifteenth Century France," *Bulletin of the Institute of Historical Research*, xx (1943–4), 181–5; but he finds no evidence of indentures such as those described by W. H. Dunham Jr. in *Lord Hastings' Indentured Retainers, 1461–1483* (New Haven, 1955). On the relation between the great nobles and lesser nobles, see L. Romier, *Le Royaume de Catherine de Médicis* (Paris, 1922), Vol. I, pp. 208–30. On the relation between the great nobles and the royal bureaucracy, see R. Mousnier, *La Vénalité des offices sous Henri IV et Louis XIII* (Rouen, 1945), esp. pp. 64–6, 287–311, 577–611.

[18] A. Bossuat, *Le Bailliage royal de Montferrand, 1425–1556* (Paris, 1957) provides interesting examples of the activities of royal officials.

[19] Major, *The Deputies . . .*, pp. 85–6.

estate where they competed with the bourgeois oligarchy of the towns. When disputes arose the king generally sided with the bourgeoisie against his own aggressive officials, only to have the quarrel renewed the next time elections were held.[20]

The bourgeoisie, so often considered the dynamic class of the Renaissance, was unable to hold its relative position. It is true that its members almost completely eliminated the lower classes from municipal government, but except in the largest cities they soon were supplanted in turn by the local royal officials.[21] It is also true that many members of the bourgeoisie entered the ranks of the nobility of the sword or of the robe, but in doing so they abandoned not only their class but also their social outlook. Thus the ablest members of the bourgeoisie fed the ranks of the aristocracy rather than strengthened their own estate.[22]

The position of the clergy was also weakened. The Renaissance, which in its early stage saw the final recognition of the right of the nobility and bureaucracy to escape taxation, also saw the crown begin to collect large sums from the clergy in a systematic manner.[23] No fact more clearly reveals the relative strength of these respective estates. The peasants played a minor role, but a step was taken to awaken their political consciousness by permitting them to organize communities of inhabitants at the village level and to participate in elections to the Estates General in many parts of France.[24]

If there was a dynamic nobility and bureaucracy in Renaissance France and if, as I have suggested, the crown had neither the army

[20] For numerous examples of the activities of the local royal officials in regard to the towns, see Major, *The Deputies.* . . .

[21] Documents on the elections to the Estates General reveal that the bourgeois oligarchy dominated most of the towns, but in return were challenged by the local royal officials. See Major, *The Deputies* . . ., esp. pp. 123–7.

[22] Braudel, *op. cit.*, pp. 619–24; Major, *Representative Institutions* . . ., pp. 11–13.

[23] A study of when and how the nobility and bureaucracy came to escape taxation is badly needed. On clerical taxation, see Doucet, *op. cit.*, Vol. II, pp. 831–46; and Carrière, *op. cit.*, Vol. III, pp. 249–86, 396–434.

[24] Major, *The Deputies* . . ., esp. p. 124.

nor the administrative organs to compel obedience, what was the basis of monarchical power? The answer to this question may be found in the fifth characteristic of the Renaissance monarchy. The Renaissance monarchs were obeyed when they got the support of their subjects. They usually had this support for a number of reasons. They were restorers of order after a long period of warfare and there was no safe, logical alternative to their rule. Most of the highest offices of the church lay at their disposal and the wealthiest bishoprics and abbeys went to their faithful supporters. Government positions, fiefs, patents of nobility, and nearly every type of privilege could be granted by the monarch. He who served the crown loyally could hope for untold riches. He who did not could hope for few rewards.

One last way of winning popular support was through the use of assemblies. It is true that meetings of the Estates General were rare, but provincial estates continued to meet regularly in most of France and we should not lose sight of the smaller assemblies that were frequently held at the national level for a wide variety of purposes. If a king wanted to revoke alienations of the royal domain, he might summon the great nobles and prelates in hope of winning their support; if military matters were causing concern, he might order the "captains and chiefs of war" to assemble with the council to give their advice; if it was the church, he might convoke the "archbishops, bishops, abbots, prelates and other notable clerics"; if it was judicial, he might call members of the sovereign courts; if it was economic, he might tell the towns to send deputies. The number and variety of these meetings was great and no king held them more frequently than Louis XI. Thus the Renaissance monarchy was popular and consultative because of the need to have the advice and to win the support of the people. If the king was a strong, able man, he could make the system work. If he was too young or too weak, it quickly collapsed. This is why revolts were so frequent during royal minorities. Not until Louis XIV established a reasonably adequate bureaucracy and a large loyal standing army was the crown able to maintain order without a vigorous adult as head of the state. But by the reign of the "sun king" the Renaissance monarchy had come to an end and the crown was attempting to weld the decentralized conglomeration of duchies, counties, and provinces of the earlier period into a centralized well-ordered state.[25]

[25] Major, *Representative Institutions* . . ., esp. pp. 14–20, 52–3.

2 The Administrative Structure of the State in the Sixteenth and Seventeenth Centuries

J. VICENS VIVES

ONE of the most brilliantly presented and heatedly discussed papers at the Tenth International Congress of Historical Sciences held in Rome in 1955 was that of Professors Roland Mousnier and Fritz Hartung, "Some Problems of Absolute Monarchy."[1] Nevertheless, the following considerations have led us to restate the whole problem of the origins of the modern state: the nature of the discussion, which in the opinion of many was left unfinished; the series of interesting research projects which since 1955 have been devoted to clarifying essential aspects of the structure of states on the threshold of the modern age; and the fact that the reading of that paper and the subsequent discussion scarcely touched on so essential an element for the comprehension of the subject as the dynamics of the politico-administrative organization of the Spanish monarchy, and, what is still more important, its expansion into the New World. We hope that this paper will result in a full exchange of views which will permit the opening of new paths in the comprehension of an extremely important phenomenon in the history of the last five centuries.

The theme of the authority of the state, which so closely affects social relationships, falls naturally within the sphere of religious, philosophical, and ideological speculation. This explains the importance given during the first stages of research on absolute monarchy to political theory and to the intellectual reactions which were necessarily provoked after the Renaissance by the affirmation

---

[1] "Quelques problèmes concernant la Monarchie absolue," *Relazioni del X Congresso Internazionale di Scienze Storiche, IV, Storia Moderna* (Florence, 1955), pp. 1–55, and *Atti del X Congresso Internazionale* (Rome, 1957), pp. 429–43. Especially interesting were the contributions to the discussion by L. Bulferetti, A. Meusel, and S. D. Scaskin.

of the supremacy of the state. This was a preliminary task and obviously a most useful one. But historians have come almost to the end of this particular line of investigation, in the information that is available as well as in methodology; they have even gone so far as to reduce political doctrines to mere symbolic diagrams.[2] Philological research, allied to transcendental idealism, has frequently vitiated the historical attitude toward absolute power, which above everything else was a reality of command, a reality lived daily by those who had to govern and those who wished (or did not wish) to be governed in this way. The history of the political and juridical principles of absolute monarchy has been seen to be inadequate, if not actually erroneous, for the purpose of uncovering this reality and giving us an accurate view of it.

This conviction explains the more recent tendency to examine the origins of the modern state from the point of view of other historiographical possibilities. Thus we owe considerable progress to the school of historical materialism. It has shed much light on important aspects of absolute monarchy from the stimulating angles of economic development and social dynamics in the sixteenth and seventeenth centuries. It has placed at the disposal of research workers an indispensable body of facts. Such facts constituted a palpable, even a measurable, reality during that period, from which it has been possible to sketch the origins of the inner structural articulations of state authority. There is still much to be done along these lines. But on the other hand the interpretative possibilities of the proposed [Marxist] model appear to be exhausted, in so far as they make it dependent on a model of social and economic process which involves not only the historical reality studied but the projection into it of a philosophical system.[3]

The attention of scholars has been concentrated during the past

[2] Such was the influence exercised by the German school just before World War II, whose traits are very evident in W. Näf, *Die Epochen der neueren Geschichte*, 2 vols. (Aarau, 1945), and especially in A. Ferrari, *Fernando el Católico en Baltasar Gracián* (Madrid, 1945).

[3] See Mousnier's defence in response to S. D. Scaskin's views, in *Atti del X Congresso Internazionale*, pp. 438–9.

few years on humbler (and perhaps more instructive) aspects of research on the origins of state power in modern times. Since the act of governing is in fact carried out by human agency, the focus of modern working hypotheses tends to illuminate the bureaucratic apparatus which made absolute monarchy possible. Such investigation into the vicissitudes of administrative institutions is one of the classic themes of legal history of German inspiration. Substantial progress has also been made along these lines, though naturally there are many areas which have not been studied as yet, and a pattern of resemblances and connections, or differences and exceptions, has not yet been established. But the history of institutions is not history properly speaking; it is the description of the condition of the power apparatus at a given moment, a description which ignores its genesis, and which in particular disregards the tumultuous reality contained in it. Thus it has been necessary to delve more deeply into the human element which constituted the framework of absolute monarchy, and to consider the ministers and officials of the ruler in their role as the props of state authority and instruments in its progress. Thus historians have begun to develop an analysis of the bureaucracy of the sixteenth and seventeenth centuries as a basic element determining the internal structure of the states of the period, and characterizing—as Frederico Chabod has said[4]—the transition from the doctrinal absolutism of the Middle Ages, which was not put into practice, to the actual and fully realized absolutism of the western European states in the sixteenth and seventeenth centuries.

The present paper follows this line. Its author is convinced that when research into the internal organization of the state at the beginning of the modern period is completed, when all the necessary data are available concerning the birth of the civil service and the accumulation of the social, economic, intellectual, and ideological factors which moulded the attitudes of the bureaucrat,

[4] "Y a-t-il un État de la Renaissance?," *Actes du Colloque sur la Renaissance organisé par la Société d'Histoire Moderne* (Paris, 1958), pp. 57–74, especially p. 73. [Translated in H. Lubasz (ed.), *The Development of the Modern State* (New York, 1964), pp. 26–42.]

we will have taken a great step forward towards understanding modern state authority and applying correctly the results acquired through the history of political doctrines and of economic and social events.[5]

The first point to be examined is that of the *effective structure* of state power in the sixteenth and seventeenth centuries. We believe that there are two factors here which have obscured, and continue to obscure, proper comprehension of this phenomenon. One is the identification between absolute monarchy and state power; the other is the confusion between the monarchy itself and the so-called nation state.

The monarch of the Renaissance and the Baroque period, who emerged from the doctrines supporting imperial authority in late medieval schools of Roman law and from the empiricism of fifteenth-century Italy, tended to assume full royal authority and the government of the state without making any distinction between them. Throughout the period we are examining, this tendency was reinforced by the impact of humanism, which in politics was frankly royalist, and by the development of the religious and social crises of the sixteenth century, during which society was forced to entrust the role of supreme arbiter and organizer to the person of the monarch. All this led to the deification of the ruler; this is particularly apparent in chancery documents, political propaganda, and the lucubrations of thinkers, philosophers, and theologians. But this defence of the monarch was an abyss away from the institutional organization of the state, and another abyss separated this organization from the simple practice of government. Failure to observe this methodological distinction has caused many scholars to commit gross errors, such as that of describing monarchical authority as absolute solely on the strength of the theories of a few jurists placed at the apex of the governmental system.[6]

[5] This premise clearly indicates that we do not intend to give this paper a bibliographical character, which is in any case precluded by lack of space. However, the reader will find the most important bibliographical information in the works cited in the notes.

[6] This has generally been the case in Spain. However, in his *Historia de la*

In the agrarian Europe of the Renaissance and the Baroque period, even in the western monarchies where some concentrations of commercial or industrial capital existed, authority was stratified in at least three separate areas. The largest of these was direct government of the peasant masses by the seigneurial lords, either lay or ecclesiastical. It was the world of villeins and semifreedmen, and even in certain places of serfs. Within this area there survived the remnants not only of the feudal world but of still older systems connected with Roman colonization and even with previous tribal organizations. Contrary to what is usually believed, a closer examination of this seigneurial world leads us to believe that at the time it was still in a state of expansion, or at least in a period of successful consolidation.[7] This is at the root of one of the important contradictions in absolute monarchy, especially in the Mediterranean countries, where absolutism was accepted by the great lords and ecclesiastical proprietors only in exchange for the monarchy's recognition firstly of their particularist jurisdiction,[8] and then of the intervention of these same landed proprietors in the mainsprings of state power.[9] It would be extremely revealing to chart the results of a documentary study of exempt seigneuries or privileged jurisdictions in the sixteenth and seventeenth centuries. Then we should probably be able to envisage the geographical limitations to the real power of the ruler.[10]

Administración española e hispanoamericana (Madrid, 1958), J. Beneyto has avoided applying the term "absolute" to the monarchy of the sixteenth and seventeenth centuries.

[7] In his well-known work on La Méditerranée et le monde méditerranéen sous Philippe II (Paris, 1949), F. Braudel clearly states this fact ("L'État et la montée seigneuriale," pp. 628–37).

[8] As in the case of the Catholic monarchs in Castile, where the expansion of royal justice was not an obstacle to the consolidation of a seigneurial system with great jurisdictional privileges. The argument needs to be developed in more detail.

[9] Especially noticeable from the beginning of the seventeenth century onwards. In the first half of this century, the great ministers of the Spanish crown were all members of the landholding aristocracy.

[10] S. Sobrequés has made an attempt of this kind for northern Catalonia, in an unfortunately unpublished thesis on the Margarit family. [See now A. M. Guilarte, El régimen señorial en el siglo XVI (Madrid, 1962).]

The second area—or stratum depending on how one looks at it —was composed of the group of autonomous jurisdictions within the ambit reserved for the direct authority of the monarch. It corresponds to the different bodies, organizations and privileged colleges which had arisen out of the commercial revolution and the establishment of the urban middle class. These institutions had greater or lesser influence on the activities of state power according to the intensity of their medieval heritage or the forms taken by its development. Sometimes they are considered to be an offshoot of the so-called state of orders, of the dualist state authority which characterizes the transition from feudal to absolute monarchy.[11] However, in this sphere, as in the seigneurial one, there was no questioning of the titular sovereignty [of the ruler], or even of the applicability of the clause proclaiming absolute power which figures in the proclamations and edicts of the princes: all sovereignty belonged to the monarch.[12] But [the existence of this second layer] led much more importantly to the creation of a geographical area where the ruler could not control money, troops, or the administration of justice except by means of or through the acquiescence of such bodies, whether or not they were represented in the institution of the Cortes, parliaments, or Estates General. The overlapping of these jurisdictions with the seigneurial ones produced a multiplicity of situations in the different European countries which cannot be reduced to a single formula. We shall emphasize this point later.

Lastly, the third stratum corresponds to the princely level itself, and reflects the attitudes of the bureaucracies (not always identified with the evolution of the principle of absolute monarchy) which were used by the royal power to carry out policy. Throughout the

[11] This is, as is well known, the thesis of Näf, so sharply contested by F. Hartung since 1932: "Die Epochen der absoluten Monarchie in der neueren Geschichte," *Historische Zeitschrift*, CXLV (1932).

[12] In Spain it was obligatory to refer to "absolute royal power" from 1418 until the beginning of Philip II's reign; the phrase then disappeared, since it was considered a principle recognized by all: L. Sánchez Agesta, "El 'poderío real absoluto' en el testamento de 1554," *Carlos V. Homenaje de la Universidad de Granada* (Granada, 1958), pp. 439–60.

sixteenth and seventeenth centuries there was a dynamic of monarchical power which was a phenomenon independent of the evolution of government on the two levels we mentioned before. This dynamic did not represent continual progress. It depended on the possibility of the monarchy solving the economic, social, and political contradictions posed by its past and reflected in its present. No case is more typical than the internal contradiction of the sixteenth-century Spanish monarchy, based on the maximum concentration of power at the summit and the minimum irradiation of that power downward.[13]

The second methodological error to which we alluded is the confusion between absolute monarchy and the nation state. It derives from an idealistic political philosophy which exalted state authority as a realization of freedom, and the nation as the perfect expression of the social community. Thus the illusion arose of the nation state as a definitive form of the historical process. According to this view, such a state had begun to appear in western Europe at the end of the fifteenth and early in the sixteenth century, as a result of the concentration of supreme power in the ruler. Save in one country, France (and even in this case we would have to make a number of geographical and jurisdictional exceptions), nowhere did absolute monarchy embody a national tradition. It represented an association—imposed by force, freely accepted, or arising from diplomatic necessity—of differentiated, sometimes totally disparate, communities which only a slow process of coexistence would forge, in the most favourable cases, into a common sentiment; in others, into a resigned and passive acquiescence; and in yet others into an antagonism which could only be resolved by violent separation. This was the reality in which the sixteenth and seventeenth centuries lived, so obvious a reality that there is no need to give examples of it. Therefore the ruler was conditioned, in his political capacity as an absolute monarch, to respect the juridical conditions on which the union

[13] This interpretation of the history of state power in Spain under the Habsburgs finds verification in J. Lalinde's recent thesis, "La institución virreinal en Cataluña (1479-1716)," submitted in 1958.

or association of his patrimonial estates had arisen; hence the presence of a number of serious obstacles to his power, and the need for regional adaptations for the exercise of command. These adaptations were not always easy, for they often altered and interfered with the programme of absolutism.

It would be well, then, to clarify the exact relationship between state authority and state power (authority, as a theory; power, as governmental practice), and to promote a series of investigations into the stratification and regionalization of the power sources of absolute monarchy in the different European areas. Thus we should be able to obtain a true idea of the internal structures of the different states during these centuries.

The Renaissance state in western Europe arose as a result of the international conflicts in which the different monarchies had been engaged since the twelfth century. This statement may seem one-sided, as one-sided perhaps as the theory of the establishment of the absolute state through the mechanism of the class struggle. In fact we are not trying to beg the question, but to investigate the problems on the basis of empirical facts.

It is clear that within the different feudal monarchies, various factors connected with neither war nor diplomacy contributed to the first cracks in their structure and prepared the way for a progressive evolution. The first of these was the demographic expansion of the western European world, the first great wave of humanity loosed after the eleventh century.[14] Thanks to it, internal colonization, the resettlement of vast territories, the development of the cities and, in consequence, a parallel expansion in agriculture, industry, and commercial life were made possible. This demographic and subsequently economic movement was

[14] The demographic factor continues to attract the primary interest of scholars, in spite of the fact that little attention was paid to it at the Tenth Congress of Historical Sciences. Since the excellent paper presented by Cipolla, Dhondt, Postan and Wolff (*IXᵉ Congrès International des Sciences Historiques*, Vol. I, *Rapports* (Paris, 1950), pp. 54–80), studies of demographic history have developed considerably, and should lead to important statements on the subject with which we are dealing here.

related in its turn to the possibilities for technical and cultural innovations; it spilled out of the framework of the institutions of feudal monarchy, showed up their internal contradictions, and prepared the conditions for their transformation into authoritarian and absolutist states. But before these possibilities could be realized, an atmosphere of tension was needed which would put to the test both the resistance of the feudal structure and the strength of the new forces which were to create the structure of the Renaissance state. This atmosphere was induced by the constant wars unleashed in the thirteenth, fourteenth and fifteenth centuries, whose object was to create some territorial possibilities in preference to others. [Yves] Renouard has charted this process exactly. The present-day map of western Europe is the result of a selection among various possibilities,[15] and what eventually prevailed was the will of those human groups which were the most compact and powerful from a triple point of view: demographic, economic, and spiritual. The permanent state of war in western Europe made certain military, diplomatic, and financial demands on the monarchies which eventually caused them to burst out of their feudal framework, and pulled them towards a growing concentration of power; and in this movement the monarchies were supported by the intellectual class trained in Justinian [Roman] law.

From the work of Sombart we know the causal relationship between war and capitalism.[16] But what we are interested in just now is not to dwell on this point of view, which has been treated by all historians and by Mousnier himself in his 1955 paper, but on the revolutionary quality of these conflicts from an internal standpoint. For such wars were not a succession of military encounters between homogeneous states, like the "national" wars of the nineteenth century, but penetrating onslaughts in which the discords and internal conflicts of each incipient political structure played an important part. This complex phenomenon acquired

---

[15] Y. Renouard, "1212–1216. Comment les traits durables de l'Europe occidentale moderne se sont définis au debut du XIIIᵉ siècle," *Annales de l'Université de Paris*, xxvIII (1958), 5–21.

[16] [Now disputed by historians, see e.g. J. U. Nef, *War and Human Progress* (Cambridge, Mass., 1950).]

its greatest intensity from the middle of the fourteenth to the end of the fifteenth century. France, Burgundy, England, Castile, Portugal, the crown of Aragon, Italy, and Germany were swept along by a swift politico-military whirlwind, in which civil war was often more important than external conflicts. Suffice it to recall the final decades of the fifteenth century, when each state aspired to prevail on the international chessboard with the aid of social and political forces which it was combating on its own soil— whether these were the aristocracy or the middle classes—and which it supported on the soil of its adversaries.[17]

This is why the triumph of the authoritarian monarchy[18] of the Renaissance was always achieved on two planes: externally, by annihilating or reducing a dangerous enemy; internally, by leading one faction in its own civil wars. Hence the fabulous increase in the power of the prince and its justification as a double guarantee to maintain both order within the state and its invulnerability against foreign powers which had developed by a similar process. Both of these were tasks which could be accomplished only by the creation of a permanent army, independent of all feudal ties,[19]

[17] I believe that I have demonstrated this phenomenon in the relations between France, Aragon, Castile, and Naples in *Juan II de Aragón* (Barcelona, 1952).

[18] In order to avoid the adjective *absolute*, which cannot be applied to the monarchy between 1450 and 1550, the exact expression would have been *pre-eminent monarchy* (that is, one which attempts to defend its "pre-eminence" above all, as in the case of Spain under the Catholic monarchs and Charles V), which appears in the documents of the period: see my *Ferran II i la Ciutat de Barcelona* (Barcelona, 1936), Vol. 1. But the relative disuse of this term in the modern world led me, and continues to lead me, to use this terminology, even though I am aware of its possible confusion with modern political authoritarianism, an expression of superabsolutism.

[19] The "army of mercenaries," comparable according to Chabod to the "bureaucracy of mercenaries" of the same period, *loc. cit.*, p. 66, n. 4. The point of view of V. C. Kiernan is also worth mentioning—"Foreign mercenaries and absolute monarchy," *Past and Present*, XI (1957), 66–83—though his theory that mercenary armies were formed to avoid arming the populace seems excessively one-sided. In reality, if the princes wished to count on mercenaries it was to assure their position as victors in the civil war to which we have alluded in the text. The entry of Charles V into Spain in 1522 with an army of 3,000 to 4,000 Germans and 74 cannon, mentioned by Kiernan, was devoted to this purpose and not to that of controlling "the populace".

whose chief aims were to make the ruler's sovereign pre-eminence respected within the territory of his own state and to establish an administrative structure strong enough to assure the financial resources required for the maintenance of that army.

Such were the conditions under which the monarchy of the sixteenth century grew and developed. But though the tendency was the same, the development of each state varied according to circumstances arising out of its previous history, and especially according to whether the autonomous forces described above, were they those of social stratification or of regional structure, had survived to a greater or lesser extent. The concurrence of such factors, added to the contingencies of international politics and the different kinds of opportunities created by the economic expansion of the century, promoted the complexity of the institutional picture and the disparity between the effective sources of power in the various European monarchies. The most widely divergent cases were those of France and Spain, countries which are usually pointed to as the first fruits of the absolute nation state of the Renaissance. While in France progress toward the consolidation of absolutism was accomplished by surmounting internal social and political conflicts, in Spain the unified monarchy of Castile and Aragon received the decisive impulse toward absolutist forms from an external circumstance: the arrival of American treasure. The gold and silver of the Indies was to permit the Spanish monarchs an exceptional freedom of movement in the management of the apparatus of the state, and an unquestioned affirmation of their authoritarian position with the fewest possible obstacles from regional or social groups;[20] but at the same time

---

[20] This fact explains the decline of the Castilian Cortes during the reign of Charles V, especially after 1538, when the crown had more than ample resources to meet its growing financial needs. Previously, the Cortes' position was one of uncompromising resistance: J. Sánchez Montes, "Sobre las Cortes de Toledo de 1538–1539," *Carlos V. Homenaje de la Universidad de Granada*, pp. 595–663, and two [cyclostyled] papers presented to the Third Congress of Intellectual Co-operation [1958]: G. Maura, *Las Cortes Castellanas no compartieron ni secundaron la idea imperial de Carlos V* and J. Martínez Cardós, *Carlos V y las Cortes de Castilla*; references in *Indice Histórico Espanol*, nos. 27661–2.

they were to witness throughout the length and breadth of their possessions the survival of the firmest bases of resistance to the ruler throughout western Europe.

The tendency toward a definitive solution by means of the concentration of power in the hands of the monarch reached a point of crisis in the middle of the seventeenth century. Four chief factors, working in a contradictory but effective manner, contributed to this: economic contraction, which forced a readjustment in the power relationships between the monarch and existing social forces; the dislocation of these same forces following a century of economic expansion and changes in the distribution of landed property and in the social classes who derived revenue from it; the financial sacrifices entailed by the need to equip and modernize armies in accordance with the new tactics arising in the course of the international conflict in which the states were engaged during this period; and the demands of bureaucracies which had arisen as the expression of the new state and now often practiced a policy of containing or distorting the ruler's wishes. The social, administrative and political crisis brought on by the clash of these factors was resolved everywhere in Europe between 1640 and 1660, and its results—there is no reason to be surprised by this—were different in each country.[21] While in England the tendency was toward a limited monarchy, and in France toward functional absolutism, in Spain there was a regression toward the bases of the feudal and regional system. The more modern solutions, the French and English ones, were to prevail eventually, especially in the case of France in the short term, as a result of the example of efficiency presented by her administration. But even so, the true situation of absolute state power in France was very far from being what the apologists of the court of Versailles claimed it to be.

[21] I cannot go into the general discussion of the political and social problem posed by this crisis, as it has been debated recently in England by a group of scholars: "Seventeenth-century Revolution," *Past and Present*, XIII (1958), 62–72. However, we will note in passing the general agreement that the European revolutions of this period were unleashed by the financial pressures caused by military and diplomatic expenditures during the Thirty Years' War.

Army and administration worked together, therefore, to promote the pre-eminence and centralization of royal power as an effective force during the sixteenth and seventeenth centuries. Each act of war brought the need for more men, equipment, supplies, and money in a given place,[22] and especially the need to co-ordinate this process of concentration in order to make it more efficient.[23] Money was needed to recruit specialized personnel, to buy arms and provisions, to supply equipment at the proper time, and to satisfy the continuing needs of military operations. All this exerted pressure on governmental institutions and required an effort by the administrative personnel, all the more so because military mobilization raised many problems of a social, juridical, and political kind. Pursuing this line of thought, we may say that the impulse toward an administrative monarchy of a modern type began in western Europe with the great naval operations undertaken by Charles V against the Turks in the western Mediterranean, beginning in 1535.[24] The threat which the Sublime Porte annually held over this area (the result of various political and social circumstances, but translated into a formidable concentration of offensive power) obliged the imperial chancery to set in motion a complicated and powerful naval and military operation, in which the different kingdoms which [the emperor] governed or controlled took part either directly or indirectly. An armada is an undertaking in which the technical and financial factors handled

[22] The most accurate estimate of the increase in the public debt during the reign of Charles V is given by F. Braudel and G. Bellart, "Les emprunts de Charles-Quint sur la place d'Anvers," Charles-Quint et son temps (Paris, 1959), pp. 191–200. Each international conflict brought about a sharp increase of the imperial debt in Antwerp: from £500,000 to £1,000,000 in 1521; an additional million in 1528–9; from half a million to more than six millions (!) in 1551–5.

[23] R. Mousnier, in his well-known work La Venalité des offices sous Henri IV et Louis XIII (Rouen, 1945), points out the rhythm of the sale of offices in France and the development of the apparatus of the state in relation to expenditure for war. Culminating moments were probably 1532, 1554, 1586, 1597, 1620–2, 1627 and 1633. The relationship of these dates to specific military campaigns is obvious.

[24] F. Braudel informs us that from 1534 to 1575 naval armaments increased at least three times, La Méditerranée . . ., p. 666.

by the administration are more important than the heroic or individualistic action of the Renaissance warrior, who still retained some of the motivation of his predecessor, the medieval knight. The war machine was no longer improvised; it became a regular concern of the administration. It is possible that an investigation in depth would prove the working hypothesis that the development of royal bureaucracies in the countries along the Mediterranean littoral in the middle of the sixteenth century coincided with the culmination of the Ottoman offensive.

During this same period the Spanish monarchy (and we use it as an example to show the scope of its problems, but without forgetting the parallel cases of other colonizing powers, such as Portugal) had been obliged to create an administrative structure for the New World. From the colonization of the West Indies arose a number of problems which are of supreme interest for the evolution we are examining. Perhaps the most important of these was the problem of "just titles," from which were derived not only the right of conquest—a problem of political philosophy— but, concretely, the right to rule over the aborigines.[25] But here we are interested only in analyzing the channels of the process by which the administrative apparatus was expanded and adapted. One aspect of this problem was the transfer of institutions to the New World, which has been taken up by a number of authors from conflicting points of view. It is very possible that there was a transfer from the Mediterranean across the Atlantic, with a direct transplanting of institutions and even methods of colonial administration. This is the thesis of Verlinden.[26] But a subsequent dislocation of functions must also have taken place, so that a different exercise of state power and a distinct administrative structure in the New World went under the same name [as in

[25] See C. Verlinden's recent contribution, "Pax Hispánica en la América colonial," *Historia* (Buenos Aires), IV (1958), which does not supersede the fundamental work by S. A. Zavala, *Las instituciones jurídicas en la conquista de América* (Madrid, 1935).
[26] The work which summarizes Verlinden's thesis is *Précédents médiévaux de la colonie en Amérique. Période coloniale* (Mexico, 1954).

Spain]. This seems to have been so in the case of the viceroyships.[27] Another aspect was the presence of new administrative institutions which arose from the contingencies of the government, conquest, and exploitation of the New World. And still another was the behavior of the colonial bureaucracy, at a great distance from the centres of princely power and consequently with a tendency to develop new characteristics—especially in the sphere of independent judgement and ease of movement—whose influence on the mother country is very probable.

This dual phenomenon—a military crossroads in the Mediterranean and colonial expansion across the Atlantic—places the Spanish monarchy in the very centre of interest for those who are studying the development of modern bureaucracy. We find ourselves in fact in the presence of a great political body subject to formidable internal contradictions: one of them, as we have said, was the contradiction between the monarchy, apparently omnipotent, and the regional and local powers, in large part alive and active; another was the profound contrast between a regional bureaucracy deeply rooted in the old formulas and resisting all attack from the early years of the sixteenth century onwards (as in the case of the duchy of Milan[28]) and the new bureaucracy, detached from any contact with medieval political institutions because it had arisen by decree of the ruler in exotic American places. The interminable conflicts between the different concepts of effective state power in the Spanish monarchy should shed light on many unknown aspects of the formation of the attitudes of modern bureaucracies.

It seems to us that one of the most important aspects to be

---

[27] There is still no study defining the link between the institutions of viceroy of the crown of Aragon in the Mediterranean and those of the same type in America, nor is there a study comparing the functioning of the Spanish viceroyships in America and Europe during the sixteenth and seventeenth centuries. We do not find very convincing the opinion of S. Radaelli, *La institución virreinal en las Indias* (Buenos Aires, 1957), which denies all resemblance, except for the name, between the American viceroyship and the European one.

[28] C. Santoro, *Gli uffici del dominio sforzesco (1450–1500)* (Milan, 1948).

investigated is the differing process of formation and the diversity in development in the structural model of the Spanish and French states in the sixteenth and seventeenth centuries. As predominant types of the administrative apparatus of authoritarian monarchy— each essentially different from the other—their comparison presents an interesting set of problems.

The root of both administrative structures is to be found in the same feudal principle of a council which was at once the monarch's advisory body and a high court of justice. Central institutions appeared in a confused and embryonic form, linked to important personages in the household (especially in the chancery), while provincial administration began timidly, as a product of two spheres of interest: the maintenance of public order and the administration of the royal treasury. This unifying seed of the apparatus of the state reached a maturity favorable to germination, in France as well as Castile, about the middle of the fifteenth century; in France after the Hundred Years' War, in Spain as a result of the conflict for authority between the monarchy and the nobility at the time of John II's favourite, Alvaro de Luna. The expansionist policies of both monarchies at the end of the fifteenth century, directed toward a single objective, predominance in Italy, resulted in the rapid development of modern administration: the central agencies became specialized, while the provincial ones displayed a greater subordination to the monarch's directives. In France four great areas of specialization appeared within the single body of the Royal Council: the Council of State, the Council of Finance, the Privy Council, and the Council for Foreign Correspondence; four distinct versions of the same kind of institution:[29] In Castile the process was the same, with the appearance of the Councils of the Royal Chamber, the Military Orders, the Inquisition, the Crusade, and Finance; but in this case it was both adulterated and masked by the sudden addition of two new factors at the very outset of the united Spanish monarchy: the administrative procedures of the crown of Aragon and the

[29] Mousnier, op. cit., pp. 79 ff.; J. Ellul, Histoire des institutions, Pt. II, Institutions françaises, Vol. I (Paris, 1956), pp. 297–8.

methods of government necessary to meet the problems of expansion across the Atlantic. This dual circumstance resulted in very different orientations of the machinery of state in Spain and in France; it was more precocious in Spain in solving the general problems of empire, more effective in France for internal matters.

The crown of Aragon contributed both plurality of institutions and the separate rule of many territories as administrative principles. Subjected to the pressures of a triple administration in the Iberian realms of Aragon, Catalonia, and Valencia, and to the need of a government for its separate Mediterranean possessions [in Italy], it overcame them by adopting more or less new and original administrative principles. Without going into administrative details, we may say that these principles were in any case unique in so far as they functioned within a single political community. Three of these are worth noting: affirmation of the principle that the bureaucracy was independent of the old royal household; the coexistence of central organs of administration with private spheres of government in defined territorial areas; and the presence of high officials to whom royal power was delegated. This creative process developed throughout the fifteenth century, and its most important stages were the formation of the Catalan chancery in 1424, the development of judicial *Audiencias* [supreme courts], and the creation of viceroyships, lieutenancies, and captaincies-general in the Mediterranean possessions.[30]

These principles, incorporated by Ferdinand the Catholic into the old Castilian unitary tradition, were reflected in the series of councils established by him and his wife to govern the Spanish monarchy, a clear case of multiplicity of councils, as well as in the system devised for the administration of the newly discovered West Indies. The most significant moment was the creation of the Council of Aragon (1494), reflecting the admission of the plural principle into the upper levels of the administration of the state. This circumstance forced the conversion of the old Castilian royal

[30] There is no modern bibliography on this subject. The study by Lalinde, to which we referred in note 13, is unpublished; our remarks are based on his information and on our own research.

Council into the Council of Castile (reorganized in 1480) and the improvisation of a Council of State, a consultative organ of the monarch for common matters, especially foreign policy and war. Almost at the same time, and by virtue of the Capitulations of Santa Fe in 1492, the principle of administration through viceroys and captains-general, and even through *Audiencias* of justice and government (1511), was accepted for America.[31]

After the establishment of this principle no important changes took place until the third decade of the sixteenth century, when the Spanish monarchy was confronted with the twofold problem of war with France and the enormous expansion of its conquests in Mexico, really the single problem of supporting the European war with American treasure.[32] This was the moment of the creation of the Council of the Indies,[33] which was separated from the Council of Castile in 1519, but did not receive legal recognition until 1524. This was a further development of the system of many councils, but went beyond it in administrative functions, as the Council of the Indies was granted very broad powers, among which were the right to act as a court of appeal, to propose appointments of bishops and officials, to organize the fleet and the discoveries in the New World, [and to control] colonial finance, legislation for the Indians, etc. It was also the council which received reports from America and despatched the appropriate decisions on general policy. When the office of viceroy was reestablished in the Indies (1535), the links in the chain of upper colonial administration were firmly riveted.

[31] A good summary of the classic studies, such as those by C. H. Haring, "El origen del gobierno real en las Indias espanolas," *Boletín del Instituto de Investigaciones Históricas* (Buenos Aires), III (1924–5), and L. E. Fisher, *Viceregal Administration in the Spanish-American Colonies* (Berkeley, 1926), will be found in J. M. Ots, *Manual de Historia del Derecho Español en Indias* (Buenos Aires, 1945), and in C. H. Haring, *The Spanish Empire in America* (New York, 1947).

[32] This relationship is brought out in the article by A. Rumeu de Armas, "Franceses y españoles en al Atlántico en tiempos del Emperador," *Charles-Quint et son temps*, pp. 61–75. For the general problem, see R. Carande, *Carlos V y sus banqueros*, 2 vols. (Madrid, 1943–9).

[33] E. Schäfer, *El Consejo Real y Supremo de las Indias*, Spanish trans. in 2 vols. (Seville, 1935–47).

The obvious imperial purpose which underlay the activities of the Council of the Indies had no equivalent in the ensemble of European states ruled by Charles V.[34] It became necessary to retreat from the imperial ideal of a Caesar to the more modest but viable dimensions of a Spanish hegemony, before the first administrative apparatus of an imperial kind since the days of Rome could appear in Europe. This is the opinion of Koenigsberger when he refers to the creation of the Council of Italy (1555-8),[35] which he considers to have been the chief advance of the century in the field of administrative technique. Separated from the Council of Aragon to make it more effective,[36] the Council of Italy supervised financial, mercantile, customs, civil and military administration, and superintended the actions of the viceroys and governors of Sicily, Naples, and Milan. Only high-level policy escaped it, being reserved for the king and the Council of State. It is very possible that the experience gained in the working of the Council of the Indies had an influence on the foundation of the Council of Italy; it is also possible that there was a reciprocal effect: in 1569 the Council of the Indies was reorganized as the supreme authority in the government and the administration of justice in America.

The final stage of conciliar development in the Spanish monarchy occupied the last two decades of the sixteenth century: new territorial councils were created for Flanders in 1588 and Portugal in 1580 and a specialized Council for Finance in 1593. Their foundation is explained by the international conflict in which Spain was engaged under Philip II, with its war, diplomacy, and financial crisis. But by these crucial years the system of many councils was showing signs of exhaustion. The dispersion of

[34] The debate on whether Charles V's imperialism was the result of humanist, Castilian, or Flemish influence was considerably advanced on the occasion of the commemoration of the quater-centenary of his death. A summary of the opposing views is given in the articles signed by R. Menéndez Pidal and J. Vicens Vives in *Charles-Quint et son temps*, but the articles by F. Braudel, P. Rassow, R. Konetzke, and R. Clavería, among others, should also be noted.

[35] *The Government of Sicily under Philip II of Spain* (London, 1951), p. 72.

[36] Rather than from a desire to break the unity of the territorial empire of the crown of Aragon in the Mediterranean, as suggested by Batista i Roca in the introduction to *The Government of Sicily under Philip II of Spain*, pp. 21-2.

governmental tasks resulted in administrative inefficiency, in delays which piled up mountains of paper; confusion over the responsibilities of the various councils delayed the expedition of business and diluted responsibility at critical moments. The mediocrity and conservatism of the councillors, the majority of them holders of law degrees, perhaps assured the impartiality of judicial decisions,[37] but it also impeded the establishment of a modern administrative system. Thus the Spanish pattern of many councils remained as a balancing system between semi-autonomous, if not antagonistic, forces, and all the remedies applied by the monarchy after the beginning of the seventeenth century to cure its anachronistic lethargy were doomed to failure: the introduction of more manageable members into the councils, e.g. councillors "of robe and sword," that is, nobles, in 1603; the growth in the role of the secretaries of state, achieved through the system of *consultas* [reports, usually written, from the councils to the king]; and finally, the supreme and dangerous recourse to an overall, omnipotent minister, the confidant or favourite. . . .

Many doubts about the validity of any structural model for the evolution of European absolute monarchy from the sixteenth to the seventeenth century . . . arise if we consider the human element, the bureaucrat, of whom there were so many in the administrative channels we have described. The broad sweep of administrative history is governed by monarchies, advisory bodies, the great officials of the crown, and representative institutions; its trivial details are made up of the narrative accounts and the day by day records of all these; straightforward administrative history is the attitude, the temperament, or the outlook—call it what you will—of the administrative officer toward the exercise of his office. By following this last and difficult line of investigation we come to the whole problem of the nascent state bureaucracy, to which several well-known scholars have dedicated valuable studies in recent years.[38] Given the importance of this task and the

[37] *Ibid.*, p. 68.
[38] Besides Mousnier's studies, already cited, we must mention those of F. Chabod, "Stipendi nominali e busta paga effettiva dei funzionari dell'

repeated requests for collective and simultaneous studies in this area, it seems appropriate for us to present to the Congress the discussion of the following working hypotheses.

The difficulty of the medieval official in adapting to the role of the modern civil servant

More than a working hypothesis, this seems to be a fundamental conclusion reached by recent historiography. While the monarchical state was developing new forms of administration to cope with the pressure of the economic, social, and military circumstances which encompassed it in the sixteenth and seventeenth centuries, the majority of the people who held offices preserved an almost totally medieval outlook. Certainly the authors of treatises had been speaking of "public office" since early in the seventeenth century, but those using the term understood by it a personal advantage of a hereditary kind. This derived, according to Mousnier,[39] from the fact that the monarch himself continued to think of the state as his patrimony, in spite of the fact that the theoreticians pointed to his role as usufructuary and administrator; when he granted an office, a part of his property was detached and passed into the possession of the beneficiary. Perhaps even more intense was the survival of feudal practice, which impregnated administration in the first centuries of the modern centralized state. This is Chabod's thesis of office as a pension granted by the sovereign.[40] Ownership of an office, and the office as a patent of juridical monopoly and an instrument of plunder[41]

---

amministrazione milanese alla fine del Cinquecento," *Miscellanea in onore di Roberto Cessi* (Rome, 1958), Vol. II, pp. 188–363; "Usi e abusi nell' amministrazione dello Stato di Milano a mezzo il '500," *Studi Storici in onore di Gioacchino Volpe* (Florence, 1958), pp. 95–154; and in the now classic studies of K. W. Swart, *Sale of Offices in the Seventeenth Century* (The Hague, 1949), and J. H. Parry, *The Sale of Public Offices in the Spanish Indies under the Hapsburgs* (Berkeley, 1953).   [39] *Op. cit.*, p. xxviii.
[40] "Stipendi . . . e busta paga . . .," *loc. cit.*, pp. 251–3.
[41] This definition can be found in J. van Klaveren, "Die historische Erscheinung der Korruption, in ihrem Zusammenhang mit der Staats- und Gesellschaftsstruktur betrachtet," *Vierteljahrschrift für Sozial- und Wirtschaftsgeschichte*, XLIV (1957) and XLV (1958).

are two principles opposed to the very essence of modern bureaucracy. And yet without them we could understand nothing about the administrative machinery of the sixteenth and seventeenth centuries, especially about the forms of venality we shall discuss below.

The middle class as the source of administrative personnel

According to one theory the bureaucracy of the sixteenth and seventeenth centuries was recruited from among the middle class and was a class instrument which supported authoritarian or absolute monarchy against the nobility.[42] It is possible that this was the case in countries which underwent a real economic expansion, such as France. Given the large increase in the number of posts in the administration of the state, it is very logical that the monarchy should have looked for specialized and competent personnel on the one hand, and for persons who would be politically and socially loyal on the other. The middle class fulfilled both of these requirements. Moreover, through the system of purchase of offices, the middle class was irresistibly attracted towards the administration as a means of meeting the financial requirements of the state. Because of its education, its social attitude, and its money, the middle class must have carried the weight of the bureaucratic transformation of the feudal state toward modernity. But the historical realities allow us to uncover problems which do not conform exactly to these assumptions. In the first place, it would be necessary to define what type of middle class is being referred to; to consider whether it was not, in fact, a question of an already well-developed urban middle class whose chief aspiration was to become absorbed into the aristocracy of blood or landed inheritance. In this case the sense of privilege and pre-eminence arising out of the feudal world would permeate the administration, giving it the feudal cast mentioned before. It

---

[42] This is the thesis of B. F. Porchnev, *Die Volksaufstände in Frankreich vor der Fronde* (Leipzig, 1954), contested by R. Mousnier, "Recherches sur les soulèvements populaires en France avant la Fronde," *Revue d'Histoire Moderne et Contemporaine*, IV (1958), 81–113.

is very possible that the members of the middle class who rose to offices and became identified with them may have been previously assimilated to the noble class, at least in their outlook on life. It would be interesting to make a sociological investigation of this in several countries. The results of such studies as have been made to date seem to show that the middle class, as a source of bureaucratic personnel, did not have the revolutionary strength which is attributed to it. Detailed examination of the great crisis of the state in western European countries between 1640 and 1660 suggests that the administrative personnel of middle-class origin prudently limited themselves to serving the reactionary cause of the great aristocratic proprietors.[43]

It is very possible that this statement may have different connotations depending on the country we are talking about. . . . In the Mediterranean peninsulas and especially in Spain, even in the most mercantile and industrial regions, the aspiration of the rich burgher was to make his children members of the noble class through the purchase of property and the acquisition of public office. On the other hand Braudel[44] has shown that in Castile public officials were largely recruited from among the poor and the semi-proletariat. Was not the mental attitude of this sort of official very different from that of a man who had emerged from the French middle class? Even so, both men would have had to uproot themselves from the social group out of which they had arisen.

We should like to summarize our thought briefly here. In states with a strong medieval tradition, the administrative personnel of middle-class origin tended to enter the noble class quite quickly by means of their office, and to maintain the privileged positions of the feudal or pre-eminent oligarchies, including their own; in those where the evolution was more

---

[43] In the English colloquium published by *Past and Present*, XIII (1958), the theory of Mousnier was accepted: that the French public official, confronted with the Fronde, was faced with the dilemma of whether to return to the feudal system, or to fight on behalf of absolute monarchy. Both solutions were equally repugnant to him.

[44] *Op. cit.*, pp. 526–7.

modern, the official was able to aspire to other things, especially if he had the support of the social structure of the new "manufacturing" middle class. In any case, throughout the seventeenth century a process of refeudalization was going on in Europe, in which the aristocratic classes took advantage of the administrative mechanism established by the authoritarian monarchy of the sixteenth century and tried to recover a leading role within the state; and for this purpose they must have counted on the complicity of the bureaucracy of middle-class origin. This seems to us to be the case with Spain; did the same thing happen in other countries?

The difficulties of recruiting competent administrative personnel

Koenigsberger points out that the great problem of administration for the Spanish monarchy during the second half of the sixteenth century was the difficulty of finding honest and capable officials. The cause of the mediocrity of councillors and officials is to be found, according to him, in the small number of university graduates.[45] This subject should be discussed and studied in depth by a team of researchers. However, there appears to be no doubt as to the incompetence of the bureaucrat in the exercise of most of the posts of the period, even the highest ones. Qualification for office was obtained with an academic degree, but all the more easily if a man could count on good patronage or ample funds, either his own or his family's. This is the conclusion that can be drawn from Chabod's detailed study of the Milanese bureaucracy of the sixteenth and seventeenth centuries.[46] In this case there is no proof of middle-class pressure from below to convert the bureaucracy into the mouthpiece for their class interests, as in the nineteenth century, or of the monarchy's interest in encouraging recruitment of specialized personnel to defend its interests. Often the burgher with academic qualifications was more of a hindrance than an effective aid [to government].[47]

---

[45] Op. cit., pp. 70, 91.
[46] "Usi e abusi . . .," loc. cit., pp. 145 ff.
[47] As in the case of opposition by the degree-holding councillors of the Council of Aragon to the absolutist policy of Charles II in Spain.

Material gain as the chief incentive of administrative office

In principle, an office was desired in the sixteenth and seventeenth centuries for the "dignity" that went with it. By dignity I mean status and privilege, a portion of power synthesized in an attitude toward life. In certain cases and certain countries the tendency toward status and hierarchization, transplanted into the practical administrative sphere, was to constitute a hindrance to the normal functioning of the apparatus of state; this is what happened, for example, in Spain.[48] But everywhere the civil servant aspired to a higher style of life as an outward reflection of his position.[49] This fact very obviously impinged on the bureaucrat's attitude toward the adequate profitability of public office.

In principle, the acceptance of an office in the feudal world was an integral part of the homage owed by the vassal to the lord. During the sixteenth century we can still find cases where this sentiment prevailed;[50] we can even say that the civil servant had to be faithful primarily to the monarch rather than to the public weal. But this attitude of mind was gradually disappearing by the end of the sixteenth century, and in the following century the theory generally prevailed that the loyalty and integrity of the official was measured by the "just salary" he received from the prince. Chabod has demonstrated this by collating the doctrines of a Spanish moralist and an Italian moralist of the period, Luis de Molina and Giacomo Menochio, who published their works in the last decade of the sixteenth century.[51] The demand for a "just salary" is related, of course, to the price revolution of the sixteenth century and the drop in real wages until about 1600, but it also possibly indicates the separation of the administrative function from the old feudal concept of loyalty, and the appearance on the

[48] Disputes over status, for example the discussion over precedence in seating arrangements at council meetings, sufficed to paralyze its proceedings for months (information by courtesy of E. Asensio).

[49] Chabod, "Stipendi . . . e busta paga . . .," *loc. cit.*, p. 210.

[50] Chabod, "Usi e abusi . . .," *loc. cit.*, p. 181.

[51] Chabod, "Stipendi . . . e busta paga . . .," *loc. cit'*, pp. 205–9.

scene of the mechanization of the relations between the state and its employees. Discussion on this point is still open.

Corruption can be considered as a system imposed by the need to correct the deficiencies of an outworn administrative machinery

The abuses of medieval officials passed over in large measure to the bureaucrats of the authoritarian-absolutist state of the sixteenth and seventeenth centuries. It is possible that abuses increased rapidly during periods of acute monetary changes, as was the case during the inflations of the third and sixth decades of the sixteenth century, but any firm conclusion on this point would be most premature if made today. We should probably limit ourselves to accepting the criterion that in the sixteenth century the abuses of the feudal official continued, and that by the end of that century corruption had begun to develop as an administrative system, as a result of the crisis produced by the abrupt decline in the purchasing power of money. . . . Perhaps this distinction between abuses and corruption could be challenged. The official who, in addition to the emoluments traditionally associated with his office, accepted a gift or took money to pervert the course of justice or speed up its action to the detriment of a third person, simultaneously committed an abuse and an act of corruption. But we have to fall back on established terms to designate two different bureaucratic attitudes of mind: that of the official who occasionally stepped outside his moral limits, in an individual and isolated action, and that of the administrative service which ordinarily functioned according to the principle of corruption. The second half of the sixteenth century formed a rough dividing line between abuse in medieval administration and corruption in modern administration, "fraud elevated into a system."[52]

Recently van Klaveren has proposed certain theories about corruption and has tried to systematize its origins and development. His theories are interesting, especially when he tries to generalize about its historical development. His chief contention is that there was a struggle for the distribution of certain sources

[52] Van Klaveren, *loc. cit.*, p. 294.

of national revenue between the monarch, the bureaucracy, and the oligarchy. Lack of authority in the state or the least variation in the standing of the officials led the oligarchs—the pressure groups—to exercise their corrupting function. The oligarchy, obviously, could be composed of the intermediate classes mentioned by van Klaveren—evidently referring to the middle class—or of the upper aristocratic classes firmly established on the fringes of state power. In any case, oligarchs and officials both acted in a single upward thrust and were closely linked, although the nobles operated on their own level and the officials vertically [via the hierarchical channels of the bureaucracy]. In the distribution of the fruits of the system, the same division can be observed: horizontal and equitable among the members of the pressure group; vertical and selective among the bureaucracy. This produced an important division between the upper and lower levels of administration and aroused jealousies in the lower ranks, with the inevitable result that there were frequent upheavals in the functioning of the system: the fall of influential persons, administrative purges, and the like.[53]

These working hypotheses can be accepted. They lead us to restate our own in the form that corruption occurs when a government tries to control an important economic development with a closed and archaic type of legislation. This was the situation of the Spanish crown when economic expansion in the American colonies completely burst through the monopolistic limits and the instruments of action which it had created during the first half of the sixteenth century. The fact that during the sixteenth and seventeenth centuries Spain was the epicentre of corruption[54] cannot be completely explained by any propensity of the Castilian administrator toward moral relativism. The saying that if the king did not provide for his servants it was "licit for them to use other means," though written in Spanish, is by an Italian.[55] If corruption

---

[53] Ibid., esp. pp. 299 ff.
[54] Haring, The Spanish Empire in America, pp. 143–65, 298; Swart, Sale of Offices . . ., p. 35.
[55] The Milanese secretary Maona: Chabod, "Usi e abusi . . .," loc. cit., p. 137.

became deeply rooted in Spain it was because, despite the moralizing attitude of the crown and its repeated declarations against any sort of corrupt practice, the bureaucracy had to make the mechanism of American trade work *in spite of the laws*. This is the logical foundation for the "fraud psychosis" described by Chaunu and his wife in their research on American trade, a psychosis which was active from the end of the sixteenth century, unleashing chain reactions of administrative corruption.[56] The stakes were so enormous that it is understandable that a vast governmental apparatus succumbed to the temptation. When Holland and England encountered the same problem in the seventeenth century, they lapsed into the same system of administrative corruption.

Venality of offices a defense against corruption?

The conditions required by the state throughout the sixteenth century for correctly discharging an office were, in accordance with oft-repeated regulations: fitness, qualifications, personal and direct service, and efficiency in fulfilling that service.[57] This result was almost never achieved, and its failure was attributed primarily to the sale of offices, considered as the cause of evasion of duty. This has led historians to admit a fateful parallelism between venality and corruption and between venality and administrative disorganization. This was the thesis upheld by Martin Göhring in 1938 and by Koenraad W. Swart in 1949.[58]

The most recent studies have cast doubt on this thesis. In the first place, the purchase, hereditary transfer, and leasing of a public office are not phenomena which appear with the modern

[56] H. and P. Chaunu, *Séville et l'Atlantique (1504–1560)*, Vol. I, *Introduction méthodologique* (Paris, 1955), pp. 97 ff., esp. p. 121.

[57] Edicts of Charles V in 1538 and 1545: Chabod, "Usi e abusi . . .," *loc. cit.*, p. 108.

[58] *Die Ämterkäuflichkeit im Ancien Régime* (Berlin, 1938), and *Sale of Offices*. Swart strongly condemns venality, which he attributes to the exclusion of the middle class from state power, the financial ruin of the state, and the country's economic deterioration as a result of the application of revenues to "unproductive goods," and condemns this as a "primitive form of administration" (p. 123).

state, but, like the patrimonial concept of the monarchy from which such practices arose, have their origin in the feudal concept of public power. Mousnier has provided the relevant information in his well-known dissertation on the venality of offices in France.[59] From the time that modern administrations were established, princes desired to end the sale of offices and the resultant corrupt practices. But successive military situations and the corresponding pressures on the public exchequer resulted in the abandonment of this fundamental standard in the course of the sixteenth century. Then two solutions presented themselves: either to recognize and legalize the sale of offices—as was done in France from 1532 to 1604—or to ignore it officially, though tolerating it in private for certain or all administrative groups—as in the case of Spain, whose financial straits were less severe because she could count on the flow of American silver. If we compare the results of both administrative systems in the seventeenth century, not only does it turn out that the French system was able to check corruption, but France also had better results in the suitability, selection, and relative integrity of the bureaucracy.[60]

Van Klaveren's theory on this point states that in every country where venality did not exist corruption increased.[61] This working hypothesis deserves our attention, even though we do not consider that it is absolutely conclusive, for it could very easily have happened that corruption occurred as a result of defects in administrative organization, structural differences in society, and the greater attraction of material benefits, and not from any greater or lesser control of public offices by the monarchy by means of a venal system and its power of command over the administration.[62]

---

[59] Op. cit., pp. 1–12.   [60] Ellul, op. cit., p. 328.   [61] Loc. cit., p. 323.

[62] In the case of Spain, it appears that because of the country's scant financial resources venality did not take root. Apart from the practice of renunciation, which affected municipal offices, which were very much sought after in the sixteenth century, it seems that the sales of public offices made at moments of greatest financial strain, in 1557, 1619, and 1621–40, were not very successful. During this last period even the post of councillor of the Council of Castile was sold, something which had never happened before. In his Sale of Offices, Swart states (p. 32) that the population did not respond to this attempt by the govern-

We should also keep another factor in mind, this time directly related to venality and therefore favourable to van Klaveren's hypothesis: the devaluation of the salaries of public officials was compensated for in the venal system[63] but blissfully ignored in the semi-venal system,[64] by means of an immediate response in the ingenious efforts of both upper and lower officials to balance their budgets behind the back of the state, and to its disadvantage.

---

ment: from 1621 to 1641 only 90,000,000 ducats' worth were sold out of the 509,000,000 offered. These figures should be examined more fully in relation to the social and economic situation of Spain in the seventeenth century.

[63] Mousnier, *op. cit.*, p. 390. The continued price rise in the sale of offices from 1593 to 1622 can be attributed to the guarantee given to the market through the establishment of the *paulette* [in 1604, which confirmed hereditary succession to offices].

[64] As in the case of the duchy of Milan, where officials' salaries were further complicated by the practice of accounting in two currencies: Chabod, "Stipendi . . . e busta paga . . .," *loc. cit.*, pp. 211. 230 ff.

PART TWO

The Impact
of the Reformation

3 The Concordat of 1516:
A Reassessment

R. J. KNECHT

A. F. POLLARD believed that the Henrician Reformation was a "natural and inevitable" result of "the rising national spirit," which could not tolerate an allegiance divided between king and pope.[1] If he was right, then one may ask why it was that the Reformation did not also succeed in France, where "the rising national spirit" was no less lively. France was without question the most anti-papal country in Christendom, yet for some reason she chose to remain within the Roman allegiance. By summoning parliament, Henry VIII "opened the floodgates of anti-papal and anti-sacerdotal feelings."[2] What was it that induced Francis I to keep the floodgates shut in France?

The answer usually given is that the king of France never needed to break with Rome because of the Concordat which he signed with the pope in 1516. This, it is alleged, gave him full control of the French church. "By the first article of the agreement, the king received the substantial right to nominate archbishops, bishops and abbés in his kingdom, in all some 620 preferments. With this arrangement the earlier gallicanism, or rather independence, of the Church of France, which derived from its conciliar character, gave way to a royal gallicanism. At a stroke, the monarchy imposed its solution of the problem of *regnum et sacerdotium*."[3] Francis I, it has been suggested, gained so much from the Concordat, that he could not have wished for more: "Il donnait au souverain de France un tel pouvoir sur son Église qu'il n'avait

[1] A. F. Pollard, *Henry VIII* (London, 1913), pp. 227, 268.
[2] *Ibid.*, p. 251.
[3] *The New Cambridge Modern History*, Vol. II, *The Reformation, 1520–1559*, ed. G. R. Elton (Cambridge, 1958), p. 211.

guère à désirer plus."[4] By giving so much power to the king of France, the Concordat, it is said, destroyed all the inducements which led other rulers to throw off the papal yoke. "With so much gained there was no reason why the French king, unlike the English and Swedish monarchs, should ally with the reformers against the Church."[5] This interpretation of the Concordat seems all the more plausible when one remembers that it was signed soon after Francis I had won a great military victory. "It was the greatest French gain from the battle of Marignano. . . ."[6]

Convincing as the traditional view of the Concordat may appear, it does leave certain questions unanswered. State control of the church was not necessarily a safeguard against schism. The English kings controlled episcopal appointments long before the Reformation, yet this did not prevent the breach with Rome.[7] In Germany, as Jedin has shown, secular intervention in church affairs had the effect of assisting the Reformation.[8] Secondly, there is evidence that the French crown enjoyed a large measure of control over the church in France before 1516, so that the Concordat cannot be said to have destroyed its "independence." Thirdly, no one could go so far as to suggest that Francis I obtained as much theoretical authority or material benefit from the Concordat as Henry VIII did from his breach with Rome: he did not become "supreme head of the church," he was not given a free hand to confiscate ecclesiastical wealth. Some of the most important temptations of schism, therefore, remained. Lastly, it is necessary to explain why contemporaries regarded the Concordat, not as a triumph for the monarchy, but as a capitulation to the Holy See. Far from being similar to the Henrician programme, the Concordat acknowledged papal supremacy, and restored annates and appeals to Rome, which had been respectively abolished and curtailed by the Pragmatic Sanction of Bourges in

---

[4] V. L. Tapié, *La France de Louis XIII et de Richelieu* (Paris, 1952), p. 35.
[5] V. H. H. Green, *Renaissance and Reformation* (London, 1952), p. 84.
[6] A. J. Grant, *A History of Europe from 1494 to 1610* (London, 1948), p. 75.
[7] R. J. Knecht, "The Episcopate and the Wars of the Roses," *University of Birmingham Historical Journal*, VI (1958), *passim*.
[8] H. Jedin, *A History of the Council of Trent*, Vol. I (London, 1957), p. 153.

1438. Because of this, it was strongly resisted by Gallican bodies in France, notably by the *parlement* and the University of Paris. There are enough reasons for thinking that the claims which have been made for the Concordat have been greatly exaggerated. If so, another reason will have to be found for the decision of the French monarchy to remain loyal to Rome.

1

The notion that the Concordat of 1516 destroyed the independence of the Gallican church and placed it under royal control rests on a simplified view of what really took place. The crown already had an extensive control of the church before 1516; the Concordat merely extended this control within theoretical limits.

From 1438 until 1516 the church in France was governed in theory according to the Pragmatic Sanction of Bourges, which embodied twenty-four of the decrees of the Council of Basle.[9] In particular, it restored to chapters the right of electing bishops and abbots, in an attempt to remedy the confusion that existed in the system of appointing to benefices. But the Sanction could not be applied completely, for the church lacked the cohesion necessary to withstand external pressures. Within a short time electoral freedom succumbed to force and bribery. Frequent disputes arose and lawsuits flooded into the *parlement* of Paris. The church displayed "an excess of personal or collective selfishness, a state of universal and permanent war."[10]

In such circumstances it was not difficult for the monarchy, whenever it was strong, to determine the outcome of ecclesiastical elections. From 1471 onwards Louis XI freely appointed to bishoprics and abbeys. More than thirty bishops were nominated by him for the choice of chapters, or imposed if these resisted, and instituted by the pope. In effect, the elective system set up by the

[9] N. Valois, *Histoire de la Sanction Pragmatique de Bourges sous Charles VII* (Paris, 1906).
[10] P. Imbart de la Tour, *Les Origines de la Réforme* (2nd edn., Melun, 1946), Vol. II, p. 211.

Pragmatic Sanction no longer existed. "At least since Louis XI and Sixtus IV, the monarchy in France had effective control of elections. . . ."[11] The Estates General of 1484 demanded that the Sanction should be properly applied, but the government would not listen—nor would prelates like Hélie de Bourdeilles, archbishop of Tours, who owed their sees to royal patronage.[12] By 1515, when Francis I came to the throne, royal control of the ecclesiastical hierarchy was an accepted fact. He showed this in his dealings with Maximilian Sforza, duke of Milan: "And if the brother of the said Maximilian wishes to become a cleric, the said lord [king] will obtain benefices for him in a manner befitting his rank."[13] Mondot de la Marthonie, first president of the *parlement* of Paris, acknowledged the king's control of appointments, in March 1515, when he asked: "that it please the king to provide men of worthy life and sufficient years to bishoprics, archbishoprics and prelacies, and likewise good persons of religion to the abbeys and monasteries of his kingdom and territories."[14] Equally significant was Chancellor Duprat's reply that "no bishoprics, archbishoprics and prelacies have fallen vacant since his accession and, if any vacancies do occur, he hopes to fill them with worthy persons, and the abbeys likewise."[15]

Royal control of the French church before 1516 was not confined to episcopal or monastic elections. The *régale*, the king's right to a bishop's inheritance including the right of presenting to benefices, was already established in the fourteenth century. During the fifteenth century various legal subtleties were invoked to extend the *régale* beyond the strict limits of an episcopal vacancy. It was made to last as long as a bishop had not taken his oath of fealty and homage to the king and received his temporalities. The *régale* was also applied to all territories which had been under

[11] G. Loirette, "La première application à Bordeaux du Concordat de 1516," *Annales du Midi*, LXVIII (1956), 319.

[12] A. Renaudet, *Préréforme et humanisme à Paris pendant les premières guerres d'Italie (1494–1517)* (Paris, 1953), p. 5.

[13] *Journal de Jean Barillon*, ed. P. de Vaissière (Paris, 1897), Vol. I, p. 89.

[14] Renaudet, *Préréforme et humanisme . . .*, p. 578.

[15] *Ibid.*

English occupation: that is to say, the Île-de-France and Champagne till 1436, Normandy till 1449 and Guyenne till 1451. All appointments made by bishops and abbots during the English occupation were declared null and void. The frequent deaths or translations of prelates under Louis XI meant that most churches passed under royal control. There was no diocese where the king did not claim the right to appoint to benefices. Between 1468 and 1471 Louis XI appointed *en régale* to most of the archdeaconries of Paris, Sens, Orléans, Laon, Rouen, Chartres, Thérouanne, Bayeux, Meaux and Beauvais. He also disposed of canonries and prebends in the cathedral chapters.[16]

All this is not to suggest that royal control of ecclesiastical appointments was accepted without resistance. The Poitiers election of 1507, in which violence broke out between supporters of the royal candidate, Claude de Tonnerre, and those of his rival, Florent d'Allemagne, was not untypical.[17] Under Louis XII there were disputed elections at Arras, Rodez, Soissons, Vienne, Aleth, Tarbes, Angoulême, Comminges, Pamiers and Limoges.[18] Royal collations also provoked frequent quarrels and an enormous amount of litigation. The king's nominees were always challenging ancient rights and trying to dispossess the existing holders of benefices. In the diocese of Noyon appointments dating back to the English occupation were still being disputed in 1464. Louis XII's attempt to check the amount of litigation by forbidding the *régale* to be taken back more than thirty years had little effect.[19]

The condition of the French church was chaotic by the end of the fifteenth century; but amidst all the confusion the crown enjoyed a substantial measure of control over all ranks of the clergy. The Concordat cannot, therefore, be wholly blamed for the appointment of "men of high rank and infrequent vocation whom the king wished to reward."[20] Ex-courtiers, soldiers and diplomats were being given bishoprics and abbeys, often in plurality, long before. The list of cardinals who held the post of

[16] Imbart de la Tour, *op. cit.*, Vol. II, pp. 233–4.
[17] *Ibid.*, Vol. II, pp. 222–3.   [18] *Ibid.*, Vol. II, p. 230.
[19] *Ibid.*, Vol. II, p. 234.   [20] Green, *op. cit.*, p. 84.

first minister did not begin in 1516; it went back to the fifteenth century and included the names of La Balue, Briçonnet and Amboise.

However, it would be wrong to imply that the Concordat did nothing to increase the crown's control of the church. By discarding the elective principle to a large extent and by conferring on the king the right to nominate to most benefices, it certainly helped to strengthen his hand. Whereas before he had often had to take the unpopular step of disregarding the Pragmatic Sanction, he could henceforth do so without feeling any legal inhibitions. But the Concordat did not give him an unlimited power of nomination. The pope reserved to himself the right of instituting the king's nominees and of setting aside those whose qualifications fell short of the canonical requirements. He also kept the right of nominating to benefices vacated at the Curia and to those which remained vacant beyond a specified time. Moreover, the Concordat did not abolish the elective system completely; a church which could produce evidence that it had been granted the privilege of election by the papacy was allowed to keep it.[21]

If the limitations embodied in the Concordat had been strictly enforced, the crown would not have gained as much control over the church as it did. Almost immediately Francis I disregarded the privilege of election claimed by many churches. When the chapter of Troyes tried to hold an election in November 1518, it was compelled to accept the royal nominee, Guillaume Petit.[22] In the same year, Jean de Magdeleine, who had been elected by the monks of Cluny as their abbot, was ousted in favour of Aymar Gouffier, the king's protégé.[23] The papacy did try on one or two occasions to enforce the Concordat. In 1520, for example, there was a dispute between François de Bueil, who had been elected archbishop of Bourges, and Guillaume Petit, the king's nominee.

[21] Many editions of the Concordat exist. The best will be found in *Ordonnances des rois de France: François Ier*, Vol. I, p. 434, no. 91.

[22] Imbart de la Tour, *op. cit.*, Vol. II, pp. 479–80.

[23] *Ibid.*, Vol. II, p. 480; J. Thomas, *Le Concordat de 1516, ses origines, son histoire au XVIe siècle* (Paris, 1910), Vol. III, pp. 105–6. Jean de Magdeleine was bought off with a pension of 4,000 *livres*.

The pope decided in favour of de Bueil.[24] But usually the king got his way, and in June 1531 he obtained from the pope an annulment of the privilege of free election, except in the case of heads of religious orders.[25]

The crown also disregarded the canonical requirements of nomination laid down by the Concordat. In theory a bishop was to be at least twenty-seven years of age and an abbot twenty-three, but the practice proved quite otherwise. Martin Fournier de Beaune became archbishop of Tours at twenty-three; Louis de Husson bishop of Poitiers at eighteen; Gabriel Le Veneur bishop of Évreux at fourteen; and Charles de Guise archbishop of Rheims at nine.[26] The ruling that a bishop or abbot should be a man of learning and of worthy life was also often overlooked. The letters which Francis I wrote to the pope after 1516 recommending his nominees paid lip service to the canonical requirements but gave some idea of the real reasons that had determined his choice. Arnauld-Guillaume d'Aydie was described as "a most learned man, endowed with good morals, virtue and knowledge," but, even more important, he was "a loyal and devoted councillor, reliable and stable." Another episcopal nominee, Thomas Duprat, was picked, "considering the many great and virtuous services which our chancellor, his brother, has given to us in the past and continues to give us now." Charles de Villiers was appointed to Limoges not only because he was "a person endowed and qualified with good morals and learning," but also on account of his belonging to "a great and noble house," and of his "many good, virtuous and commendable services" to the crown.[27] Very occasionally the pope refused to institute a royal nominee. He objected to Jean de Buz, who had been nominated first to Chalon, then to Meaux in 1535; and also to Dominique de Saint-Séverin, nominated to Maurienne in 1544.[28] But again these were

[24] *Ibid.*, Vol. III, p. 101.   [25] *Ibid.*, Vol. II, pp. 349 ff.
[26] *Ibid.*, Vol. III, p. 204.
[27] *Ibid.*, Vol. III, pp. 184–5. The depths were reached when Henry III gave the see of Amiens to Captain du Guast, who sold it for 30,000 *livres* to a lady of easy virtue: *ibid.*, Vol. III, p. 206.
[28] *Ibid.*, Vol. III, p. 196.

exceptional cases. Normally the crown's nominees were duly instituted.

There is no doubt that the independence of the French church vis-à-vis the monarchy suffered as a result of the way in which the Concordat was applied. But an assessment of the Concordat must take into account the relations that existed between church and state before 1516 and the limitations on royal control which the agreement embodied. On both counts it would seem that the Concordat has been misunderstood. It has been shown that the state had an effective control of elections before 1516 and that the right of nomination conferred by the Concordat on the crown was subject to limitations. Yet historians are still saying that the Concordat destroyed the independence of the French church and handed it over to royal control. It is easy to see how this distorted interpretation has come about. The way in which the crown misapplied the Concordat in its own interest produced many protests in the sixteenth century. As memory of the state of affairs that had existed before 1516 faded away, the Concordat was blamed for all that was wrong in the church. At the Estates General of 1560 Jean Quintin demanded a return to the Pragmatic Sanction.[29] The idea that the church had been able to conduct free elections before 1516 was implicit in the request made by the Third Estate in 1576 "that elections should be conducted according to the procedure observed before the Concordats."[30] During the Wars of Religion criticism of the monarchy intensified the attack on royal nominations. Gradually the idea took root that the Concordat had destroyed the independence of the French church. Only a few people realised that the *grandissima servitú* of the church noted by the Venetian ambassador Giustiniano was the result, not of the Concordat, but of its distorted application by the monarchy.[31] In 1591 and 1595 the clergy showed a better understanding of the situation by asking Henry IV to remedy

[29] *Ibid.*, Vol. III, p. 123. The ordinance of Orléans of January 1561, while it did not denounce the Concordat, seriously modified its provisions, but it was not applied.

[30] *Ibid.*, Vol. III, p. 145.   [31] *Ibid.*, Vol. III, p. 183.

abuses by applying "what is provided for in the Concordat."[32]

II

So far only the relations of church and state in France have been examined. In order to get the Concordat into proper perspective, it is essential also to examine Franco-papal relations before 1516. The abuse of the Concordat by the monarchy and the protests which this aroused in the sixteenth century have led historians into thinking that the Concordat was originally conceived as an instrument of royal absolutism and that it was opposed for this reason. An examination of Franco-papal relations may suggest a different conclusion. The assumption that royal nominations were the main objective of Francis I in his negotiations with the papacy fails to take into account the earlier motivation of royal policy in relation to Rome. The Concordat must be seen not as an isolated phenomenon, but as the culmination of a traditional policy. Moreover, the notion that the opposition to the Concordat was mainly due to fear of royal absolutism overlooks the much deeper loathing which Gallicans felt of papal absolutism.

The Pragmatic Sanction of Bourges, which the Concordat repudiated, was anti-papal in theory and practice. It rested on the doctrine that a general council of the church was superior in authority to the pope, and, as well as attacking the papal right of nomination, it abolished annates and restricted appeals to Rome. The Sanction could not always be applied, for the French monarchy only chose to support it when and where its own interests were not adversely affected by it.[33] Even so, the Sanction was bitterly resented by the papacy. For years it repeatedly demanded the removal of this "thorn driven into the eye of the Church."

At first, Charles VII seemed willing to come to terms with the papacy, but the Sanction proved too useful politically to be readily discarded. In 1450 the forged Pragmatic Sanction of St. Louis was produced to buttress it, and in 1453 and 1454 Charles

[32] *Ibid.*, Vol. III, p. 223.
[33] Renaudet, *Préréforme et humanisme . . .*, pp. 2–5.

issued ordinances confirming it. Pius II complained bitterly of French policy in a two-hour speech at Mantua in 1459.[34] It was not until the reign of Louis XI, however, that the Sanction was fully exploited politically. By alternately suspending and reviving it, the king tried to win papal support for his policy in Italy and elsewhere. In 1462 he proclaimed its abrogation to win Pius II over to the Angevin cause in Naples. But Louis was soon dissatisfied with the pope, and so he promulgated a series of Gallican ordinances in 1463 and 1464 which had the effect of nullifying the abrogation. During Paul II's pontificate, Louis XI continued his tortuous policy: in 1467 he made a declaration against the Sanction, but did not abolish it. Under Sixtus IV the Sanction was replaced, again for political reasons, by a Concordat (1472) which gave the papacy a half-share with the ordinaries of appointments to benefices. After 1475 Franco-papal relations deteriorated once more, and in May 1479, following another spate of Gallican ordinances, the Sanction was reaffirmed by an assembly of the French church at Lyons. The war of nerves which Louis XI waged on the papacy was not unlike that later conducted by Henry VIII by means of the Act in Conditional Restraint of Annates.[35] Until 1515 the papacy continued to demand the abolition of the Pragmatic Sanction, the climax being reached in December 1512, when its supporters were ordered to appear before the Lateran Council.[36]

The Pragmatic Sanction was not the only means used by the French crown for putting political pressure on the papacy; it also made a practice of periodically threatening to call a general council of the church. The doctrine that such a council was superior in authority to the pope was an important element in Gallicanism. France was the cradle of conciliarism. Long before d'Ailly and Gerson, the Dominican John of Paris had put forward the view that a council, since it represented the whole church, was above

[34] Thomas, op. cit., Vol. I, pp. 223–42.

[35] Ibid., Vol. I, pp. 243–56; R. Aubenas and R. Ricard, L'Église et la Renaissance (1449–1517) (Paris, 1951), pp. 56–7, 70–2, 78–81.

[36] Thomas, op. cit., Vol. I, pp. 284–5.

the pope and could depose him if he misused his authority.[37] It was at the suggestion of the French Cardinal Fillastre that the Council of Constance had issued the decree *Sacrosancta* to the effect that a council derived its authority directly from Christ and that everyone, including the pope, should obey it.[38] And it was an archbishop of Tours who said that, if the papacy could not be wrested from the Italians, it would have to be so "plucked" that it would not matter where it was.[39] Even after the Holy See had triumphed over the conciliar movement, the theory of conciliar supremacy continued to have adherents in France. It was kept alive by the general desire for reform and by the increase of anti-papal feeling provoked by the administrative methods of Sixtus IV. During the fifteenth century "Gallican France was the real stronghold of the strict conciliar theory and the University of Paris its citadel."[40]

Conciliarism was closely associated with the monarchy's political use of the Pragmatic Sanction, for whenever the king threatened to suspend this, Gallican opinion appealed to the authority of the conciliar decrees which it embodied. This meant that the king had two weapons in his diplomatic armoury: if suspending the Sanction did not achieve the desired result, he could threaten to demand a general council.[41] This was the course followed by Louis XI in his dealings with Pius II.[42] In 1476 he announced the imminent convocation of a general council to deter Sixtus IV from favouring Charles the Bold. Two years later he used the same threat when the Pazzi conspiracy gave him a pretext for interfering in Italy. Charles VIII wielded the conciliar cudgel to prevent Alexander VI recognising Alfonso II as king of Naples.[43] But no general council was actually summoned until the reign of Louis XII. In 1510 Julius II, after being his ally, reversed his policy with a view to expelling the "barbarians" from Italy. The king retaliated by calling an anti-papal council at Pisa

[37] Jedin, *op. cit.*, Vol. I, p. 7.
[38] *Ibid.*, Vol. I, pp. 14–15.
[39] *Ibid.*, Vol. I, p. 19.
[40] *Ibid.*, Vol. I, p. 32.
[41] *Ibid.*, Vol. I, pp. 54–55.
[42] Aubenas and Ricard, *op. cit.*, p. 79.
[43] Jedin, *op. cit.*, Vol. I, pp. 55–8.

in November 1511, which declared the pope suspended. But the council turned out to be a wretched fiasco: its predominantly Gallican and French character alienated support; the emperor failed to send any representative to it; and the local population proved so hostile that it had to move to Milan, where it could be protected by the French army. Even within Louis XII's entourage, opinion about the council's prospects was divided. Not even the French victory at Ravenna was able to save it. Julius II's decision to call the fifth Lateran Council finally sealed the fate of the Council of Pisa: it was compelled to evacuate Italy and dissolved itself at Lyons.[44]

Two conclusions can be drawn from an examination of Franco-papal relations before 1516: first, the Concordat satisfied a long-standing demand of the papacy by revoking the Pragmatic Sanction of Bourges; secondly, it was part of a traditional policy on the part of the crown of alternately suspending and reviving the Sanction to put political pressure on the papacy.

III

The Concordat of Bologna was approved by the pope on August 18, 1516. It consisted originally of three bulls which were ratified by the Lateran Council on December 19 following.[45] But before it could become law in France, it had to be registered by the *parlement* of Paris, and Francis I was allowed six months in which to have this done. It is sometimes assumed that the *parlement* was merely a ratifying body with no mind of its own, but this is a misrepresentation of the court as it existed in the early sixteenth century. Though ultimately it could not resist the royal will, it did hold strong opinions and could prove obstructive when it disapproved of a policy. This was clearly shown in the matter of the Concordat. The *parlement* was fervently Gallican

[44] *Ibid.*, Vol. I, pp. 106–12, A. Renaudet, *Le Concile gallican de Pise-Milan* (Paris, 1922), *passim.*

[45] The bulls were *Pastor aeternus*, which abolished the Pragmatic Sanction, *Divina providente gratia*, which promulgated the Concordat, and *Primitiva illa Ecclesia*, which contained its text: Renaudet, *Préréforme et humanisme . . .*, p. 581.

in outlook and viewed Francis I's negotiations with the pope with grave misgivings. Although it was asked on February 5, 1517 to register the Concordat, it was not until March 22, 1518 that it complied under protest. Because of the delay, Francis had to obtain from the pope an extension of the time he had been allowed for getting the agreement registered.[46]

For more than a year the *parlement* tried to wear down the king's resolution by delaying tactics. Francis was so infuriated that in June 1517 he ordered his uncle, the Bastard of Savoy, to attend its debates. The court protested at this infringement of its liberties, but had to submit when the king threatened to banish its members and to replace them by "worthy persons." In spite of the Bastard's presence, the *parlement* decided on July 24 that it would not register the Concordat and that the Pragmatic Sanction should be maintained. This provoked a paroxysm of rage on the part of Francis. Declaring that there would be only one king in France and no senate as in Venice, he threatened to turn the *parlement* into a nomadic institution and to make it "trot after him like the members of the *Grand Conseil*." "Concern yourselves with justice," he told its representatives, "it is as ill administered as it was a hundred years ago." When they applied for permission to stay at court until local floods had subsided, they were told that if they were not gone by six o'clock the next day, they would be thrown into a pit by twelve archers and left there for six months.[47] On March 6, 1518, La Trémoille, the king's chamberlain, appeared before the *parlement* and again demanded the registration of the Concordat, letting it be known that he had authority to punish disobedience severely. It was rumoured that Francis I planned to set up a new *parlement* at Orléans. Royal intimidation achieved its purpose. On March 22, the *parlement* at last registered the Concordat, albeit with the significant qualification "on the repeatedly made behest and command of our lord the king." At the same time it drew up a secret protestation to the

[46] R. Doucet, *Étude sur le gouvernement de François Ier dans ses rapports avec le Parlement de Paris*, Pt. I, *1515–25* (Paris, 1921), pp. 84, 123, 133.

[47] *Ibid.*, pp. 91–7, 115–17.

effect that it had only yielded through fear of being dissolved, and that it would continue to apply the Pragmatic Sanction in judging ecclesiastical causes.[48]

The *parlement* had no sooner capitulated to the crown than the University of Paris began to agitate against the Concordat. It decided to suspend its courses, to forbid the printing of the Concordat, and to appeal against it to a future general council. On March 27, the appeal, which took the form of a violent attack on the papacy, was drawn up. A memorandum against the Concordat was also sent to preachers so that they might derive inspiration from it for their Lenten sermons. Placards—some of them inviting the English to invade the kingdom—were put up in the colleges and public thoroughfares. Members of the university approached the archbishop of Lyons to obtain an assembly of the French clergy without royal intervention.

Alarmed by these developments, which threatened to turn a hitherto exclusive opposition into a popular movement, Francis I ordered the *parlement* to enquire into the disorders and to end them, "for otherwise we shall deal with the affair in a manner which will make it memorable for all time." A few days later, seeing that the court had not yet done anything, he humiliated it by transferring the enquiry to a special commission. This remonstrated with the college principals, ordering them to keep their students within bounds. On April 25 a royal edict forbade the university to meddle with state affairs under pain of losing its privileges and of banishment from the kingdom. Some suspects were arrested and a commission was appointed to try them, but their case was eventually referred to the king and allowed to lapse. Now that Francis had got what he wanted—the registration of the Concordat—no purpose could be served by making martyrs of the opposition.[49]

IV

The main contemporary arguments for and against the Concordat of 1516 are to be found in three documents: namely

[48] *Ibid.*, pp. 117–23.   [49] *Ibid.*, pp. 125–39.

Duprat's speech to the *parlement* of February 5, 1517; the *parlement's* remonstrances of January 1518; and Duprat's memorandum replying to these, also of January 1518.

When Francis I first asked the *parlement* to register the Concordat on February 5, 1517, his chancellor, Duprat, who was the real author of the agreement, explained why it had been signed.[50] He claimed that Francis had done everything to defend the Pragmatic Sanction, but that he had been overruled by the prejudice based on avarice of the papal negotiators. If he had resisted Leo X's demand for the abrogation of the Sanction, his kingdom would have been placed under an interdict, and other kings and princes would have been free to invade it and share it among themselves. To drive the point home, Duprat reminded his audience of the disasters that resistance to the papacy had brought down upon Louis XII's head. If, on the other hand, Francis had decided to submit to the pope without negotiating, the French church would have succumbed to papal arbitrariness and the abuses which the Council of Constance had eradicated. Wisdom had therefore dictated that he should negotiate an agreement which preserved the interests of the kingdom. In short, Duprat presented the Concordat, not in the eulogistic terms which historians have lavished upon it, but as a *faute de mieux* bred of political necessity.[51]

The *parlement* was not impressed by the chancellor's case. In its remonstrances of January 1518 it rejected the notion that resistance to the pope would have led to the destruction of the kingdom. The king, it argued, held his authority of God, had no superior in secular matters, and possessed strength enough to repulse any attack from outside. But the *parlement* was concerned not so much to demolish Duprat's excuses, as to reveal the weaknesses of the Concordat itself, notably the restoration of annates, the full resumption of appeals to Rome and the replacement of election to benefices by nomination. In every case it declared that the pope would gain more from the agreement than the king: annates

[50] For Duprat's role in the negotiations leading to the Concordat, see A. Buisson, *Le Chancelier Antoine Duprat* (Paris, 1935), pp. 113–14.

[51] Doucet, *op. cit.*, p. 85.

would drain the kingdom of money; appeals to Rome would affect all benefices, especially bishoprics and abbeys; and royal nominations would be subject to papal control. As for the annulment of the Pragmatic Sanction, the *parlement* saw this as a blow struck at the king's authority and as an affirmation of papal as against conciliar supremacy. After suggesting that the king should either ask the pope to call a general council or himself summon an assembly of the Gallican clergy, it concluded that the Concordat was "contrary to the honour of God, the liberties of the Church, the honour of the king and the public weal of his kingdom."[52]

Faced by this detailed criticism of the Concordat, the crown was obliged to produce an equally detailed justification. In a memorandum intended solely for the king's use, Duprat repeated his earlier account of the political situation which had necessitated the Concordat, alluding to secret reasons which the *parlement* should accept without demanding explanations. The king had tried to preserve the Pragmatic Sanction and the elective system, continued the chancellor, and he had succeeded to a large extent, for the Concordat preserved the content, if not the form, of the Sanction, "so that the only difference is that what was once called Pragmatic is now called Concordat." The elective system had had to go, however, because of the abuses which it had engendered. The pope, asserted Duprat, was within his rights in getting rid of it, for his authority was superior to that of a general council. The king would use his right of nomination so well that the pope would not be given any pretext to interfere. As for annates, they were not even mentioned in the Concordat and would not be restored; nor would the existing system of ecclesiastical jurisdiction be changed.[53] Having expressed his belief in papal supremacy, the chancellor did not feel that it was necessary for him to reply to the *parlement's* criticism of the repudiation of

[52] *Ibid.*, pp. 99–104. The remonstrances of 1518 repeated arguments used by the *parlement* in 1464 against Louis XI's threatened abolition of the Pragmatic Sanction, but their tone was more anti-papal.

[53] Annates were specifically mentioned in a bull of October 1, 1516, which Francis I submitted to the *parlement* after the Concordat had been registered, thereby giving the lie to Duprat's statement: Doucet, *op. cit.*, p. 133.

the Sanction. In conclusion, he rejected the need for a general council, and declared that Francis would call an assembly of the French clergy, but only after the Concordat had been registered and given a chance to demonstrate its worth. Duprat's memorandum was not an impressive document: his indictment of the abuses caused by the elective system was inconsistent with his statement that the king had tried to keep it; his denial that annates would be restored was soon proved false; and only a simpleton would have been deceived by his argument that the Sanction and the Concordat were essentially alike, considering their diametrically opposed theoretical premises.[54]

An examination of the debate over the Concordat yields two conclusions. First, the *parlement*'s opposition was of an essentially anti-papal character. Its criticisms of the king were few and temperate, and centred upon his weakness in having succumbed to papal pressure. Secondly, the crown, far from seeming proud of the Concordat, adopted the line that it had been compelled to sign it as the only way out of a political impasse. It has been suggested, however, that neither side was sincere in its statements: that the *parlement* used anti-papalism to conceal its fear that the Concordat would open the way to royal absolutism; while the crown justified it on every ground except the real one that it was intended to strengthen the king's control of the church.[55] This view is plausible: the *parlement* may have foreseen the arbitrary application of the Concordat by the crown and been too timid to express openly the real motive of its opposition; and the government would have been unwise to confirm the worst suspicions of its critics by explaining the Concordat's real purpose. However, we should remember that the crown already had an almost complete control of the church, and that the *parlement* seemed to acquiesce in this. Moreover, while Duprat's defence of the Concordat was largely specious, there are reasons for thinking

[54] *Ibid.*, pp. 106–15.
[55] *Ibid.*, pp. 105–6, 114. C. Terrasse writes (*François Ier* (Paris, 1945), Vol. I, p. 138) that the councillors of the *parlement* "saw in the Concordat a formidable instrument of power in the hands of the king."

that he may not have been entirely dishonest in admitting that it had been a result of political necessity.

V

Certain assumptions are commonly made about the Concordat: first, that having won the battle of Marignano, Francis I was sufficiently strong to impose his own terms on the pope; secondly, that his main purpose in the negotiations was to increase his authority over the Gallican church. Both assumptions are questionable.

Marignano was an important battle from the military point of view: it was the first defeat suffered by the Swiss pikemen, who had hitherto been reputed invincible.[56] It also gave Francis I control of the duchy of Milan. But he still had a long way to go before he could call Italy his own. Though defeated, the Swiss might still launch a counter-attack from their homeland. The Emperor Maximilian was soon raising with English financial assistance a large army to drive the French out of Italy, and but for his own fecklessness he would probably have succeeded.[57] The king of France could depend on Venetian support, but he also needed to protect his southern flank by gaining the alliance of the pope. Francis was certainly not in a position to impose his own terms on Leo X. Duprat's account of the political difficulties which had obliged the king to sign the Concordat was not far from the truth.

In 1515 Francis I was only twenty-one years old and had almost no experience of government. He was "as ill informed on the affairs of the Church as on canon law."[58] His main preoccupation was the conquest of Italy. He felt that he had a just claim to the duchy of Milan and to the kingdom of Naples and wanted to succeed where his predecessors had failed by permanently

[56] Sir C. Oman, *A History of the Art of War in the Sixteenth Century* (New York, 1937), p. 171.

[57] F. Mignet, *La Rivalité de François Ier et de Charles-Quint* (Paris, 1876), Vol. 1, pp. 101–7.

[58] Doucet, *op., cit.* p. 146.

establishing his authority south of the Alps. But before attempting this, he had to prepare the ground diplomatically. Recent events had shown that France could not achieve a lasting foothold in Italy without the co-operation of the Holy See. Louis XII had been successful only as long as he had enjoyed the support of Alexander VI and Julius II. As soon as the latter had turned against him he had been driven out of the peninsula. From the start of his reign, therefore, Francis I tried to get on friendly terms with Pope Leo X: he promised French sees to Cardinal Cibo, and confirmed with only minor modifications the wide powers of the legate Canossa. When the *parlement* in an excess of Gallican zeal tried to scrutinize these powers, the crown intervened, saying that "it was a question of pleasing the pope for good reasons and in order to achieve matters of far greater importance, which cannot be revealed to everyone. . . ."[59] But the king's first efforts to ingratiate himself with the pope failed. In June 1515 Leo joined Spain, the duke of Milan and the Swiss in a coalition for the defence of Italy.[60]

Though disappointed, Francis did not bear Leo X any grudge, and immediately after Marignano redoubled his efforts to gain his friendship. The king needed Leo more than ever now, not merely to safeguard his gains in north Italy, but also with a view to acquiring more territory farther south. Having gained Milan, Francis wanted Naples. On learning of the death of Ferdinand of Aragon in February 1516 he "decided to set to work to regain the kingdom of Naples."[61] But this required the pope's help. As temporal ruler of the papal states and as a member of the house of Medici which ruled Florence, Leo X controlled the overland route to Naples. Moreover, as suzerain of the kingdom of Naples, he alone could deny or grant its investiture. Thus, writes Barrillon, "in order to carry out this enterprise, the king had to have the aid of the Pope."[62]

As a gesture of goodwill Francis I released the papal commander Prospero Colonna, who had been captured shortly before

[59] Renaudet, *Préréforme et humanisme* . . ., p. 579.   [60] *Ibid.*, p. 580.
[61] *Journal de Jean Barrillon*, Vol. I, p. 194.   [62] *Ibid.*

Marignano.[63] But more was needed to secure the pope's friend-ship. The Pragmatic Sanction, which was currently under fire from the Lateran Council, remained as a major obstacle in the path of a Franco-papal *entente*. Unlike his predecessors Francis was unable to ring the changes on the Sanction and the threat of a general council. For after the disastrous Council of Pisa he would merely have exposed himself to ridicule had he revived the conciliar threat. This meant that he only had the Sanction with which to bargain. Even if the king did not know much about ecclesiastical matters, Duprat would have been able to advise him that its revocation would not only not diminish his authority over the French church, but would probably increase it. So Francis decided to risk offending his Gallican subjects in the hope of gaining the pope's help in Italy. The spirit in which he approached the Concordat was similar to that in which Louis XI, Charles VIII and Louis XII had exploited the ecclesiastical situation. Although he may have been aware that the Concordat would tend to increase his own absolutism, what he mainly wanted to get from it was papal support for his Italian policy. "The settlement of religious quarrels a century old was a condition of success for the Italian policy of Francis I, and without doubt this entirely secular aspect of the question of schism influenced his resolve."[64] To the *parlement* and the University of Paris the conquest of Italy must have seemed a poor return for the surrender of the conciliar doctrine and the acceptance of papal supremacy—hence the bitterness of their opposition.

As a purely political move the Concordat was a failure. It is true that Leo X supported for a time Francis I's candidature for the Empire, but he subsequently turned against him. In May 1521 he signed an alliance with Charles V and in June granted him the investiture of the kingdom of Naples and papal recognition of his election as Emperor.[65] In 1522 the French were driven out of Italy, and the Pope is said to have died of the joy that he felt on

[63] *Ibid.*, Vol. i, p. 196.
[64] Doucet, *op. cit.*, p. 145.
[65] Mignet, *op. cit.*, Vol. i, pp. 163–5: Terrasse, *op. cit.*, Vol. i, pp. 248, 253.

receiving the news.[66] When Francis I was defeated and captured at Pavia three years later, his mother, Louise of Savoy, expressed doubts about the Concordat, even blaming it for her son's misfortunes.[67] Yet the king was never tempted to revoke it: as long as he entertained the hope of conquering Italy, he wanted to remain on the best terms possible with the papacy. Moreover, by cancelling the Concordat he would have humiliated himself in the eyes of the Gallican opposition, and lost the incidental advantages which he had gained from his agreement with the pope. As it happened, the Reformation also provided Francis with alternative means of exerting pressure on the Holy See: he could ally with the German Protestants, tolerate or persecute heretics in France, according to whichever way papal policy fluctuated.[68] After 1525 the papacy tended to side with Francis because of its fear of Charles V's power, but it was never prepared to help him dominate Italy.

VI

The Concordat of Bologna was not, therefore, the unqualified triumph for the French monarchy which it has generally been acclaimed to be. For more than half a century before, the kings of France had exerted political pressure on the papacy by using the Pragmatic Sanction or the threat of a general council to further their Italian ambitions. The Concordat was part of this traditional policy. As such it failed to achieve its object; for the pope never would allow Francis I to become master of Italy. Within France, the Concordat did not produce the revolutionary changes that have been ascribed to it: the independence of the Gallican church was already a thing of the past. All that the Concordat did was to give the pope's blessing to an already Erastian situation. Because

[66] *Ibid.*, Vol. I, p. 253.
[67] Thomas, *op. cit.*, Vol. III, p. 109.
[68] V. L. Bourrilly, "François Ier et les Protestants: Les essais de concorde en 1535," *Bulletin de la Société d'Histoire du Protestantisme Français*, XLIX (1900), 348; V. L. Bourrilly and N. Weiss, "Jean du Bellay, les Protestants et la Sorbonne (1529–35)," *ibid.*, LII (1903), 97–127.

the price of this blessing was the surrender of the Pragmatic Sanction, the agreement was a capitulation to the doctrine of papal supremacy. To suggest that the Concordat was a kind of substitute for Henry VIII's "supreme headship" is to misunderstand its theoretical basis: if it confirmed the king's control under the supreme direction of the pope, it was also the reverse of the Henrician programme in that it restored annates and appeals to Rome. The idea that Francis I desisted from schism because the Concordat gave him as much authority over the church as Henry VIII or Gustavus Vasa enjoyed is, therefore, untenable. Among the factors which may have strengthened Francis I's resistance to the temptations of schism was the knowledge that if he broke with Rome he would never fulfil his Italian ambitions. In other words, it was not the Concordat so much as the political situation that produced it which deterred Francis from going the same way as Henry VIII. If the latter had also had territorial designs south of the Alps he might have thought twice before giving rein to "the rising national spirit" and the "anti-papal and anti-sacerdotal feelings" of his subjects.

4 The Role of Parliament in the Henrician Reformation

G. W. O. WOODWARD

I PROPOSE in this paper to touch briefly upon two aspects of the work of the parliaments of Henry VIII of England: first the part played by parliament in bringing about the Anglo-papal schism, and in particular, in this connection, the work of the Long, or Reformation Parliament of 1529–1536. and, secondly, the share of parliament in maintaining the ecclesiastical arrangements then made and in governing the *Ecclesia Anglicana*, now independent of Rome.

I should however make it clear, before I proceed any further, that I do not intend to produce any new or startling evidence. In that respect I make no claim to originality. All I propose to do is to reconsider briefly some of the evidence already available in an attempt to determine how far it supports, to the exclusion of any other view, the conventional interpretation of this period in the history of the English parliament.

The story of the English Reformation in the reign of Henry VIII is generally told in some fashion similar to the following: the king, being balked by the papacy in the matter of his marriage, turned to parliament for assistance, first in bringing pressure to bear upon the pope, and, when that failed, in rejecting papal jurisdiction in England altogether. In making use of parliament in this manner, King Henry was enlarging its powers, widening the scope of its activity, and creating precedents which his successors were unable to live down. Hence, the modern history of parliament as an institution which developed steadily in strength until it challenged and overthrew the monarchy, can be said to begin with this Reformation Parliament.

But do the facts together support this interpretation? Was

parliament, for instance, summoned in 1529 to assist the king in the matter of his marriage? Certain facts certainly lend colour to this suggestion. It is true that the legatine court at Blackfriars in London, tardily and reluctantly established by Pope Clement VII, had ended its sitting on July 27, 1529, having achieved precisely nothing. This was greatly to the displeasure of the king, and the writs for a new parliament were in preparation within a fortnight of that date. It is true also that that same parliament was eventually to provide the king with the means of solving his domestic difficulties. But it was not to do so until 1533 when the pregnancy of Anne Boleyn made swift action essential. Until then parliament was not even permitted to discuss the king's affair. Admittedly parliament was to have read to it in 1531 the carefully gathered opinions of the universities about the marriage, but only in order that the members of the commons might report what they had heard to the country at large when they dispersed upon prorogation. The ill-timed attempt of certain members in the following year to offer the king unasked-for advice about his personal affairs earned a swift and severe rebuke, which made it abundantly clear that they had no right to meddle with such high matters. There is certainly plenty of room for doubt that the parliament of 1529 was summoned primarily to attend to the King's Great Matter.

Of course, if one is prepared to believe that every ecclesiastical statute of the seven sessions of the Reformation Parliament was part of a preconceived and well-laid plan, then it is arguable that the work of the earlier sessions was necessary to prepare the way for the more drastic measures of the later sessions. According to this view, the first session (1529) established the right of parliament to legislate for the church; the second (1531), and the third (1532) saw the church at home brought low and the first tentative anti-papal measure passed (First Annates Act, 23 Henry VIII cap. 20).[1] Then when this failed to move the pope to favour the king's suit,

---

[1] All references to statutes are by regnal year and chapter. Those of the reigns of Richard II and Henry V may be found in Vol. II of *Statutes of the Realm*, Record Commission edition (London, 1810–28). Those of the reign of Henry VIII are in Vol. III of the same series.

the fourth session (1533) made arrangements to solve the whole affair without reference to His Holiness (Restraint of Appeals, 24 Henry VIII cap. 12), and the fifth and sixth (1534) completed the breach.

But there are many difficulties in the way of accepting this view. I need only mention a few. We must, for instance, bear in mind the long intervals between the sessions of parliament. Was it really necessary to proceed so slowly if the ultimate course of action was from the first decided? Was it really necessary to establish parliament's legislative sovereignty by enacting a series of minor ecclesiastical reforms before attempting such a measure as the Act in Restraint of Appeals?

Then again we must remember that the duke of Norfolk and Stephen Gardiner, who replaced Wolsey in the king's confidence after the fall of the cardinal in 1529, were themselves gradually being replaced by Thomas Cromwell during these early years of the 1529 parliament. A change of ministers suggests a change of policy. Indeed if there was any master plan in this parliament, most authorities would agree that it cannot be seen in action until 1532 at the earliest, when Cromwell was established as the chief influence in government, and when the statutes passed begin to acquire a more forceful tone, and to have a more direct bearing upon the king's case. In comparison with the acts of the later sessions, those of 1529 and 1531 seem disconnected and haphazard.

No, it is difficult to accept the work of the earlier sessions of the Reformation Parliament as a deliberately planned preliminary to the eventual solution of the marriage question.

But why then was parliament summoned in 1529, if not immediately to deal with the king's affairs? Clearly not for the purposes of taxation, for no grant of supply was made until the sixth session in the autumn of 1534 (Subsidy Act, 26 Henry VIII cap. 19. First Fruits and Tenths, 26 Henry VIII cap. 3). The first session, it is true, had seen the passage of an act converting the forced loan of previous years into an outright gift (21 Henry VIII cap. 24) but such a measure could well have been held over until other reasons occasioned a parliament. Indeed the fact that a grant of a fifteenth [a levy on moveable property] was proposed in the third session in 1532, but was allowed to lapse because parliament was prorogued before the necessary bill had passed through all its stages,[2] and was not renewed in the following session, argues no great financial urgency on the part of the crown.

Some suggest[3] that this parliament was summoned primarily to deal with the fallen Cardinal Wolsey by act of attainder. But in the event, an indictment in king's bench proved sufficient to secure the necessary legal condemnation, and no attainder was necessary. Acts of attainder were weapons increasingly used in this parliament, but generally only in those cases where it might have been difficult otherwise to secure conviction. Were this parliament then summoned to deal with the cardinal, it seems strange that the writs should have been issued before the more normal judicial processes had been attempted.

No, any explanation of the summoning of this parliament in terms of a specific programme is in some way unsatisfactory. But is such an explanation necessary? Could it not be that it was the normal practice at that period to summon parliaments from time to time even if there was no important official programme ready to be laid before the houses? The fact that nearly every sixteenth-century parliament made a grant of taxation to the crown has inclined us to think in terms of the need for taxation alone. The autocratic Tudors, we tend to think, would have liked very well to manage without parliament had it not been that from time to time that financial assistance which parliament alone could give them made it necessary to summon the houses. And so when we come face to face with this parliament of 1529, when financial urgency cannot account for its being summoned, we look, and look perhaps in vain, for another immediate reason for its appearance.

Significant in this connection is, I think, the demand that was to be made by the rebels participating in the Pilgrimage of Grace in 1536, for the holding of a parliament to remedy their grievances.

[2] *Hall's Chronicle*, ed. Sir H. Ellis (London, 1809), p. 786.
[3] A. Ogle, *The Tragedy of the Lollards' Tower* (Oxford, 1949), pp. 175–8.

If they were accustomed to regard parliaments primarily as royal taxing machines, they would scarcely have placed their hopes for redress so surely in parliament.

Significant too is the very general wording of the speech made by the chancellor, Sir Thomas More, at the formal opening of the parliament of 1529. Parliament, he said, had been summoned because "divers laws . . . were made now by long continuance of time and mutation of things, very insufficient and imperfect, and also, by the frail condition of man divers new enormities were sprung amongst the people."[4] Was any specific programme intended, his words would surely have been less general and have given some allusive hint of the government's plans.

Significant too is the amount of legislation of this parliament which is in no way connected with the church. Economic and social regulations fill 70 of its statutes; another 37 are concerned with the amendment of the law, both criminal and civil. In this respect this parliament was no different from its immediate predecessors. The proportion of economic and social statutes amongst the measures passed by Henry's first four parliaments is almost exactly the same.

And so, quite apart from the financial needs of the crown, or the urgency of any national crisis, there would seem to be a very adequate occasion for the periodic meeting of parliament in the need to keep abreast of the nation's economy. Once you embark upon a policy of governmental economic regulation, you cannot hope in any age to construct a system of rules which will not be in need of periodic overhaul as the needs of the nation change. And so, if parliament was to be the instrument of national economic control, then parliament must continue to meet at not too infrequent intervals.

Now in the autumn of 1529, more than six years had elapsed since the last brief session of parliament in 1523, an intermission between parliaments as long as any save one since the accession of Henry VII. That last parliament had been the one which had stood on its privileges in the face of the displeasure of Cardinal Wolsey.

4 *Hall's Chronicle*, p. 764.

Now Wolsey was gone—perhaps the time was ripe for another parliament.

Finally, in this connection, it is noticeable that no contemporary thought that there was anything impending out of the ordinary when the parliament of 1529 first met. It is true that one chronicler, Hall, gives it a little more attention than some previous parliaments. But then it is very likely that he was a member of this one, and in a position to know more about its activities than about the activities of any of its predecessors. And even he has nothing to say about the causes for its summons, treating its meeting at that date as a perfectly natural occurrence.

Thus there is good reason to suggest that perhaps it is vain to search for some outstanding specific reason for the meeting of this parliament, or to attempt to postulate a contemplated programme of legislation for it. By that I do not mean to imply that the crisis in the king's personal affairs had no connection at all with the summoning of parliament. Undoubtedly that crisis created a situation in which it might be desirable to have a parliament in being. But it is not necessary to suppose that there was any definite plan of action in the mind of the king and his advisors when the writs were sent out. I would however venture to suggest that, crisis or no crisis, parliament would probably have met soon in any case.

It was only in 1532, when this parliament had lasted for three sessions (the maximum length of any other parliament of the reign), and requested a dissolution, only to be denied it, that it began to acquire a character worthy of contemporary notice.

But I must pass on to my next point. If the summoning of parliament in 1529 was not necessarily the revolutionary step it is sometimes held to be, was the ecclesiastical legislation of that parliament any more revolutionary in its implications? To have the temporal legislature dealing with matters clearly spiritual, such as probate (21 Henry VIII cap. 5), tithes (27 Henry VIII cap. 20), benefit of clergy (23 Henry VIII cap. 1) and even heresy (25 Henry VIII cap. 14), was this not a revolution? A triumph of the temporal over the spiritual?

But once again, contemporary observers, if revolution there was, were blind to its occurrence. They all note the curtailment by this parliament of papal powers, but none comments upon the manner of its curtailment. Argument there was in plenty, and opposition too to the passage of many of the ecclesiastical measures. That cannot be denied. But that opposition was to the contents of the measures rather than to the principle involved in their passage. Even Bishop Fisher of Rochester, when protesting against the probate and mortuaries bills of the first session, did not take his stand on principle, or suggest that parliament had no authority to meddle thus with clerical matters. The burden of his protest was that the measures before the house all tended "to the destruction of the church."[5] How? By limiting its fees and restricting its perquisites. The crucial question of whether parliament had power over the church does not seem to have been argued then, or at any time in the reign; not even in 1515 when the abbot of Winchcombe preached his famous sermon which touched off the great debate about the statute of 1512 (4 Henry VIII cap. 2), which had restricted the operation of benefit of clergy. Though he said plainly enough that the act was "clean against the law of God," he never suggested that it had been beyond the power of parliament to make it. That issue does not seem to have been faced at that time by either party.

The best argued defence of the spiritual power which we have at this period is the answer[6] of convocation to the commons' supplication of 1532. But even in this answer, the question of the competence of parliament is not touched upon. The clergy zealously defend their own right to make canon law without the assent of king or laity, but are not called upon to discuss the cognate question of the limits of the authority of the temporal legislature.

But then were the ecclesiastical measures of the Reformation Parliament really sufficiently unprecedented to force into the open the question of the authority of parliament to enact them?

---

[5] *Ibid.*, p. 766.
[6] D. Wilkins, *Concilia Magnae Britanniae et Hiberniae* (London, 1737), Vol. III, p. 750.

Some of the more important of these statutes were not properly acts of parliament at all, but merely statutory confirmations of acts of convocation. For example, the Act of Supremacy (26 Henry VIII cap. 1) did not make Henry head of the English church. It merely acknowledged an allegedly existing fact that the king "is, and ought to be Supreme Head," and, more important "so is recognised by the clergy in their convocations." That clerical recognition had been given three years before. Now parliament merely confirmed it in a declaratory form.

Likewise the Act for the Submission of the Clergy (25 Henry VIII cap. 19) was in form a statutory confirmation of the act of convocation when, in 1532, it yielded to the crown the right to veto its existing and future legislation. Similarly the Act of Succession (25 Henry VIII cap. 22) added the authority of the voice of parliament to the decision of Archbishop Cranmer's court about the validity of the king's first two marriages, and imposed forceful penalties for any refusal to accept that decision, but did not expressly claim for parliament any right to determine such cases.

For other acts there was good precedent. The Act in Restraint of Appeals (24 Henry VIII cap. 12), which terminated the appellate jurisdiction of the court of Rome in causes matrimonial and testamentary, and in suits for tithe, could look back to statutes of previous centuries such as the "Great Statute of Praemunire" of the sixteenth [year] of Richard II which had restricted papal jurisdiction over advowsons. The act for the suppression of the lesser monasteries (27 Henry VIII cap. 28) had some sort of counterpart in the fifteenth-century suppression of alien priories (1 Henry V cap. 7). The act for the punishment of heresy (25 Henry VIII cap. 14) made express reference to certain statutes of Richard II (5 Richard II st. 2 cap. 5) and Henry V (2 Henry V st. 1 cap. 7), which it purported to re-enact, whilst those concerned with benefit of clergy (23 Henry VIII cap. 1) and clerks convict (23 Henry VIII cap. 11) looked back to 1512.

Most of the remaining acts were concerned with the revenues of the church, limiting fees, transferring papal revenues to the king, or providing for the assistance of the secular arm in the collection of tithe. Parliament's concern with clerical fees might be defended on the grounds that the object of the statutes was to defend the laity from excessive exactions, though there was also precedent for the limitation of probate fees (4 Henry V cap. 8); the tithe acts were designed only to make collection more sure. The transfer of papal revenues was favoured by many of the clergy, and so all passed without serious question.

But one can say all this, and still be left to wonder how such blatant invasions of the proper territory of the spiritual power as the grant to the king by parliament of a tenth of all spiritual incomes (First Fruits and Tenths, 26 Henry VIII cap. 3), or the statutory deposition of the absentee bishops of Salisbury and Worcester (25 Henry VIII cap. 27), or the arrangements made for the appointment and consecration of bishops without reference to Rome (23 Henry VIII cap. 20, First Annates; 25 Henry VIII cap. 20, Second Annates; 26 Henry VIII cap. 14, Nomination of Suffragans), were allowed to pass without serious challenge from the spirituality.

Archbishop Warham did register in February 1532, six months before his death,[7] his determination not to obey any statute prejudicial to the papacy or the church; but even he did not attempt to argue that parliament had no competence to make such statutes. Only Sir Thomas More seems to have been prepared to insist that there were limits to the legislative powers of parliament, though his profound sense of duty to the state obliged him to keep silent on that point until after his conviction.[8]

For the rest, contemporaries believed with Stephen Gardiner that "men must conform themselves to the more part in authority,"[9] without speculating whether there were any limits to what the "more part" could do. We should be mistaken if we were to attribute to the men of this period too clear an idea about

---

[7] *Ibid.*, Vol. III, p. 746.

[8] W. Roper, *The Lyfe of Sir Thomas Moore Knighte*, ed. E. V. Hitchcock (Early English Text Society Original Series No. 197, London, 1935), p. 92.

[9] *The Letters of Stephen Gardiner*, ed. J. A. Muller (Cambridge, 1933), p. 350.

the respective limits of spiritual and secular authority. And partly for that reason, and partly because there was something like a precedent for so many of the acts of the 1529 parliament, that assembly which seems so momentous to us looking back at it from the present day, performed its work without exciting constitutional comment at the time.

Once the authority of the pope had been ousted from England, and the sovereignty of the crown over both church and state clearly enunciated, what part did parliament then play in governing the *Ecclesia Anglicana?*

In dealing with this point, even more than in dealing with the previous two, it is as well not to be too categoric. One can argue from certain texts that the effect of the Henrician ecclesiastical measures was to maintain in England the powers of church and state separate and distinct, united only at the summit in the dual capacity of the sovereign as supreme head of both bodies. That is to say the Reformation Parliament deposed the pope, and put the king in his place, but otherwise left the church in possession of its old theoretical independence of the state. The best statement of this idea is to be found in the preamble to one of the major statutes of this very parliament, the Act in Restraint of Appeals (24 Henry VIII cap. 12). "The realm is a body politick compact of all sorts and degrees of people divided in terms and by names of Spiritualty and Temporalty . . . the body Spiritual . . . having power when any cause of the law Divine happened to come in question . . . the Laws Temporall for trial of property and land and goods," and the conservation of the peace being administered by the temporality. This definition of the relationship between church and state seems so clear as to leave no room for diversity of interpretation. This preamble prescribes the theoretical separation of the two powers which Elizabeth I tried in vain to maintain when she repeatedly warned her parliaments that church matters must be left to her and the clergy. The same theory was acknowledged in the submission of the clergy to Henry VIII (25 Henry VIII cap. 19), when convocation accepted the royal summons as the only valid occasion of its meeting, and the royal assent as necessary to all its legislative acts, and thus put itself in the same relationship towards the monarch as parliament already enjoyed. Henceforth parliament and convocation were to be equally dependent upon the king, but neither was to be dependent upon the other, an arrangement which had more theoretical than practical virtues if any dispute were to arise between the two jurisdictions.

Now it is clear that some effort was made to maintain this theoretical separation of church and state in the working out of the new arrangements for the church in England. For instance, the king, in the person of his vicar-general [Thomas Cromwell], presided over convocation, and with its advice and assent a number of things were done; articles of faith were issued, and the number of saints' days curtailed in 1536. Again it was by a commission of convocation that the fuller credal statement contained in the King's Book of 1543 was compiled, and by another that a handbook of ceremonial was prepared, though this latter was not adopted. In 1535 and 1536 royal visitations of monasteries were held, and in 1536 and 1538 royal injunctions issued to the clergy. All this was done by king and clergy alone without reference to parliament, save that its assistance was required in enforcing adhesion to the King's Book (34–5 Henry VIII cap. 1).

But there were other occasions when this theoretical equality of parliament and convocation was not so consistently maintained. There was a tendency, seemingly, to regard parliament as the superior power, and statute as being of more force than canon, so that on occasions it was thought advisable to confirm an act of convocation by an act of parliament. For example we have the case of the King's Book just quoted, a text compiled and agreed upon by convocation, but endorsed by parliament and backed up by statute. Or again, to revert to something already mentioned in another connection, the submission of convocation to the crown in 1532 was confirmed by statute two years later (25 Henry VIII cap. 19). Likewise with the supreme headship: acknowledged by convocation in 1531, it was restated in statutory form in 1534 (26 Henry VIII cap. 1).

This early practice of reinforcing an act performed by convocation with a complementary statute was later extended even to clerical taxation, and from 1540 onwards all clerical subsidies, granted in convocation, were confirmed by statute. From this practice, too, there developed by degrees the legal doctrine that no act of convocation had any binding force upon the laity unless confirmed by parliament.

Why add statute to act of convocation, unless the former added something to the force of the latter, by being enacted by a superior authority?

But there were yet other occasions where the part played by parliament in the government of the Henrician church was not just one of assisting the clergy in the enforcing of their will. In the matter of the Act of Six Articles of 1539, for example, parliament was the sole authority concerned, and convocation was not consulted at any stage. The task of finding a means to put an end to diversity of opinions in religion was at first entrusted to a committee of the lords, a committee entirely composed of men exercising spiritual jurisdiction, the king's vicar-general and eight bishops, but nevertheless a committee of the House of Lords and not of convocation. But in the end, it was the duke of Norfolk, a member of the royal council and a layman, who produced the first draft of the six articles of faith which were to be the test of orthodoxy in England and, though it was the bishops who monopolised the subsequent debate, it was the temporal legislature, the two houses of parliament, which had power to accept or reject these articles and to impose or not impose them upon the nation.

And of course it had been parliament which a few years earlier, again without reference to convocation, had decided that bishops consecrated without papal approval would be as validly bishops as any of their predecessors (Annates Acts, 23 Henry VIII cap. 20, 25 Henry VIII cap. 20).

These were occasions, and they were not the only ones (see also e.g. 28 Henry VIII cap. 16; 32 Henry VIII cap. 15; 33 Henry VIII cap. 31; 37 Henry VIII cap. 17; 37 Henry VIII cap. 31—some of the more notable examples), where the proper division between temporality and spirituality postulated by the Act in Restraint of Appeals (24 Henry VIII cap. 12) was totally ignored. Indeed, the exceptions to the rule prescribed in that act are so many as to incline one to doubt whether it was ever other than accidentally observed; whether, that is to say, there really was any attempt to maintain the separate existence of church and state once the royal ecclesiastical headship had been established. Was the king, or were his advisors at this period, given to niceties of constitutional thinking? Or did they act through whatever institution they considered a suitable instrument for the occasion regardless of the theoretical division of function between parliament and convocation?

This is not an easy question to answer. On the one hand, it is impossible to dismiss the preamble of the Act in Restraint of Appeals as merely so much propaganda, because the theory of church and state contained in it is too carefully thought out. On the other hand, that theory is so often ignored in subsequent legislation that one is led to doubt whether any real attempt was made to keep within its terms. Parliament's control over the Henrician church seems haphazard and irregular, and sometimes against the principles enunciated by itself. Yet it was sufficiently a reality to provide later generations with strong precedents for parliamentary intervention in church affairs, and to make it impossible ultimately for the crown to keep the hands of parliament off the church.

5 King or Minister? The Man Behind the Henrician Reformation

G. R. ELTON

THE question whether Henry VIII or Thomas Cromwell supplied the ideas and the policy which underlay the break with Rome is of more interest than may be imagined. Until it is answered neither the men nor the event can really be understood. The English Reformation gave to England, the English monarchy, and the English church a character quite their own: this makes it important to know just how and why· and through whom it happened. It may perhaps be thought strange that so well-worked a part of English history should be supposed to retain some mysteries still. Yet the last full-scale accounts of it are, on the Protestant side, Froude's great but partisan work published in 1862–70;[1] on the Anglo-Catholic side, Canon Dixon's weighty, condemnatory, and sometimes misleading volumes (1878–1902),[2] or James Gairdner's even more hostile and unreliable writings (1902–13);[3] and on the Catholic side, the much briefer recent book by Dr. Hughes.[4] To take the accounts more commonly used, there is Fisher's, written in 1913,[5] Professor Mackie's, which after forty years adds nothing in interpretation,[6] and the overpraised work of Constant, now also some twenty years old.[7] The standard

[1] J. A. Froude, *History of England from the Fall of Wolsey to the Defeat of the Spanish Armada*, 12 vols.

[2] R. W. Dixon, *History of the Church of England from the Abolition of the Roman Jurisdiction*, 6 vols.

[3] J. Gairdner, *The English Church from the Accession of Henry VIII to the Death of Mary* (1902); *Lollardy and the Reformation*, 4 vols. (1908–13).

[4] P. Hughes, *The Reformation in England: The King's Proceedings* (1950).

[5] H. A. L. Fisher, *The Political History of England*, Vol. v, *1485–1547*.

[6] J. D. Mackie, *The Earlier Tudors, 1485–1558* (1952).

[7] G. Constant, *La Réforme en Angleterre: Le Schisme Anglican* (1930; English trans. 1934).

lives of Henry VIII and Thomas Cromwell appeared in 1902.[8] On the face of it, a new study of those critical years in the 1530's might, to say the least, not be without reward. Here I shall attempt only to elucidate the true relationship between the two leading personalities of that age, for the prevailing notions seem to me to do scant justice to the genius of the minister and vastly to overrate the genius of the king. One's opinion of Henry VIII must stand by one's view of his part in the Reformation. The positive achievements of his long reign were crowded into its middle years; if he deserves the high opinion of his skill and understanding which so many moderns seem to hold, it must be because he was "the architect of the Reformation." But whether he was that remains to be seen.

Since it is the purpose of this paper to set up Thomas Cromwell as the moving spirit in the early Reformation, it will be of assistance to recall that this view is far from original. It was held, to begin with, by some of Cromwell's contemporaries—by Cardinal Pole, for instance, by the imperial ambassador Eustace Chapuys, and by John Foxe.[9] It was adopted outright—mainly in reliance on Pole and without proper investigation—by many nineteenth-century historians.[10] But then came Pollard, who held that the Reformation was a natural development from discoverable causes which was given its particular direction by the king himself;[11] and he had the support of the other early-Tudor pundit of the day, Gairdner, who ascribed to Cromwell at best outstanding execu-

[8] A. F. Pollard, *Henry VIII* (first published 1902, new edn. 1905); R. B. Merriman, *Life and Letters of Thomas Cromwell*, 2 vols. (1902).

[9] Reginald Pole, "Apologia ad Carolum Quintum Caesarem", *Epistolarum etc.: Pars Prima*, ed. Quirini (Brescia, 1744), pp. 66 ff.; *Letters and Papers, Foreign and Domestic, of the Reign of Henry VIII* (hereafter cited as *L.P.*), Vol. IX, no. 826; John Foxe, *Acts and Monuments*, ed. Pratt (1870), Vol. V, p. 366.

[10] *E.g.* Dixon, *op. cit.*, Vol. I, pp. 50 ff.; Merriman, *op. cit.*, Vol. I, pp. 89 ff.; A. D. Innes, *Ten Tudor Statesmen* (1906), pp. 127 ff. Similarly, Froude, *op. cit.*, Vol. I, p. 588; Vol. II, pp. 82 ff.

[11] This view underlies Pollard's general argument in his *Henry VIII, Thomas Cranmer and the English Reformation* (1905), and *Factors in Modern History* (first edn., 1907).

tive skill with perhaps some independent advice.[12] Not everybody, however, has been completely convinced by Pollard's picture of the "pilot who weathered the storm."[13] Both Fisher and Dr. Hughes have sat judiciously on the fence,[14] while Dr. Parker has recently suggested in general terms that the plan for the Reformation may have come from Cromwell.[15] A general reinterpretation of the period was attempted a few years ago in a book whose weaknesses of proof and argument have caused it to be too much neglected;[16] its general thesis is not dissimilar to the one which I had formed before I read it and which is the basis of this paper. In tilting at Pollard—with all the deference due to so great a historian and fully conscious of my temerity in attacking one of his fundamental tenets—I am not, therefore, altogether without company both past and present.

It is time to turn from what has been said about Cromwell and Henry to what can be found in the evidence. Is it, in fact, possible to come to conclusions in this matter which are more than opinions? Can one decide with any degree of certainty whether Thomas Cromwell or Henry VIII evolved the plan which led to the schism and the establishment of the royal supremacy, especially since both men must have worked together and much of the story must lie for ever hidden in unrecorded conversations, council meetings, and even private thoughts? I believe that despite these obstacles an answer is possible. In the first place, we can investigate the relations between king and minister to see whether they permit an insight into their position towards each other. Secondly, a reinterpretation of the course of the Henrician Reformation collated with Cromwell's career will, it is hoped, offer a solution of the problem.

[12] In his *Dictionary of National Biography* article on Cromwell, and in *The English Church* . . ., pp. 100 ff.
[13] *Factors in Modern History* (1926 edn.), p. 80.
[14] Fisher, *op. cit.*, pp. 295 ff.; Hughes, *op. cit.*, p. 195.
[15] T. M. Parker, *The English Reformation to 1558* (1950), p. 56; cf. also his "Was Thomas Cromwell a Machiavellian?," *Journal of Ecclesiastical History*, I (1950), esp. p. 63.
[16] A. Ogle, *The Tragedy of the Lollards' Tower* (1949).

No attempt to ignore or despise Henry VIII could ever be successful. Whatever may be thought of his character, he dominated the history of his time: he was a mighty king, no man's puppet, and never ignorant of what was done in his name. He took much active interest in the running of the realm, decided what policy was to be followed, made and unmade ministers and servants, and kept in his head and hand the strings of government. To suppose that Cromwell's was the real mind behind the great revolution is not to suppose that Henry had no mind at all. But the events of the reign—its confusion, its changing character, Henry's dependence on ministers, and so forth—all go to show that his was definitely an unoriginal and unproductive mind, intelligent indeed and capable of the swift assimilation of ideas, but unable to penetrate independently to the heart of a problem and its solution. Henry had the qualities of a first-rate politican— especially a remarkable opportunism—without the equipment of a first-rate statesman. Moreover, he was lazy: he took little part in the detailed business of government and surrendered the kind of prime-ministerial position which Henry VII had occupied.[17] Between them, his unoriginality and his laziness made him less really decisive than his personality and the deference of others would suggest. For the king's part in government is the harder to assess because his servants constantly protested that they were merely carrying out his orders. In theory the king determined everything: his pleasure was invariably vouched in warranty. How meaningless this could be is well illustrated by a case in which two rival claimants in some land dispute both pleaded the king's pleasure,[18] or again by Cromwell's habit of obtaining royal warrants for expenditure he himself had authorized, long after the payments were made.[19] We must never be so simple as to accept unquestioningly some Tudor politician's statement that he had his sovereign's orders for his doings, even as we must not be so subtle as always to disbelieve him. Sixteenth-century ministers did not

---

[17] Cf. G. R. Elton, *The Tudor Revolution in Government* (1953), pp. 66 ff.
[18] *L.P.*, xv, no. 36; cf. Elton, *The Tudor Revolution in Government*, p. 122.
[19] *Ibid.*, pp. 154 ff.

proclaim their independence of the crown, but their prudent citation of authority is not proof that they were not after all acting on their own initiative.

Cromwell's relations with Henry are the more obscured by this difficulty because Cromwell was normally careful to give no grounds for such accusations of independent action as had helped to bring Wolsey low. Instead he cultivated a sedulous obsequiousness in his letters to the king which contrasts strongly with his upright and straightforward address to all others. Advice which would involve the king in doing some work he wrapped up in apologies for his "bold audacite."[20] Though he had the king's ear, he knew Henry well enough to disclaim all ability to rule the king's wishes. Gardiner, on embassy in France, blamed Cromwell's alleged interposition for every sign of disfavour to himself, thereby moving Cromwell several times to point out that Henry VIII was not that kind of ruler. In private matters, Cromwell wrote, he would never act without orders.[21] (He did not say what his practice was in public affairs!). Nor could he pretend to "that which is not in me, that is that I shoulde be hable to doo what I wold."[22] He had no illusions about a favour which could never be taken for granted; in April 1536 he commented to Chapuys with unusual frankness on the mutability of things of which, he said, he had had a recent "domestic" example in the fall of Anne Boleyn.[23] Henry VIII was hard to manage, as Wolsey's successors discovered before they learned how to do business with him.[24] Great care was the more necessary because his reliance on others might at any moment give place to personal intervention. He surrendered his kingship to nobody.

However, that the whole truth does not lie in this picture of an active king to whom all things are deferred is sufficiently indicated in Cromwell's own correspondence. He summarized letters from abroad because they were too "long and diffuse" to trouble the king with;[25] he habitually drafted the instructions and

[20] Merriman, *op. cit.*, Vol. II, p. 177.   [21] *Ibid.*, p. 20.
[22] *Ibid.*, p. 68.   [23] *L.P.*, x, no. 601.
[24] *Ibid.*, IV, no. 6019.   [25] Merriman, *op. cit.*, Vol. II, p. 190.

other state papers which the king simply accepted by signing them;[26] he interviewed ambassadors and conducted most of the negotiations.[27] He could act without specific authority, as when he "thought better" to send instructions "by my priuate letteres then to put your highnes to the payne to have writen and troubled your self with thesame," a delicate way of excusing his omission to apply for orders.[28] In April 1539, ill with fever, he recited a long list of things done on his own responsibility which would ordinarily exhaust the energies of a man in the best of health.[29] Writing from the Tower after his fall, he summed up his essential liberty of action:

> I haue medelyd in So many matyers vnder your Highnes that I am not hable to answer them all . . . but harde it ys for me or any other medlyng as I haue done to lyue vnder your grace and your lawse but we must daylye offende.[30]

Unless we wish to suppose that Cromwell meant to accuse the king of authorizing breaches of the law—and of course he did not —it follows that he was accusing himself of often acting in affairs of state without the king's knowledge or authority.

The question here is whether it was Cromwell's mind or Henry's that evolved the plan for breaking the deadlock created by Wolsey's failure to get the king his divorce. What has been shown so far is that there is no justification for the frequent assertion that Cromwell was a mere "instrument";[31] in government and affairs he followed his own mind. But while this makes it possible to see in him the maker of the Reformation if further proof is forthcoming, it does not do so by itself. The answer can only be found in a reinterpretation of the meaning, and especially of the chronology, of the Henrician Reformation.

The whole interpretation depends on chronology because

[26] *Ibid.*, p. 216.
[27] *Ibid.*, p. 176; cf. Elton, *The Tudor Revolution in Government*, p. 327, n. 1.
[28] Merriman, *op. cit.*, Vol. II, p. 102.
[29] *Ibid.*, pp. 216 ff.   [30] *Ibid.*, p. 266.
[31] E.g. Pollard in his article on Cromwell in *Encyclopaedia Britannica* (11th edn.), or C. H. Williams in his in *Chambers' Encyclopaedia* (1950).

Cromwell did not immediately succeed Wolsey as the king's chief minister.[32] If he represented a policy of his own one might expect to see it appear with his arrival in power in 1532; and this is what happened. It is necessary to keep in mind what the "Henrician Reformation" really meant: the break with Rome—the withdrawal from the papal obedience—the creation of a schismatic English church—the setting up of the royal supremacy. All these are different, and in part tendentious, descriptions of one thing: the definition of independent national sovereignty achieved by the destruction of the papal jurisdiction in England. There lay the supremely important constitutional achievement of the 1530's. It came about because of the king's desire for a divorce from his first wife; it was greatly facilitated by the dislike of clergy and papacy which prevailed among the English laity; it may even have been assisted by the supposed spread of new and reformist ideas, whether Lutheran or humanist, though here the present writer would advocate the utmost caution. But in none of these things lay the essence of the change. Henry's campaign to have his marriage annulled is one thing; his break with the pope is another. The break was the means by which in the end the marriage was annulled; but Henry tried other means, and the historical importance of the break did not consist even mainly in the accomplishment of the divorce. To understand the years 1527–34 one must indeed start from the divorce, but one must try to follow events without allowing one's knowledge of the outcome to influence interpretation. One must attempt to discover what the king was up to as time went on.

This goes counter to Pollard's view that "the general course of the Reformation was a perfectly natural development from existing circumstances which it is idle to attribute to the influence of any one man."[33] It was his opinion that Henry knew from the beginning where he was heading, though he had hopes that he would not be driven all the way but might compel the pope to surrender before the break came. In Pollard's own metaphor, the

[32] Elton, *The Tudor Revolution in Government*, pp. 76 ff.
[33] *Thomas Cranmer*, p. 47.

outworks were sapped and the fortress taken step by pre-determined step.[34] Gairdner, too, thought that Henry from the first "claimed spiritual as well as civil supremacy in his own kingdom" since he never intended "to accept the jurisdiction of the Roman Curia," an extremely doubtful statement indeed.[35] This I believe to be now the accepted view: it credits the king both with farsighted plans and with an immediate ready radicalism of action. But it cannot be reconciled with those six long and tire-some years spent over the business. More than sixty years ago, Brewer rightly asked why Henry did not assert his own supremacy as early as 1529 but continued to prosecute the divorce at Rome even after Wolsey's failure.[36] He answered that Henry "never, in the first instance, seriously contemplated separation from Rome." This view makes better sense. Unable to see how he could legitimately marry Anne without the pope's connivance, and unaware of the possible implications of a royal supremacy in the church, Henry did not at first plan anything as extreme as a break with Rome. The ideas on which the revolution rested only ap-peared in the course of time.

To make the disagreement plain: Pollard held that a policy which relied on bringing Clement VII to compliance was the natural preliminary to a policy which solved the problem by ignoring the pope altogether. Put like this, it surely looks as though there were two radically different lines of approach rather than one naturally developing single line. With dubious logic, Pollard argued that the ultimate outcome, being inevitable (which one may doubt), was therefore envisaged from the first. What proof is offered? The Reformation was "so far dictated by circumstances that intelligent observers could predict its general tenor" even before November 1529.[37] "General tenor" is a question-begging phrase; of course, intelligent observers could foresee some of the issues that were going to be raised, but did they forecast, and did Henry show signs of aiming at, something

---

[34] *Henry VIII* (1905 edn.), pp. 276 ff.   [35] *L.P.*, v, introduction, p. xv.
[36] J. S. Brewer, *The Reign of Henry VIII* (1884), Vol. II, pp. 462 ff.
[37] *Thomas Cranmer*, p. 68.

very like the royal supremacy and break with Rome ultimately established? The alleged evidence—commonly cited from a calendar [*Letters and Papers . . . of the Reign of Henry VIII*] which at times mistranslates tendentiously—will not bear this out. There is Campeggio's report in October 1529 of Wolsey's warning that failure to give the king his divorce would result in the ruin of the realm, of Wolsey, and of the reputation of the church in England.[38] He cited Germany to show what a cardinal's intransigence could do and repeatedly asserted that this would shatter the authority of the Apostolic See which he had served so well and with which all his greatness was linked.[39] These last words, omitted by the calendar, are the clue to the whole: Wolsey knew his own fate and in his desperation painted things as black as he could to make Rome take action. If he had any idea how the authority of Rome would be "shattered" he seems to have thought it possible—quite wrongly—that Henry might turn Lutheran. He thought, in fact, only that ecclesiastical influence would decline; there is nothing to prove that he ever considered the likelihood of England breaking all ties with Rome.

Nor is the proof to be found in the reports of various French envoys, especially Jean du Bellay, bishop of Bayonne, who was in England in 1529. He wrote in August that parliament would meet in winter and that then "they would act of their own unfettered power" if the pope failed to oblige.[40] Again the calendar misleads; it renders *de leur puysance absolue* as "absolute power," a term too full of later shades of specific constitutional meaning to be employed with safety.[41] Of course, everyone knew that parliament was called and everyone rumoured that it was intended to get the king what he wanted; one cannot fairly read into these vague phrases a foreknowledge of the parliamentary history of the next seven years. In October Du Bellay wrote that the lay

[38] H. Laemmer, *Monumenta Vaticana Historiam Ecclesiasticam Saeculi XVI Illustrantia* (1861), p. 30: "presta et total ruina del Regno, di Sua Sign. Rev. et della reputatione ecclesiastica in questo regno."

[39] "Perche con questa ha congiunta tutta sua grandezza."

[40] J. Le Grand, *Histoire du Divorce de Henri VIII* (1693), Vol. III, p. 342.

[41] *L.P.*, IV, no. 5862.

lords dreamed of accusing the clerical estate and of sequestering its goods; instead of foreseeing how accurately these plans would be realized he called them fantasies and added ironically, *je croy qu'ils feront de beaux miracles* ["I believe they will perform beautiful miracles"].[42] The calendar's translation replaces a contemptuous remark by an apprehensive forecast, and—by translating the general *ils defferent* as the specifically legal "to impeach"—suggests a foreknowledge of the praemunire charge [a comprehensive indictment of invasion of royal powers by ecclesiastics] of 1530–1531; it turns Du Bellay's scepticism into accurate prophecy.[43] A little later the envoy noted that no priest was likely to hold the great seal again and that the clergy would have "terrible alarms,"[44] a correct interpretation of the prevailing anticlericalism but not a forecast of the break with Rome. That there was talk in government circles of settling the divorce without the pope—even loose talk of "provincial" independence—is not surprising and is vouched for by another French envoy, De Vaux, who reported in April 1530 that Henry spoke of dealing with the matter in his realm by the advice of his council and parliament without recourse to Rome.[45] But it was only talk, even to the king himself. When he tried, several months later, to find means of turning words into deeds, he was told by a committee of canon and common lawyers, which had investigated the question, that parliament could in no way circumvent the pope and order the divorce to be decided by Canterbury.[46] As Chapuys added, Henry was continuously threatening the pope with the power of parliament; yet there was so little genuine understanding or purpose in the threats that the solution later adopted without question was in 1530 ruled out as quite impossible. One cannot ask for better proof that in 1530 the government had not yet arrived at the policy of the break with Rome; the vigorous language of the disappointed king and his

[42] Le Grand, *op. cit.*, Vol. III, p. 374.
[43] *L.P.*, IV, no. 6011.
[44] Le Grand, *op. cit.*, Vol. III, p. 378 (*L.P.*, IV, no. 6019).
[45] Le Grand, *op. cit.*, Vol. III, p. 418 (*L.P.*, IV, no. 6309).
[46] *Calendar of State Papers, Spanish*, Vol. IV (i), p. 758 (Chapuys to Charles V, October 15, 1530).

ministers was backed by no design or practical project. It is fair to say that no one can be shown to have prophesied in 1529, or even in 1530, the complete separation of England from the papacy, though many expected attacks on specific forms of papal authority. Among them was the Venetian envoy, also put in evidence by Pollard, who in December 1530 remarks that the English government were trying so to arrange affairs that they no longer needed the pope in administrative matters.[47] Charles V similarly heard that Henry would "degrade" the pope, whom he allegedly called heretic.[48] The king was thought to desire a reduction of English dependence on Rome such as had long been achieved in France, not the overthrow of the pope's entire temporal and spiritual authority. After all, England, having been the most papalist and pope-ridden of countries in the fifteenth and early sixteenth centuries, had some way to go to attain the relative independence of France or even Spain. Henry's continued stand against Lutheran heresy made plain that he was not following the German example, and no one as yet—including Henry—could visualize a Catholic country without the pope.

What matters are not the words of observers but the deeds and intentions of Henry's government. Wolsey's failure to free Henry from Catherine of Aragon by means of the legatine court at Blackfriars was followed by the revocation of the case to Rome (July 1529), and for the three years after that everything turned on the issue whether Henry could be compelled to attend a trial at Rome or persuade the pope to let the case be decided in England. All the manœuvres on the king's part revolved around this central point. His intention was clear throughout: he wished to impress on Clement VII how much more comfortable it would be if he complied with the king's wishes. As a first step he called parliament. Left to themselves, the commons could be trusted to attack the church; they had shown their temper in 1515 and had been restive in 1523. The anti-clericalism of that first session was neither king-imposed nor king-inspired; at most it was permitted by the king. The commons' spontaneous action put pressure on

[47] *L.P.*, IV, no. 6774.   [48] *Ibid.*, no. 6142 (January 11, 1530).

the church and supplied Henry with ammunition for his attack at Rome—at Rome but not on Rome, for it is patent that Henry thought a divorce not sanctioned by the papacy insufficient to secure a legitimate succession. The real purpose of parliament was to overawe the church; it is too readily forgotten that Henry could no more afford opposition among his own clergy if the pope permitted them to try the case in England than if he acted (as ultimately he did act) entirely without the pope. Attacks on the independence of the English church were not synonymous with attacks on Rome: hitherto king and pope had more commonly joined hands against the liberties of the English church.

To start with, therefore, Henry's policy was to bring the clergy to heel in anticipation of their being called upon to adjudicate in the divorce, and to put pressure on Clement to permit them to do so. It continued in 1530. Parliament stood adjourned and rumours abounded. The general threats which were reported back to France and Venice have already been noticed: in words Henry was certainly growing fiercer. In October 1530, repeating that by the customs of the realm an Englishman could not be compelled to stand trial outside England, he warned the pope that his continued refusal would raise the whole question of his authority; what right had he so to treat a prince of such dignity *ut superiorem in terris non agnoscamus* ["that we recognise no superior on earth"]?[49] Lest we think that Henry had at last found a way out of his difficulties, let us remember that he had claimed to have no superior on earth as early as 1515,[50] six years before he committed himself to exceedingly high views on papal authority in the *Assertio Septem Sacramentorum*. He was ready to make resounding claims, but he had no idea how to give effect to them. His only action, a proclamation forbidding the procuration of papal bulls designed to interfere with the reforming legislation of 1529, attacked the authority of papal legates only and not that of the Roman Curia at all;[51] it did not touch the

[49] *State Papers of Henry VIII* (Record Commission, 1830–52), Vol. VII, pp.261 ff.
[50] Fisher, *op. cit.*, p. 215.
[51] N. Pocock, *Records of the Reformation* (1870), Vol. II, pp. 49 ff.

divorce in the very least. Despite all his brave words, Henry could do no more than spend a profitless year pursuing Cranmer's donnish suggestion by collecting the opinions of the universities on the two points at issue—the rights of the divorce suit and the plea that Englishmen were privileged to have their cases tried in England—in the hope that the weight of authoritative pronouncements would change the pope's mind. When it did not, Henry contented himself with a vigorous protest and an appeal to general councils and unnamed English laws; there is no particle of a threat of schism.[52]

The session of 1531 was preceded by another crop of rumours that something would be done concerning the divorce; Chapuys, who in September 1530 had reported the duke of Norfolk's promise to the papal nuncio that the king would not bring the matter before parliament if the pope did nothing,[53] had heard from a "well-informed man" in January that the divorce would "undoubtedly" be accomplished in the next session.[54] Norfolk proved better informed than Chapuys' anonymous friend: 1531 brought the king no nearer his divorce than 1529 or 1530. Parliament discussed no single measure in any way designed to promote the King's Great Matter, a fact which reminds one that a few months earlier the experts had decided that parliament could not help. The contrast with those busy later sessions needs no comment. Some four years had passed since Henry first determined to exchange Catherine for Anne, but there was still no sign that anything had occurred to him except the hopeless plan of forcing the pope to agree to a trial in England which Catherine and her Spanish supporters refused to contemplate. One thing 1531 did produce— the surrender of the clergy to the threat of praemunire and their recognition of Henry as "their singular protector, only and supreme lord, and as far as the law of Christ allows also supreme head." Unable to make Rome do his will, the king at least succeeded in his other ambition of bringing the English clergy firmly

52 *L.P.*, IV, no. 6759 (December 6, 1530).
53 *Calendar of State Papers, Spanish*, Vol. IV (i), pp. 719, 725.
54 *L.P.*, V, no. 24.

under his control. Contrary to the accepted view, this title of 1531 looked back to the earlier vague claim that the kings of England had no superior on earth, rather than forward to the precise and effective position of jurisdictional and political authority which the same title was to imply in 1534. Canon Dixon could see no point in a phrase which, as he rightly said, added no new authority to the crown: "it was a piece of folly to surprise the clergy and the country by strange language."[55] Perhaps it was less folly than a reflection of the fact that the new adviser in whose hands the title was to assume a formidable reality was then busy with the management of the convocations,[56] but as far as the king's own understanding of the matter went Dixon's view seems sound enough. The reservation which Fisher and Warham had inserted made nonsense of any claims more extreme than those which the English monarchy had steadily asserted over the church for centuries. Certainly the words "as far as the law of Christ allows" were not meaningless; Henry himself interpreted them as excluding all spiritual authority and with it the one thing that mattered to him, the divorce. Replying to Tunstall's protest against the title, the king wrote that the words *supremum caput* ought to be qualified by the addition of *in temporalibus*. That the king is the temporal head of spiritual persons in his realm, he continued, appears from history: in the temporal sphere of

> the persons of priests, their laws, their acts, and order of living . . . we . . . be indeed in this realm "Caput"; and because there is no man above us here, be indeed "Supremum Caput."[57]

It may seem, and probably is, a disingenuous defence, but it is clear on one point: the king's title does not expressly deny the pope's spiritual headship or justify the withdrawal of England

---

[55] *Op. cit.*, Vol. I, pp. 67 ff.

[56] *L.P.*, v, no. 224 (dean of York to Cromwell, May 2, 1531).

[57] Henry's answer is printed in D. Wilkins, *Concilia Magnae Britanniae* (1737), Vol. III, pp. 762 ff. The date there assigned to it (1533) is wrong. This letter differs from the one summarized in *L.P.*, v, no. 820, but there is no real reason for supposing that the latter document was a reply to Tunstall (*ibid.*, no. 819), or that it belongs to 1531.

from the papal jurisdiction. As yet there is no policy of a "break with Rome."

It would be tedious and pointless to follow the negotiations at Rome which throughout 1531–2 turned on the small technical point whether the Curia should hear Edward Carne, sent to Rome as *excusator* to plead that Henry should not be compelled to appear in a foreign court, in person or by proxy.[58] For two more years the pope held off both parties, refusing to let the case proceed in England, but also refusing to decide against Henry in Rome as the Spaniards demanded. All this time Henry continued his policy of convincing the pope of the justice of his case, showing so little decision that hostile observers repeatedly concluded that he would give in, put Anne away, and return to Catherine.[59] Reginald Pole heard similar reports: he alleged that Cromwell's advice rescued Henry from a fit of depression induced by his inability to see any way out.[60] The king was bankrupt in ideas. He knew what he wanted; that neither he nor his ministers knew how to obtain it is proved by those years of bootless negotiations. Strong words having failed, he was less violent in language in 1531 than in 1530. In July he again suggested that Canterbury might be allowed to adjudicate;[61] so far from wishing to withdraw from the Roman obedience, he still hoped to get papal approval for a trial in England. New envoys were despatched, only to report the obvious fact that nothing could be hoped for from Rome.[62] By December 1531 Henry was so far reduced that he was ready to have the case tried in France, a safe enough compromise no doubt, but an astonishing surrender of his claims as a sovereign prince and greatly at variance with the high language of 1530.[63] The letter ended in threats so vague as to lack all import: if the king knew what he meant he carefully hid his knowledge. Early in 1532, when the pope seemed at last about to pronounce, Henry was desperate to have the case deferred;[64] throughout 1531 and

[58] *L.P.*, v, introduction, p. ix.   [59] *Ibid.*, nos. 70, 1448, 1459.
[60] Pole "Apologia...," p. 116.   [61] *State Papers*, Vol. VII, p. 310.
[62] Bryan and Foxe to Henry VIII, September 22, 1531 (*L.P.*, v, no. 427).
[63] Pocock, *op. cit.*, Vol. II, pp. 148 ff.   [64] *L.P.*, v, nos. 691–2.

1532 there run like a thread the silly machinations designed to bribe some cardinals to Henry's side and so prevent a decision in consistory.[65] As late as this Henry was so firmly stuck in the mental processes of the past that he hoped to obtain his ends by the bestowal of English sees on Italians. Small wonder that early in 1532 Norfolk and Gardiner allegedly counselled the king to give up: it was about the only piece of advice they had left.[66]

By this time, however, Norfolk and Gardiner were no longer the leading advisers, and diplomatic pressure at Rome was no longer the only policy. Late in 1531 Cromwell was at last admitted to that inner circle of councillors who really advised the king and governed the realm.[67] Possibly the use of the term "empire" by Norfolk in conversation with Chapuys in January 1531 reflects the beginning of Cromwell's real influence;[68] it can be shown—though not here—that it was he who introduced the notion of empire (=sovereignty) into the controversy. There are signs from that time onwards that the doomed policy of forcing Rome to act as England wished her to was being accompanied by steps of another kind. The clergy's surrender to the praemunire charge gave the king some positive gains, in particular the subsidies voted in an effort to propitiate the royal wrath; this was more than had resulted from all the energy spent in beating at the gates of Rome. However, the king's ultimate aims remained as unrealizable as before. If a new policy is to be discerned in the imposition of the title of supreme head, it is also clear that it was a policy pursued but half-heartedly and without a true understanding of where it might lead. In 1532 the undercurrent usurped the lead. At last parliament was turned against the pope. However harshly the sessions of 1529 and 1531 had dealt with the English clergy, they had not touched the papacy. But in 1532 parliament passed the First Act of Annates, by which an important source of papal revenues was cut off,[69] and promoted the "Supplication against

[65] Pocock, *op. cit.*, Vol. II, pp. 144 ff., 213 ff., 241 ff., 252 ff., 339.
[66] *L.P.*, v, no. 834.
[67] Elton, *The Tudor Revolution in Government*, pp. 90 ff.
[68] *L.P.*, v, no. 45.   [69] 23 Henry VIII, cap. 20.

the Ordinaries," which enabled Henry to follow up his nominal triumph of 1531 with a real triumph over the English clergy by forcing it to accept his control of ecclesiastical legislation. Since— as Maitland has taught us—the English church had no legislative independence in the later Middle Ages, this meant that its dependence was transferred from pope to king; the manœuvre based on the Supplication—the "Submission of the Clergy"—was a real though masked attack on the pope's authority in England.

Thus 1532 saw the inauguration of the policy which was to culminate in the complete destruction of the Roman jurisdiction in England and England's complete withdrawal from the Roman obedience. It also saw the first use for that purpose of the instrument by means of which the revolution was to be accomplished, a point of great significance which can only be hinted at here: there is good reason for supposing that Cromwell, who deliberately made a career in parliament, introduced the king to the potentialities of statute. In the sudden eruption of a new policy, Cromwell's hand is manifest. It was he who brought the Supplication—first started by the commons in 1529 but then not driven home—to the attention of the government, who prepared the final draft, and who managed the manœuvre involved in its employment.[70] He drafted the famous clause in the First Act of Annates which postponed its effect until the king should have tried further negotiations with Rome.[71] In itself that clause marked a defeat for the new policy; it may be conjectured, on the basis of the developments already described, that Cromwell's act proved as yet too drastic for Henry, so that his first anti-papal measure had to be adapted to the purposes of that other policy which had relied for some three years on finding means to coerce the pope into compliance.

Like all its predecessors, this means also failed: Clement was not to be persuaded by the distant power of England while the

[70] Cf. G. R. Elton, "The Commons' Supplication against the Ordinaries," *English Historical Review*, LXVI (1951), 507 ff.

[71] Cf. G. R. Elton, "A Note on the first Act of Annates," *Bulletin of the Institute of Historical Research*, XXIII (1950), 203 ff.

neighbouring power of the emperor remained hostile. And so, a year later, in the session of February-April 1533, the Act in Restraint of Appeals to Rome, with its great proclamation of national sovereignty, signalled the triumph of the radical policy— the break with Rome. The prehistory of this act provides the last proof of the two separate policies which have been traced in this paper, and of the fact that Cromwell sponsored the one that proved successful. There survive two drafts for acts of parliament in the hand of Sir Thomas Audley, who had succeeded More as keeper of the great seal in May 1532, which indicate that even late in 1532 some doubt remained as to the best way of getting the divorce legalized in the realm. One of them would have given parliamentary endorsement to a divorce pronounced by the arch-bishop of Canterbury;[72] this represented only an *ex post facto* sanction and not a parliamentary policy. The other intended to give to the archbishops parliamentary authority to act in the divorce in the pope's place;[73] it is the climax of that policy which had persistently endeavoured to get Rome to remit the case to England—the culmination of all those complaints, recitals of privileges, and vague threats of hostile action in which Henry had indulged ever since Wolsey's failure in the summer of 1529. It used parliament, but only to permit Canterbury for once to stand in Rome's stead: not based on any profound principle, it was the half-hearted sort of thing that the lawyers' decision had held up in 1530. Its preamble recites the divine law against a man marry-ing his brother's wife, laments the long delays, and accuses the pope of aspiring to usurp the rights of princes; it is throughout full of apologies, self-justification, and polite references to "the popes holynes."

The statute actually passed, on the other hand, not only provided for a general prohibition of appeals to Rome—that is, it dealt with a wide issue of general significance instead of confining itself to the particular matter of the divorce—but also included a preamble which described in unequivocal language a theory of England as

[72] Public Record Office, State Papers, Henry VIII (SP 2), Vol. N, fos. 163-4.
[73] Ibid., fos. 155-62.

a sovereign state in which no other potentate might interfere. That it was Cromwell who evolved this measure, and how he overcame some remaining fears and doubts which proclaimed themselves in apologetic and justificatory phrases, has been described elsewhere.[74] Right to the end of the long-drawn conflict the two policies—one pursued since 1529, the other introduced by Cromwell in 1532—vied with each other for the king's approval. So reluctant was Henry to take the decisive step that even towards the end of 1532 he could still toy with a partial measure designed to keep the door open at least an inch or two, even while a simple and thorough policy based on a devastating principle was offered to him. Cromwell's grandiose conceptions triumphed, but it seems to have been a near thing.

The Reformation, then, was not the inevitable development of the text-books. Whether it would have come anyway it is idle to speculate; but it came in the 1530's simply because Henry's desire for his divorce was balked by an international situation which made co-operation with the papacy impossible, and it came as it did because Thomas Cromwell produced a plan which achieved Henry's ends by destroying the papal power and juris-diction in England and by creating in England an independent sovereign state. This policy was not present from the start; it had to overcome much caution and conservatism as well as fear of the consequences before its bold simplicity was permitted to develop. The Henrician Reformation reflects the ideas—one may say, the political philosophy—of Thomas Cromwell.

[74] Cf. G. R. Elton, "The Evolution of a Reformation Statute," *English Historical Review*, LXIV (1949), 174 ff.

6 The Peace of Augsburg:
New Order or Lull in the Fighting

HERMAN TÜCHLE

I

ON September 25, 1555, at three o'clock in the afternoon, the Recess of the Imperial Diet, with the religious peace as its nucleus, was made public at the townhall of Augsburg.[1] "The universal, permanent and perpetual peace among the Estates of the Holy Roman Empire in regard to religious disputes," the goal of many negotiations "for thirty years or more," seemed at last to have been achieved. The Estates who took part may well have been united to a man behind their spokesman when he expressed gratitude to King Ferdinand "after His Royal Majesty had shown himself so graciously disposed towards the common weal and the good of the Fatherland as to take upon himself the burden of this Diet in the name of His Imperial Majesty [Charles V, his brother], to have been present for so long at the said Diet, and to have attended to its issues with the gracious, paternal industry and patience demanded by the supreme importance of the same." And the king may have been just as sincere in answering that he had acted with the authority and on the instructions of His Imperial Majesty, for love of God, and to the welfare and good of His Imperial Majesty and the entire Estates.

All the same, the king can hardly have failed to notice that this conclusion to the religious question had been brought about quite differently from all the earlier attempts to modify imperial law on this point, starting from [the Diet of] Worms [in 1521] and continuing up to the Interim of Augsburg and the "Armed Diet"

[1] The critical edition of the Peace of Augsburg is by K. Brandi (2nd edn., 1927); excerpts from it are in E. Walder (ed.), *Religionsvergleiche des 16. Jahrhunderts* (Berne, 1945).

of 1547–8. What had been achieved in Augsburg in 1555 could well be called an imperial settlement in so far as the intention behind it was to set affairs in order within the frontiers of Germany and put an end to any future contentions. But it was no longer an imperial settlement as understood in the medieval days of imperial grandeur and the theory of empire. For one thing Burgundy, Switzerland and the Netherlands remained unaffected by it; in the case of the Netherlands, the emperor declared specifically during the course of the negotiations (on July 7, 1555) that his subjects there were not obliged to accept imperial ordinances, and this at a time when both the Netherlands and Switzerland were still formally part of the Empire. More important, however, was the fact that the Peace of Augsburg came into being without the participation of the two heads of medieval Christendom, who had put in an appearance at more or less all previous settlements. This circumstance is not obscured either by Ferdinand's reference to his authorization with imperial authority or by the intermittent presence of papal representatives at Augsburg.

The Emperor Charles V[2] had already resolutely opposed the prospect of a permanent peace in religious matters at Passau in 1552. But it was he who had issued the summons to the Imperial Diet, which had first been announced for Ulm on August 26, 1553, and then, after many postponements, finally inaugurated with the arrival of King Ferdinand on December 29, 1554, and formally opened on February 5, 1555. In the summer of 1553 the emperor negotiated in Brussels with the delegation from the city of Augsburg, who, because of the inflation caused by earlier diets, were reluctant to let Augsburg be the venue for yet another.[3] In 1553 Charles appointed as commissioners to the Imperial Diet the cardinal of Augsburg, Otto Truchsess von Waldburg, the vice-chancellor of the electorate of Trier, Felix Hornung,[4] and the

[2] K. Brandi, "Passauer Vertrag und Augsburger Religionsfriede," *Historische Zeitschrift*, XCV (1905), 206–64.

[3] F. Roth, *Augsburgs Reformationsgeschichte*, Vol. IV (1911), pp. 674 ff.

[4] His protocol (*Protocollum actorum in comitiis Augustanis anno 1555 in consilio apud Regiam Maiestatem*) is to be found as Manuscript 50 in the library of the theological seminary at Trier; cf. L. von Pastor, *Geschichte der Päpste seit dem*

Swabian Lazarus von Schwendi. After months of hard work there arrived in Brussels a memorandum drawn up in Augsburg by the imperial vice-chancellor, Seld, which formed the basis of the instructions for the commissioners and provides an interesting insight into the emperor's intentions. The emperor considered that the proper way to settle religious disputes was by a general council [of the church]. He would have nothing to do with a national council. At the same time, although the emperor still set certain hopes on a religious colloquy, he would not allow it to anticipate the future decisions of the council. He acknowledged the Interim to have been a mistake and said that it should be abandoned.[5]

The emperor, however, was already determined not to attend the Diet in person.[6] On June 8, 1554, he disclosed the real reason for this in a letter to his brother Ferdinand: "It is only the matter of religion about which I have those insuperable misgivings which I set forth in detail to you by word of mouth, the last occasion being our meeting at Villach." And so he relinquished the conduct of the Diet completely to his brother, saying that he had no doubts that Ferdinand, as a good Christian prince, would give his approval to nothing which might weigh upon his conscience; his memorandum concerning all the points of possible discussion at the Diet was intended only as an indication of his interest, and as information for the commissioners who were to support Ferdinand at the Diet at his own wish, without assuming any responsibility for the course of events. The king, at all events, was unhappy about this authority given him; but all his attempts to pass the decision-making over to the emperor, even at a distance, were frustrated by the determination of Charles, who had already, on April 8, 1555, registered a protest in advance against anything "by which our true, ancient, Christian and Catholic religion might be offended, injured, weakened or disgraced," and who, in

Ausgang des Mittelalters, Vol. VI (1923), p. 564, though his information on this point is faulty.

[5] F. Siebert, Zwischen Kaiser und Papst (1943), p. 413. [The emperor's Interim of Augsburg in 1548 had imposed a religious settlement unacceptable to the majority of both Protestants and Catholics.]

[6] K. Brandi, Kaiser Karl V., Vol. I (1937), pp. 536 ff.

September, was still turning down all requests to him for advice or instruction on the religious issues. It was only at Ferdinand's request that Charles still retained the title of emperor. In the formulation of the Recess Ferdinand attached importance to making the proclamation in the emperor's name. But Charles wrote to Ferdinand on July 7, 1555, that he would know best how affairs had proceeded and should therefore do his best, in virtue of his instructions from the emperor, and as king in his own right, to see that the most grievous points were mitigated and the decline of religion averted. Even the efforts of the pope[7] to break the emperor's reserve were unavailing. As the second head of Christendom, Charles could not associate himself with the inevitable permanent peace between the old and the new believers.[8] The process of abdication which began in October 1555 was the emperor's perfectly logical and consistent reaction to the Religious Peace.

Rome, too, was less than enthusiastic about the imminent Diet, and it was intimated to the king that a diet was an extremely unsuitable way of dealing with religious questions so long as the Council of Trent was merely adjourned and not as yet concluded. That a legate was finally sent was due only to the unremitting pressure of the cardinal of Augsburg.[9] This legate, Cardinal Morone, together with the nuncio Delfino, was supposed not merely to represent the pope in religious questions, but to bring about harmony among the princes of the church. Yet it was not until March 24 that Morone first arrived at Augsburg, and a week later he was already setting off, together with Cardinal Truchsess, for the conclave at Rome. The early death of Marcellus II of course made a new election necessary as early as May, and the outcome of this was Paul IV. The new pope was the type *par*

[7] Pastor, *op. cit.*, Vol. VI, p. 567.

[8] [Notwithstanding these intentions of the emperor, the Peace of Augsburg did have his formal approval, since a phrase giving authority to Ferdinand's actions was accidentally left in the documents when they were reworded by the imperial councillors: cf. H. Lutz, *Christianitas afflicta: Europa, das Reich und die Päpstliche Politik . . . (1552–1558)* (Göttingen, 1964), p. 436.]

[9] Siebert, *op. cit.*, p. 141; Pastor, *op. cit.*, Vol. VI, pp. 564 ff.

excellence of the counter-reformer, not prepared to make even the smallest concessions. And so Delfino was recalled to Rome in July. Lippomano, who had been appointed nuncio in Poland, was told to go to Augsburg and try to persuade the king and the Catholic princes to see that the Diet dispersed without a recess or at least passed no resolutions detrimental to the Catholics. Exhortations addressed by the pope himself to the king, to Albert of Bavaria, to the archbishops of Mainz and Salzburg, and to other Catholic princes and bishops, were designed to lend weight to these endeavours. But the nuncio did not achieve much; once on the scene he recognized the king's political predicament. He did indeed hand over a memorandum to the effect that the Apostolic See was the sole tribunal for resolving religious disputes, but at the beginning of September he departed so that he would not be forced to play the inactive spectator in the event of an unfavourable outcome. Although the pope did not reply to the Peace with a solemn protest, he did send sharply disapproving letters to Ferdinand, the duke of Bavaria and the German archbishops and bishops. Even afterwards the Peace of Augsburg did not receive papal recognition.

Thus the Diet remained from the very outset a matter for the Estates among themselves. What an opportunity this might have been to clear up the religious question, without the emperor's heavily armed troops or the moral pressures of the Roman Curia! But only very few of the Estates were actually swayed by religious interests. The Catholics were spiritless and more interested in defending their property than their faith. The Protestants were mainly concerned to bully a peace out of the emperor in order to augment their power vis-à-vis the supreme imperial authority and to secure their own church government and the ecclesiastical properties they had confiscated. One Catholic bishop alone measured up to his responsibility, and only one Protestant prince rose to the same level. These were the cardinal of Augsburg and his close neighbour, Duke Christopher of Württemberg. Here at least, even though on opposite sides, powerful religious energies still flourished.

On theological grounds the cardinal would not budge from the idea of a single religion.[10] To his way of thinking, therefore, any religious peace could have validity only until an agreement had been reached at the Council. But when the Council decided, one side would have to yield; for God was a God of unity, not discord. He delivered a solemn protest on March 23, stating that he was unable to approve the suggested articles in any way and might not act contrary to his duties towards the Apostolic See, the emperor and the Empire. He would rather, he said, lose life and limb, and was determined to remain faithful till death to his vows and obligations like a true Christian and a born German. A few months later, on hearing news of the course of the negotiations, he wrote in similar vein from Rome to his brother William: "I fear indeed that God's wrath will come upon our sins, because we have set our eyes on the temporal more than on the eternal, on the worldly more than on the spiritual. Truly, truly, my most gracious Lord, His Royal Majesty should rather depart without any Imperial Recess than with such a godless and unjust peace." His chancellor, Dr. Braun, protested again in his name on the actual day the resolutions were made known.

On the other side it was the duke of Württemberg[11] who was likewise anxious for a religious compromise rather than simply a peace. Shortly before the Diet, in fact, he had exchanged proposals to this end with the bishop of Passau. It seemed to him now that the best means was a colloquy at which the most judicious theologians of both parties should seek the truth in accordance with God's Word and Holy Scripture. If they did not bring about an agreement, the Estates themselves should meet and endeavour to remove the religious discord. "For they are all baptized in the death of Christ and are living members of the Christian church." Christopher was here putting his trust in his own and the other princes' knowledge of Scripture. Only if this method also failed, he declared in the instructions for his delegates

[10] Siebert, *op. cit.*, pp. 141, 149.

[11] V. Ernst (ed.), *Briefwechsel des Herzogs Christoph von Wirtemberg*, Vol. III (1902), nos. xxxi ff., pp. 40 ff.

on April 24, could a general or national council be allowed to achieve a settlement. The city of Strasbourg, which in earlier years had been closely associated with Christopher,[12] had similarly instructed its delegates to work for a religious agreement, which was, however, to be obtained not through a general council, but through a national assembly with disputations on all controversial points in accordance with Scripture alone. The duke, who was the sole Protestant prince to take part personally in at least the first phase of the negotiations, was disappointed by the course they took. In the end he had to yield to the pressure of Saxony and Brandenburg and move towards a religious peace, but for him the whole issue still remained essentially a religious one. The question of securing firm possession of confiscated ecclesiastical property was purely secondary; he was more interested in excluding the sectarians and drawing the knights into the peace. He was somewhat impressed by the safeguards to conscience insisted on by the Catholics, and their appeal to oaths they had taken; indeed, he himself felt that the concessions made at the end to the Catholics, and particularly the ecclesiastical reservation [see p. 156], were a moral problem, and he held discussions with his theologians about how far it was permissible for a ruler to allow such things. Again it was the Strasbourgers who, on September 14, resisted any toleration of the Catholic minority in their city with an appeal to conscience. They maintained that the city, too, had an obligation to lead its citizens to heaven; since they held the Augsburg Confession for the true doctrine, any toleration of the Catholic system was a sin against God.

Otherwise, however, very little in the way of religious motives was put forward. There was no longer any interest in restoring the unity of faith, or in winning the Empire over to the religious revolution of the century. The first ecclesiastical prince of its Empire, the elector of Mainz, was conscious only of the danger threatening the church in Germany from all quarters and saw no further possibility of regaining what had been snatched away,

[12] W. Friedensburg (ed.), *Politische Correspondenz der Stadt Strassburg*, Vol. v, 1550–55 (1928), pp. 569 ff.

considering how little protection and comfort was to be expected from the spiritual and temporal heads of Christendom. New disturbances would be inevitable if the peace were not concluded. If some remnants of former possessions and secular powers were to be preserved it would be necessary to abandon all claims where there was no longer any hope of restitution.[13] Duke Albert of Bavaria, the leading Catholic ruler after the king, was of like mind. Even for the great Protestant Estates of the Empire, the electorates of Saxony and Brandenburg and their numerous body of supporters in the Council of Princes, the treatment of the religious question at the Diet was essentially a political act. The aim was to consolidate the Protestant ecclesiastical system, which was already several decades old and had lost the impetus of its early days. A period of tranquillity was desired in order to extend what had been gained, to use the fruits of confiscated church property, and to erect permanent barriers against any jurisdiction by Catholic bishops and any interference whatsoever in the internal affairs of the territorial ruler. The enthusiasm for free option for the clergy—in other words, the right of bishops to go over to the new religion—was due primarily to the fact that this was seen as the surest way of adding the central German bishoprics to their own dynastic lands. It was not a religious agreement that was wanted here, but a religious peace, and a permanent one at that. "Better no peace at all than a patched-up one" was the rigid attitude adopted by the electoral delegates in April.[14] The electors did not conduct the Augsburg negotiations in person; of the Protestant princes, only the duke of Württemberg was present. Instead they sent their delegates, who were not theologians but jurists and politicians, because [their principals] felt certain of their cause as long as matters were arranged on this plane. It was believed that it would be possible to force the emperor to grant the religious peace promised at Passau by refusing even to con-

[13] A. von Druffel and K. Brandi, *Beiträge zur Reichsgeschichte*, Vol. IV, *Briefe und Akten zur Geschichte des sechzehnten Jahrhunderts* (1896), p. 593.

[14] Friedensburg, *op. cit.*, Vol. V, p. 599; L. Schwabe, "Kursachsen und die Verhandlungen über den Augsburger Religionsfrieden," *Neues Archiv für Sächsische Geschichte*, X (1889), 216–303.

sider his plans for imperial reform or to begin negotiations over the ordinance for the public peace before the religious peace had been concluded. The Empire, of course, was in sore need of internal law and order, and the cities would have been only too glad to comply with Ferdinand's proposal that the public peace should be discussed first. They had had first-hand experience [in 1552–3] of public insecurity and the weakness of imperial authority during the predatory incursions of Margrave Albert Alcibiades [of Kulmbach-Bayreuth in Franconia]. But the higher Estates, who were able to preserve order in their own territories, feared that to agree to a public peace ordinance would provide the emperor with a weapon for his struggle against religious innovations. They therefore forced through negotiations for the religious peace before anything else and even threatened to go to war.[15] One thing, however, they had not anticipated, that the emperor would dissociate himself from the Diet, with the result that they would not be able to secure an agreement between emperor and Estates but merely a treaty among the Estates themselves. King Ferdinand naturally used every opportunity to retaliate with diplomatic pressure. When the draft agreed on by the Estates was handed to him he left them waiting over two months for his decision, and then declared that he was unable to remain any longer in Augsburg; in other words, if the Estates would not go along with his decisions, the issue would have to be postponed until a later Diet. But nobody had any desire to return home empty-handed.

It is obviously most regrettable that what was originally a religious concern should have been transformed in this way into a political matter. At the same time it should not be forgotten that every conceivable means of restoring religious unity had been exhaustively tried out over the preceding thirty-five years: outlawry and excommunication, colloquies and councils, wars and imperial decrees, all had failed. Nevertheless, it might be queried whether some other solution was not still possible besides this

[15] N. Paulus, "Religionsfreiheit und Augsburger Religionsfriede," *Historisch-Politische Blätter*, CXLIX (1912), 356–67, 401–16, pp. 408 ff.

reinforcement of particularist forces at the expense of emperor and Empire. The recognition of two faiths in the one Empire, undoubtedly the most serious consequence of the Religious Peace, meant the destruction of the Empire as understood in the Middle Ages. It ceased to be a factor in decisions of faith in Europe. In an Empire like this the emperor could no longer be protector of the church and propagator of the true faith. Charles V's abdication a few weeks after the Recess should accordingly not have been followed by a new election; what finally happened in 1806 should have taken place then and there. That this was not the outcome was due partly to the force of tradition and above all to Ferdinand's conviction that the Recess was only a provisional measure and that the Council of Trent would still settle the religious issue. The king was also encouraged in this conviction by [the Jesuit] Peter Canisius, who was at Augsburg at the time.

II

Among the particular provisions of the Peace of Augsburg which merit special attention, the most important is the right of the Estates to implement the Reformation. The late medieval system of territorial churches had taken a steadily more absolutist turn during the decades of the Reformation. The Protestant Estates would not allow the right of territorial princes to determine the religion of their subjects to be undermined.[16] Even though in March and April there was some demand for the right of free option for subjects "of both religions," the secret agreement among the Protestant Estates in Naumburg [on March 9–12] contradicted this just as much as did the instruction given by the elector of Saxony to his delegates to arrange the provisions of the peace in such a way "that we are not obliged to tolerate the papal abuses in our land." Otto Henry of Pfalz-Neuburg proposed that freedom of religious option should be demanded for the subjects of Catholic Estates, while counter-claims should be rejected on the grounds that no secular authority might permit its subjects

[16] *Ibid.*, pp. 358 ff.

to engage in public idolatry, a suggestion which shows the insincerity of the demand. One must concur here with Brandi's judgement: "There can be no doubt whatever that they were demanding a greater degree of freedom than they themselves had any intention of granting."[17] The Catholic Estates turned the proposal down. In the Council of Electors it was Mainz, in the Council of Princes Bavaria and especially Austria, who said that it was the office of the ruler to promote the salvation and eternal bliss of his subjects within the true faith. When Bavaria and Austria openly declared that they would rather see the entire negotiations collapse than accept the proposal, the other side decided not to insist on their demand for the time being. They waited until September before trying again, but even then they had no greater success.

Thus matters remained with the right of Reformation. The principle *Ubi unus dominus, ibi una sit religio* ["Where there is one lord, there should be one religion"], often enunciated in the negotiations, later became the familiar proposition *Cuius regio, eius et religio* ["He who rules the land also determines its religion"].[18] This formula, which appears for the first time in 1599 in the *Institutions of the Canon Law* by the Lutheran Joachim Stephani, evidently has quite ancient roots, despite the fact that the territorial principle was not directly expressed but only hinted at in the Peace of Augsburg, in which *religio* did not originally mean religious confession but the public practice of religion.

What was, however, expressly formulated here for the first time was the freedom of subjects to emigrate,[19] the *ius emigrandi*, which was envisaged as a limitation of the Reformation right of the Estates. If subjects who adhered either to the old religion or to the Augsburg Confession wished for religious reasons to move to other localities they were to be permitted to depart and sell their property without any hindrance. This provision is without any

17 Druffel and Brandi, *op. cit.*, Vol. IV, p. 739.
18 J. Lecler, "Les origines et le sens de la formule: cuius regio, eius religio," *Recherches de science religieuse*, XXXVII (1950), 119–31; Paulus, *loc. cit.*, pp. 404 ff.
19 *Ibid.*, pp. 365 ff.; Ernst, *op. cit.*, Vol. III, p. 312.

doubt a step forward from the medieval laws against heretics. Its exact origin is not clear. It may have received some of its inspiration from article 30 of the Imperial Recess of 1530, which had been intended as a protection for the Catholic subjects of Protestant rulers. The right of emigration was already in the draft of the Council of Princes of March 25, 1555, where it met with no serious opposition. Bavaria insisted that it be also inserted into the draft of the electors. It is true that the article was not included in the Royal Resolution of August 30, but it was commended to the king by Catholics and Protestants alike as conducive to peace, and was accepted by him.

Another restriction on the general right to reform, however, was passionately disputed—the refusal of the free option for the ecclesiastical Estates.[20] The Diet had threatened to break up over this issue on several occasions since the beginning of May, when the Protestant secular princes had declared that they would not accept any peace if it did not grant everyone the liberty to turn Protestant. But in spite of all the threats the Catholic Estates were unyielding, and their reasons reveal the deepest distrust of the bishops and those who elected them. If the right of free option could not be confined to the secular Estates alone, then the prelates who went over to the new doctrines should at least lose their offices and revenues. This "ecclesiastical reservation," as the Catholic side explained, was a matter of life and death to the Catholic church in Germany. If this proviso were abandoned it would be the simplest thing in the world for the Protestant princes to put pressure on cathedral chapters to appoint to bishoprics only such persons as could be relied upon, once installed and given papal confirmation, to go over openly to the new religion and lead their bishoprics towards it. How great this danger was can be seen from the election during the Diet of an archbishop of Mainz: the Catholic candidate had defeated the Protestant aspirant by a single vote. Were the reservation to be abandoned, Braun wrote in June to his master in Rome, then all would be lost for religion and the Empire. The bishops would lay down their

[20] Friedensburg, *op. cit.*, Vol. v, pp. 600, 630; Siebert, *op. cit.*, p. 149.

ecclesiastical dignity, marry, install a cathedral preacher as bishop, secularize all properties and make them hereditable. If there were a Protestant majority among the electors, the house of Habsburg itself would no longer hold the imperial crown secure. But the Protestants would not back down. The king had to decide; and he decided in favour of the ecclesiastical reservation. Under the threat of the Diet being adjourned, the Protestants had to reconcile themselves to this, though they did so only on condition that the dispute should be expressly mentioned in the Recess and that the king should incorporate the article in the Peace only by virtue of the imperial authority vested in him.

The Protestants, however, had already secured a number of profitable advantages from this concession. The ecclesiastical Estates, under pressure from the king, had to leave episcopal jurisdiction in the newly Protestant territories suspended at least until such time as a religious agreement was achieved, and also to reconcile themselves to the prospect that church lands already confiscated at the time of the Treaty of Passau would not be restored. Most important of all, the Protestant Estates had renewed their demand that the subjects of Catholic rulers should be granted freedom to change their religion, attempting very energetically to ensure that this applied at least to the subjects of ecclesiastical Estates. The "poor, sorely tried king" looked for a way out. In order to secure the right to determine the religion of subjects both for himself and the secular Catholic Estates, he gave way in the case of ecclesiastical Estates. Knights, cities and communes under ecclesiastical rulers who had already adhered for some time to the Confession of Augsburg might not be brought back to the old faith by ecclesiastical princes.[21] This provision was especially important in certain bishoprics in central Germany, where a number of cities had long since turned Protestant; and this was why the electorate of Saxony was among the parties strongly in favour of it. At the instigation of the ecclesiastical electors, Ferdinand's declaration was issued in a special "Supplementary Recess," being neither incorporated in the Religious Peace nor

[21] Paulus, loc. cit., pp. 405 ff.; Ernst, op. cit., Vol. III, p. 335.

printed together with it, despite the complaints made by the Protestants about this lack of uniformity. In years to come the legal validity of the *Declaratio Ferdinandei* was frequently disputed.

One final restriction on the general right to reform affected the cities,[22] which were by far the weakest of all the political forces assembled at Augsburg and were held "in little esteem." If they sat together with the electors and princes in committee, they would generally be overruled by the higher Estates. For this reason they preferred a consultation in three separate corporate bodies, with the right to seek the decision of the king whenever they were in disagreement with the other Estates. However, separate consultations among the cities themselves were obstructed mainly by their own lack of agreement on the religious issue. As a result of the Interim and the constitutional changes ([which introduced more oligarchical municipal councils known as] *Hasenräte* ["hare councils"], after the imperial councillor Hass, who had done much to push them through), the Catholic system, or at least worship according to the Interim, had been reintroduced in a number of cities which had previously turned Protestant. Many cities had in the meantime done away with the *Hasenrat* and the Interim, others were still obliged to tolerate Catholic worship within their walls, and others again had long ago decided to remain faithful to the old church. Furthermore, the cities wanted as far as possible to avoid falling out with the emperor or the king, whose protection was their one and only guarantee of existence against their covetous neighbours. In order to protect Catholic minorities in those imperial cities where Catholic worship had once again been permitted after the Schmalkaldic War, and to ensure some compensation for relinquishing their powers of jurisdiction, the ecclesiastical Estates insisted as early as May that Catholicism should continue to be tolerated in these cities until the prospective settlement. It is true that the Protestant electors and princes finally turned down this article concerning the cities, but their draft for the Religious Peace was not read out to the cities until two days before it was handed over to the king, and the cities were not even

[22] Paulus, *loc. cit.*, pp. 413 ff.; Friedensburg, *op. cit.*, Vol. v, pp. 569–654.

specifically mentioned in it, so little consideration was paid to them by the "higher" Estates. The article, however, was again adopted in the Royal Resolution of August 30. Although the cities made known their misgivings about it, they obtained no unanimous support from the higher Estates. The Strasbourgers said it was a matter of conscience and expressed their fear that the religious settlement might still be many long years off. It would, they claimed, be an outward scandal if different religions were permanently permitted in one community, and it was also to be feared that this would not in the end lead to established, peaceful civic life. Moreover, the same rights should be given to the cities as to the higher Estates. When the city delegates were able to bring their misgivings before the king, it emerged that a considerable number of cities were by no means so displeased by the article and had merely pretended to be discontented with it. When the king was asked for time for further reflection, Augsburg[23] announced that it had no further need for reflection and approved of the article: since the two religions had already existed side by side for so many years without cause for complaint, it would even now not be the city council's will and opinion that the clergy and the old religion should be expelled; there was, indeed, a general willingness to tolerate both religions in the future as in the past. Other cities asked for time to think and in the meantime endeavoured to interest the Protestant Estates in their cause. But it was explained to them that the prospects of a peace could not be wiped out for the sake of this article. Duke Christopher asked his theologians for an expert opinion on the article concerning the cities. They declared that it might well be burdensome for the cities to be expected to tolerate two religions, but because the cities themselves were not in agreement and for that reason were not disputing the article, it was all the more questionable that the other Estates should dispute it. While Frankfurt, Ulm and Esslingen wanted to ask the king to allow the arrangement to obtain only until the next assembly of the Estates, Strasbourg addressed a petition [against it] to Ferdinand during the very last

[23] Roth, *op. cit.*, Vol. IV, p. 683.

days of the Diet. The king acknowledged the loyalty of the cities to the Empire, but at the same time adduced the parable of the wicked servant (Matt. 18: 23 ff.), declaring that although he had yielded hitherto on many points, he would not do so now. He turned down the Strasbourgers' petition on the remarkable grounds that every citizen in an imperial city was directly subject to the Empire and was therefore to be given the same free option as any of the imperial Estates.[24] And in any case, he said, the article was valid only until such time as the religious issue was finally settled. Strasbourg's absence during the proclamation of the Diet's resolutions did not change matters, any more than did a document issued by the city on December 21, 1556, laying down that the few Catholic citizens there would have by rights to submit to the religious majority of the city council, as to an authority that was subject to the Emperor alone.

III

The effects of the Peace of Augsburg were not those that had been expected. The annexation of Catholic bishoprics and foundations reached its climax during the next few years, despite the ecclesiastical reservation. In the south, too, the ensuing years saw any number of local infringements by both confessions, always in the conviction that the letter of the Peace could be appealed to in justification. The Religious Peace itself contained several ambiguities. Thus there had already been disagreements in the royal Council as to who was a territorial ruler and therefore entitled to implement the Reformation.[25] On August 29 the Swabian counts and lords brought forward the following consideration: there were many who might have villages within their supreme authority and would institute in them the religion of their choice, which would be extremely troublesome to the petitioners. The Royal Council decided that this petition should not be passed on, since it would provoke much dispute; as things

24 Friedensburg, op. cit., Vol. v, p. 645.
25 Protocol (cf. n. 4 above), fo. 52 ff.

were, opinion was already divided in the Council. Whereas the king thought that it was always the possessor of supreme authority who was competent to provide for church and parish, others were of the opinion that the right to implement the Reformation belonged to whoever enjoyed the patronage to benefices in a particular place, even without the right of supreme jurisdiction; those, in other words, to whom the subjects owed both obedience and ground-rents. Since the concept of territory in the geographical sense was only then starting to develop,[26] it is hardly surprising that there was controversy in the years immediately following the Peace as to whether the right to implement the Reformation was based on supreme jurisdiction alone or on supreme jurisdiction together with manorial rights. Patronage as the criterion was increasingly on the wane. Thus the Reformation was now extended to a considerable number of parishes whose Catholic patrons had hitherto provided elements of resistance.

All this resulted in some peculiar local solutions.[27] In Deiningen the village street divided the Catholic half from the Protestant half; the city of Öttingen also had a Catholic part and a Protestant part, based on property ownership. The principality of Pfalz-Neuburg was able to implement the Reformation in the villages of Dischingen and Staufen against the opposition of the nobles. On the other hand, Hauntheim remained a Catholic enclave right up to the extinction of the Horkheim family who held capital jurisdiction there. The Protestant family of Öttingen-Öttingen could prevail neither in Herkheim nor in Hollheim against the Catholic lords of the manor. In Reimlingen the Teutonic Order prevailed over the territorial ruler with the help of patronage, manorial rights and jurisdiction. On the other hand Ehringen, which belonged to Catholic Wallerstein, was able to remain Protestant, while in Brachstadt Öttingen was unable to make any headway against the patron in Kaisheim. In Wörnitzheim, where Kaisheim possessed both patronage and manorial rights, Öttingen did not secure the victory until 1595. In several places where

[26] M. Simon, *Evangelische Kirchengeschichte Bayerns* (2nd edn., 1952), p. 263.
[27] *Ibid.*, pp. 263 ff.

ownership was divided between the two branches of the Öttingen family, agreements were reached for the simultaneous use of the parish church.

For the cardinal of Augsburg[28] the Religious Peace was a good legal pretext for restoring the Catholic religion in his territory in accordance with the convictions of his conscience. Thus he instituted proceedings before the Imperial Supreme Court to settle the question of religious sovereignty in a number of small villages in Neuburg, and took up contacts with the duke of Bavaria regarding the Protestants in Schrobenhausen and Landsberg. Since Protestant worship had never been held in Osterzell, a village near Kaufbeuren under noble rule, he refused to allow the Reformation to be introduced in the parishes of either Osterzell or Hirschzell. In the religious edict of October 12, 1556, for his provostship of Ellwangen, he made use of his powers under the law relating to the Reformation, declaring the acceptance of another religion as disobedience on the part of his subjects. He claimed that they had a straightforward choice between return to the old church or emigration. Canisius, who in 1558 had stood firm by the letter of the law and resisted the admission of Protestant worship in Straubing, was to carry out his popular mission in 1561 and 1568 for the purpose of bringing the Protestants of Ellwangen back to the old church.

In the cities the Religious Peace was implemented in a wide variety of ways.[29] Gmünd appealed to it, though admittedly not until 1574, in an attempt to threaten the Protestants with expulsion. Contrary to the terms of the Peace, the Protestant clergy of Dinkelsbühl were forced to leave the city in 1556 and the Hospital Church was taken away from the Protestants. At the command of the emperor it was made known to them that if they wished to remain faithful to the Confession of Augsburg they were perfectly free to leave the city. And this even though they formed by far the majority of the city's population. In Kaufbeuren, too, it was not until 1557 that the Catholic city council considered

[28] *Ibid.*, p. 272; Siebert, *op. cit.*, pp. 157, 322.
[29] Simon, *op. cit.*, pp. 269 ff.

the possibility of granting the city's Protestant majority a church and preacher of their own faith. On the other hand, Donauwörth sought to place increasing restrictions on Catholic worship and in the end to confine it to the Monastery of the Holy Cross. In Ulm the Catholics were at first permitted to use the church of the Franciscan friars, but in 1569 Catholic worship was forbidden altogether. The opposition of the lords of Burgau frustrated Besserer, a patrician of Ulm, in his efforts to win his village of Unterrohr near Günzburg for the Reformation, though patricians of Augsburg were able to make their villages Protestant.

The Religious Peace was violated by Memmingen,[30] where the council, immediately after the death of the preceptor of the Order of St. Anthony in 1562, made his son surrender the monastery together with the incorporated Church of St. Martin, and refused to give them back when the superiors of the Order appointed a new preceptor. Both sides later appealed to the Peace, the council using it to justify their demand that all those resident in their city should belong to their confession, the preceptor maintaining that the Peace permitted the existence of a preceptory in Memmingen, since one had been there at the time of the Peace and the preceptory was an exempt foundation. When, in 1586, Memmingen obtained from Austria sovereignty over Amendingen, Schweighausen and the lordship of Eisenberg, the purchase came about only on condition that Memmingen undertook to make no religious changes. Lindau could maintain Protestant worship only in the neighbouring villages of Äschach and Rentin; the city's protests failed to prevent the counts of Montfort, who held supreme lordship over Lindau's alms villages of Laimnau and Roggenzell, from recatholicizing them. In Leutkirch, on the other hand, it was the right of patronage enjoyed by the powerful monastery of Weingarten under the influential Abbot Gerwig Blarer which obliged the Protestants to get by without any clergy of their own until 1559. Not until 1562 was a settlement reached.

---

[30] *Ibid.*, p. 270; preference, however, should be given to the account, based on the records, in M. Sontheimer, *Die Geistlichkeit des Kapitels Ottobeuren*, Vol. 1 (1912), pp. 321 ff.

Despite all these local disputes the Peace of Augsburg remained the norm of coexistence for the two confessions within the Empire for two generations. The Council, as is well known, did not bring the expected religious settlement, and thus the Peace became a permanent one. In the end even the papal representatives at the Imperial Diet of 1566 recognized the Peace as one dictated by political necessity and as such not in conflict with the decrees of the Council.

With its principle that the two confessions had a legal right to existence the Peace of Augsburg confirmed the principle of parity within the Empire.[31] There was as yet no question of tolerance or freedom of conscience. Within the territorial boundaries it was the will of the absolutist territorial ruler which alone prevailed. It seems misguided to try and see in all this haggling over the individual provisions of the Peace any positive effort on the part of either confession to promote liberty of conscience. Both sides were still too rigidly confined in their denominational mentality for either of them to abandon in principle the violent expedient of expulsion. It is true that tolerance was being advocated at this time, but only outside the Empire, when, after Calvin had had Servetus burned at the stake, the Frenchman Castellio published his manifesto in support of tolerance and religious freedom at the beginning of 1554. It was not until a good century later, after Germany had undergone the bloody turmoils of the Thirty Years' War, that the Saxon professor Samuel Pufendorf took up once more the cry for tolerance, though this time in the name of an enlightened natural law theory unconnected in any way with revealed religion.

The Peace of Augsburg, then, was not the beginning of religious toleration; nor was it a turning point in the fortunes of the Reformation. In the following years the Reformation continued

[31] [But see the view that it only gave the appearance of parity, whereas the ecclesiastical reservation in reality put the Protestants at a serious disadvantage and in a position of grudging tolerance: F. Dickmann, "Das Problem der Gleichberechtigung der Konfessionen im Reich im 16. und 17. Jahrhundert," *Historische Zeitschrift*, cci (1965), 274.]

to make progress, and more than once the Protestants demanded that the legal restrictions imposed by the Peace should be removed. Only about ten years later, when the Catholic Estates had adopted the reforming decrees of the Council of Trent and the educational work of the Jesuits in Germany had borne its first fruits, was a halt called to the forward thrust of Protestantism.

The Peace of Augsburg did not point a way to the future. All it amounted to was a confirmation of the status quo, a final defence against the use of brute force under the pretext of religion; a mere lull in the fighting, but a necessary and perhaps even beneficial one, since it gave time for spiritual reappraisal and an opportunity to try out religious coexistence in practice, at least in the cities. That the opportunity was not taken, and that the last word was to be a religious war [The Thirty Years' War] sparked off by the religious intolerance of one city (and a Swabian city at that [Donauwörth]), in no way detracts from the value of the Peace of Augsburg.

PART THREE

Government
in Action

7 Albert of Brandenburg–Ansbach, Grand Master of the Order of Teutonic Knights and Duke in Prussia, 1490–1568

WALTHER HUBATSCH

Threatened by internal dissolution, and weakened by wars with Poland which for years had been waged intermittently over disputed territories, the Teutonic Order made a dramatic recovery in 1525 by becoming a secular, Lutheran principality and making peace with Poland. Albert of Hohenzollern, grand master since 1511, had in 1524 accepted Luther's recommendation to convert the lands of the Order into a hereditary duchy. By the Treaty of Cracow (1525), guaranteed by the entire house of Brandenburg, Albert renounced his territorial claims against Poland and agreed to make East Prussia a fief of the king of Poland.

THE functions of the territorial ruler remained unchanged at first, despite the new constitutional form of the state. In Cracow the cloak of grand master had been taken from Albert of Brandenburg by the king of Poland in person; and the majority of the Teutonic Knights had immediately followed his example. The membership of the Order, which had originally numbered over 700 in the heyday of the Order's Prussian state, had by now shrunk to fifty-six, spread out over twenty-three castles and houses. Among these there had formed a small but determined opposition group, which at first resisted the duke openly: there was, for example, Reuss von Plauen zu Bartenstein, who held out together with the neighbouring castle of Heilsberg and at first hindered the admission of Protestant preachers. . . .

Albert had been able to win over the other Knights by setting them in charge of *Ämter* [administrative districts] or by giving them places at court or confidential posts. It cannot have been easy for them to lay aside the white cloak [of the Order], but no serious resistance was offered anywhere. During the ceremony of fealty in the castle there was laughter among the spectators when the cross was publicly cut off the coat of one of the Knights. The envoys sent by the Prussian branch of the Order gave their assent to the Treaty of Cracow, just as the landed nobility and the cities had done. Consequently Duke Albert, after giving a detailed account of the Cracow negotiations, had been able without any trouble to administer the oath of allegiance to the bishops, nobles and cities at the diet held for this purpose from May 26 to 31, 1525, at Königsberg. . . .[1]

But the diet felt itself unable as yet to approve the tax so urgently needed by the duke, and referred the question to a new meeting on August 24. Albert had to be content with this much. It was then, however, that Bishop Polentz took the sensational step of transferring all secular authority in his bishopric [of Samland] to the duke; and the reason he gave was that "it is not fitting for a prelate and bishop, whose first duty is to preach and proclaim the Word of God, to rule over lands and people, or to occupy castles, territory and cities, but rather to adhere to the true and undiluted Word and render it obedience." This was the first case in German history of a bishopric being secularized for the express purpose of helping a territorial prince burdened with debts. There can be no doubt whatever that this transfer—as Polentz himself emphasized at the time—took place quite voluntarily.[2] The ecclesiastical administration here did of its own accord what was to be carried through in subsequent years in Scandinavia and England as the result of ruthless expropriation on the part of the crown. The reason why Bishop Erhard [Queis] at Riesenburg did not immediately follow this example was simply that the bishopric of Pomesanien still remained to be evacuated by the Polish occupying force in accordance with the Treaty of Cracow, and needed

---

[1] *Acten der Ständetage Preussens unter der Herrschaft des deutschen Ordens*, ed. M. Töppen, Vol. v (Königsberg, 1886), pp. 770–4; *Urkundenbuch zur Reformationsgeschichte des Herzogthums Preussen*, ed. P. Tschackert, Vol. ii (Leipzig, 1890), no. 355, p. 120; *Chronik des Balthasar Gans*, ed. F. A. Meckelburg (in *Die Königsberger Chroniken aus der Zeit des Herzogs Albrecht*, Königsberg, 1865), p. 352.

[2] Tschackert, *op. cit.*, Vol. ii, no. 356.

to recover from the serious damage it had sustained during the war; in the state in which it found itself in 1525 the bishopric would have been more of a financial burden than a help to the duke. In October 1527 Queis was at last in a position to make over the lands of the bishopric to the duke, in order to be able, like Polentz, to devote himself entirely to his religious duties. . . .

In the middle of June the duke had sent an invitation to Martin Luther to come to Königsberg in person for the diet which was to take place on August 24 for the purpose of settling the ecclesiastical affairs of the principality; he promised to send an escort of his own cavalry. Because of the social disturbances in the electorate of Saxony, however, the Reformer was unable to come to Prussia, though he wrote the duke a detailed account of his views on ecclesiastical organization (*De ceremoniis instituendis*). The problem of new ecclesiastical institutions arose: the loosely knit groups of Gospel adherents, and the preaching of the Word, had to be organized into communities, new liturgical forms and the evangelical territorial church. The contents of Luther's letter to the duke have been lost, but there is no doubt that, thanks to the offices of his confidant, Briesmann, his proposals found their way into the first Prussian ecclesiastical ordinance agreed at the Diet of Königsberg in December. It remained at first without significance, since on July 6 the duke, even before he could possibly have received Luther's reply, promulgated a printed edict, which was sent to all the principal officers of the *Ämter* and was to be affixed to the doors of churches and read out on five successive Sundays from the pulpits. This edict was the first draft of a comprehensive ordinance for the principality and its church; the continuing disturbances made it necessary to issue the edict with all haste in order to ensure that the assumption of government by the duke was acknowledged in all parts of the country. With an eye to the neighbouring powers of Ermland and Poland, the wording of the decree was kept so general that it scarcely suggested any commitment to the new doctrines. "To the praise and honour of God our Lord and all his holy elect, and for the sake of our common Christian faith," it was decreed that the parish clergy should preach the Gospel pure and unalloyed. The congregations were called upon to support their clergy as before. Strange doctrines, sects, clandestine preachers, soothsayers or any such as gave themselves over to the heathen practices of the "goat-divinity" were to be reported to the local authorities, who were to punish them by virtue of the temporal power bestowed by God upon the duke. In this decree Luther's doctrine of spiritual and temporal government became realized in political practice. Further prohibitions were placed upon the drinking of pledges, blasphemy, swearing and cursing, disorderly extramarital relationships, and the conducting of religious discussions without reverence or in unseemly places.[3]

In the heyday of the Teutonic Order, Prussia had been a densely populated land by the standards of the time, with many churches and an active and variegated religious life. The cruel wars of recent decades had led, in the cities and especially in the country, to a degeneration of public behaviour and morality unknown in earlier times. Crudity and obtuseness in religious matters, inadequate pastoral care, and deficient instruction all fostered the growth of superstition; among the old Prussian population there stirred dormant memories of sacrificial customs from pre-Christian times some three centuries before. Despite the severest penalties, peasants repeatedly gathered for the feasts of the "goat-divinity," particularly in Samland and Balga. The ancient Prussian gods Perkunos, Potrimpos and Patollu were invoked, and in accordance with a prescribed rite the *Waidelotte*, or priest, would sacrifice a goat at night and sprinkle its blood; after this the meat was cooked and consumed to the accompaniment of copious

---

[3] Strangely enough, the Reformation edict is nowhere printed complete. Tschackert (*op. cit.*, Vol. II, no. 371) still had access to the printed version in the Königsberg state archives, which today is no longer there. H. F. Jacobson, *Geschichte der Quellen des evangelischen Kirchenrechts des Preussischen Staates*, Vol. II (Königsberg, 1839), pp. 23 ff., gives only an excerpt. Here Tschackert, *op. cit.*, Vol. I, p. 119 is followed. For Luther's advice to Duke Albert, see *ibid.*, Vol. II, no. 370. In general, see C. Hartknoch, *Preussische Kirchen-Historia* (Frankfurt am Main and Leipzig, 1686) and D. H. Arnoldt, *Kurzgefasste Kirchengeschichte des Königreichs Preussen* (Königsberg, 1769).

draughts from the ceremonial cup. This custom was observed time and again, right up to the second half of the century.[4] Despite the great numbers who flocked to hear the preachers in the cities, the new Reformation preaching tended at first to spread confusion and tumult; and the shortage of clergy in the country was made even more acute by the refusal of some priests to expound Lutheran doctrines. Duke Albert realized the need for missionary work on a broad basis of popular education. The authorities saw themselves confronted with a difficult and onerous task which could only be tackled by long-term measures.

The Reformation edict had been promulgated while disturbances were widespread throughout the land. All over the country the peasants were restless beneath the burdens of labour service. The *Amtshauptleute* [chief officials of the *Ämter*] sought to raise the yield of their often ravaged areas and to restore the dilapidated and ruined castles: there was a constant demand for labour at the lowest possible rates. As a result the rural population under the authority of the *Ämter* found themselves under an increasing obligation to render unpaid services, labour service. The tenant farmers, who had been settled under the terms of Culmic law [whereby small estates, from which light military service had to be rendered, were created in the thirteenth and fourteenth centuries] and who had once enjoyed freedom, now found their services more and more heavily requisitioned as a result of wars and increasing taxes. Confused reports now penetrated the countryside that the Order had been abolished, the duke was the sole supreme authority in the land, and the divine Word of the Gospel laid down that all men were equal and free. What was

---

[4] Tschackert, *op. cit.*, Vol. I, pp. 10 ff., with references. The one-sided verdict that the Order had not yet converted the country is not to be accepted. Tschackert overlooks the disastrous consequences of the wars and devastations after 1410. On paganism, see Johannes Maletius, *Epistola de sacrificiis et idolatria veterum Borussorum* (Königsberg, 1551), reprinted in *Acta Borussica, ecclesiastica, civilia, literaria*, Vol. II (Königsberg and Leipzig, 1731), also in *Mitteilungen der Litterarischen Gesellschaft Masovia*, VIII (Lötzen, 1902), pp. 177–96; H. Meletii, "Wahrhaftige Beschreibung der Sudawen auf Samland, samt ihrem Bockheiligen und Ceremonien," *Erleutertes Preussen*, V (1742), 701–21.

spreading here was not social rebellion by the exploited and the oppressed, but a growing sense of solidarity and identity, a powerful yearning for freedom and independence, and an excitement fanned by fleeting reports that the peasants had banded together against the nobility in Franconia and Thuringia. The duke was certainly kept informed of this unrest in the land. He forbade the sale of beer at the annual fairs, imprisoned a number of ringleaders and ordered the rural population to hand over their weapons; but otherwise he attached no great importance to the movement, since such discord had for many years become a part of everyday life. The impending diet would bring in the necessary changes. In July the duke began a tour of inspection in the *Ämter*, in order to receive the oath of allegiance both there and in the cities. In the middle of the month, however, a letter arrived from Margrave George [of Ansbach, his brother] and Duke Frederick [of Liegnitz in Silesia], requesting him to go as soon as possible to see them in Silesia for urgent negotiations, and he immediately departed. . . .

Once again the prince was out of the country; once again the irascible and detested Polentz was appointed regent and empowered to continue the administration of the oath of allegiance. This dashed the hopes for better times, for peace, prosperity and conscientious government; and it also quenched the expectations of a new era without distinctions of estate. The debasement of the coinage, the confiscation of what remained of church silver, and the disarming of the rural population all gave rise to much misgiving. It needed only the slightest provocation to spark off the same rioting as in the Empire: a smallholder ill-treated by the ducal official of Kaymen, a village in Samland, where the miller also had a vision bidding him go to the aid of the impoverished peasants; a former secretary and chamberlain of the court who organized mass gatherings and composed letters and peasant articles; and a number of preachers who advocated a primitive biblicism and whipped up the mobs with their ideas of equality. The characteristic features of peasant movements elsewhere in the same year can be found here also: in their letters to the *Amtshaupt-*

leute the peasants presented themselves as "adherents of the holy Gospel":

We wish and desire only God and our most gracious Lord Duke of Prussia as our rulers, and no other authorities. Since God has created us all equal, redeemed us and promised us a Kingdom, we desire no nobles to be our overlords, but wish to be all equal as brothers and sisters in Christ. And since God created all things for men to use for their common needs, it is our desire that rivers and forests, fishes, animals and birds of the air should be there for all in common, without prohibition. And finally we ask that the pure and undiluted Gospel without any human additions be heard and preached.

They promised they would inflict not the slightest damage on the duke's property and even claimed that they were acting in the name of the Holy Spirit and the duke, whose seal they affixed without any warrant to their proclamations.[5] Their acceptance of princely rule and their desire to abolish the old intermediary powers of the Knight Commanders and the new ones of the

[5] Letter of the peasants of Samland to the administrator of the *Amt* of Tapiau, September 4, 1525, formerly in the Preussisches Staatsarchiv Königsberg, now in the Staatliches Archivlager Göttingen, Herzogliches Brief-Archiv (HBA); J. Voigt, "Geschichte des Bauernaufruhrs in Preussen im Jahre 1525," *Neue Preussische Provinzialblätter*, III (1847), 1–50, 310–15; Tschackert, *op. cit.*, Vol. II, nos. 393–406, 411–15; A. Seraphim, "Soziale Bewegungen in Altpreussen im Jahre 1525," *Altpreussische Monatsschrift*, LVIII (1921), 1–36, 71–104; W. Stolze, "Die Erhebung der samländischen Bauern in September 1525, ihre Gründe, ihr Ziel und ihre Bedeutung," *Jahresbericht des Königsberger Universitätsbundes* (1928/9), 15–38; idem, "Zur Kritik der Überlieferung von dem samländischen Bauernaufstand des Jahres 1525," *Mitteilungen des Vereins für die Geschichte von Ost- und Westpreussen*, IV (1930), 37–43; E. Wilke, "Die Ursachen der preussischen Bauern- und Bürgerunruhen 1525" (Ph.D. thesis, Göttingen, 1930, also in *Altpreussische Forschungen*, VII (1930)); *Freibergs Chronik*, ed. Meckelburg (*Königsberger Chroniken*); (Nikolaus Richau), "Historie von dem Auffruhr der Samländischen Bauern," *Erleutertes Preussen*, II (1725), 328–57, 531–66; H. Schmauch, "Ermländische Quellen zum samländischen Bauernaufstand des Jahres 1525," *Mitteilungen des Vereins für die Geschichte von Ost- und Westpreussen*, IX (1934), 1–8; F. L. Carsten, "The Peasants War in East Prussia in 1525," *International Review for Social History*, III (Leiden, 1938), pp. 398 ff.; H. Zins, *Powstanie chlopskie w Prusach ksiazecych w 1525 roku* (Warsaw, 1953); more recently, M. Biskup in *Zapiski historyczne*, XXI (1955), 242–56.

landed nobility constituted a political programme with its roots in the people themselves. When the detested official of Kaymen had been bound fast by the peasant mob, he was greeted with the song of the German peasant insurrection: "Da Adam reut' und Eva spann, wo war dann der Edelmann?" ["When Adam delved and Eve span, where was then the gentleman?"]. By the beginning of September the revolt had broken out in Samland and had soon spread to [the province of] Natangen; the nobles, whom the peasants were demanding should be handed over to them, took refuge in the fortified cities and castles. But just as the peasants, now several thousand strong, were advancing on Königsberg, and sections of the city population were declaring themselves in support of their demands, Richau, the burgomaster of the old city, succeeded in securing a provisional truce until the return of the duke. . . .

[It was while Albert was at the court of the king of Bohemia and Hungary that] he first heard the news of the peasants' revolt in Prussia, whereupon he immediately hastened home. His regent, Polentz, who had broken off his tour and retired to the uneasy atmosphere of the capital, advised the duke to bring Silesian and Polish cavalry with him and mete out punishment with a rod of iron, "so that all be made to tremble at the name of Your Princely Grace when they hear it spoken. If this fear is not instilled into the people Your Princely Grace will rule ill and will not have his subjects in his power." On October 29, 1525, the duke arrived back in Königsberg with 540 cavalry. The peasants had finally quietened down; Albert arranged a meeting with them before the city gates and ordered them to lay down their arms and renew their oath to the territorial ruler. He confirmed their right of complaint against the nobles and the officials of the Ämter. Three ringleaders were executed on the spot and twelve others in the Ämter; Hans Gericke, ducal treasurer and a descendant of the Samland nobility, fled to Sweden: he had sided with the peasants, but had done much to hold them back from excesses.

The punishment was mild compared with the measures taken by the princes of Franconia, Württemberg and Thuringia, but severe considering the insignificance of the insurrections. The duke appeared to be giving his blessing to the nobles; and at the same time greater burdens than ever were imposed upon the only class of the population which did any really useful work and laid the foundations of the country's reconstruction. Surely the duke must have realized that the rebellious peasants were loyal to him? Might this not have been an opportunity of introducing the Swedish peasant kingship of Gustavus Vasa in Old Prussia? After all, Albert was advised not only by advocates of drastic measures, such as Polentz, Klingenbeck and Besenrade, but by those who urged understanding and clemency, like Miltitz. But there were two things which decided the course Albert took against the peasants. First there was the way in which his invariably ruthless brother Casimir had dealt with the insurrection in Franconia, detailed accounts of which he had received from Casimir himself. But more decisive than this were Luther's urgent appeals that the divinely willed ordinances of territorial rulers should not be imperilled by insubordination, and the more so when the rebels used the Gospel in support of their cause. The duke, whose name had been wrongly used by the rebels, found himself in complete agreement with the Wittenberg Reformer, whose writings against the unlawful assemblies of the rural population had soon made their way to Königsberg, where their drastic severity met with the complete approval of Johann Pollander, the city's most influential theologian.[6] In punishing the peasants the duke was simply conforming to the ideas of other contemporary princes and to the new theological justification for secular government. He had shown the nobles that they were dependent on the central authority, and during the early years of his reign this put him in a favourable position for dealing with the particularist aspirations

[6] Tschackert, op. cit., Vol. II, no. 391, pp. 130 ff.; cf. P. Althaus, Luthers Haltung im Bauernkrieg (Lutherjahrbuch (1925), 1–39, reprinted by the Wissenschaftliche Buchgesellschaft (Tübingen, 1952)); "D. Johann Polianders Leben," Erleutertes Preussen, II (1725), 432–47; the duke's instructions to the Amtleute after the end of the Peasants Revolt, November 15, 1525 (HBA). As late as September 6, 1530, Gustavus Vasa put in a word for the return of the exile Hans Gericke, at that time in the service of the count of Hoya (HBA).

of the Estates. But he had no thought of using the opportunity to exert greater pressure on the nobles by strengthening his position with the rural population. The legal procedure for dealing with complaints and grievances envisaged only individual cases coming to the duke's attention, as indeed happened. Albert was seriously determined to reign as a just prince and may have been able to secure redress for his subjects in particular cases, but he could achieve very little against the concerted opposition of the Estates. . . .

At last, on December 10, 1525, the diet which had been postponed since August took place in Königsberg. Its main purpose was to pass the *Landesordnung* [a comprehensive piece of legislation for the whole principality] in eighty articles, of which thirteen were printed at the beginning of the next year.[7]. . . This began with a brief reference to the earlier edict, a general exhortation to observe public order, and a threat of penalties for failure to comply with the regulations; and the first two articles regulated the appointment and maintenance of the clergy. The patron of the benefice, with the agreement of the parishioners, was to choose the minister and present him for the approval of the bishop responsible, who was to test him for suitability. The same procedure was to be observed in those parishes in the duke's territories which still belonged to the diocese of the bishop of Ermland, except that the examination was to be carried out by commissioners of the duke. All church livings were to be equally provided for, and they were to be distributed over the country in such a way that a village with a church could be found at least every two [Prussian] miles [about 9½ English miles]. The ministers' stipends were to be paid by patrons and parishes on the basis of fixed contributions, though all other fees were to be abolished. A common fund was to be opened for the building of churches

---

[7] Tschackert, *op. cit.*, Vol. II, nos. 416–18. The eighty articles of the *Landesordnung* contain a "provisional ecclesiastical ordinance" with liturgical appendix, which was separately printed in March 1526: E. Sehling, *Die evangelischen Kirchenordnungen des XVI. Jahrhunderts*, Vol. IV, *Das Herzogtum Preussen* (Leipzig, 1911), nos. 2–3, pp. 30–41. On Luther's recommendations, see above, note 3.

and the payment of the schoolmaster, to be used also for the relief of the poor and for emergencies. On every Sunday and at every festival the people should be given a "Christian exhortation, reminding them with all kindness and friendliness" of their duty to attend church, because "in this way their souls are nourished and faith is implanted in their hearts." Indifference or recalcitrance were placed under severe penalties. Details of ceremonies would remain to be decided on. Church estates were to be broken up and their revenues diverted to the common fund. The people were once again enjoined to inform on all magic and heathen customs, as well as to ensure that babies were not inadvertently suffocated while asleep. This section dealt finally with the responsibilities of the *Ämter* and parishes for the maintenance of roads and bridges, and laid down regulations for inns. It is clear from all this how greatly concerned the prince was to rebuild the country in the light of the Gospel. There is a joyous sense of hope and confidence about it; Albert was inspired by a solid faith and firm conviction, which he succeeded in passing on to his assistants. The authorities at all levels were to co-operate in setting up the territorial state on Protestant lines; to this end it would be necessary not merely to issue ordinances but to subject these to continual revision and ensure that as broad a section as possible of the population came within their scope. On March 31, 1526, instructions were issued for the first Protestant visitation: the duke's commissioners, the evangelical preacher Speratus and Adrian von Waiblingen—a former Knight of the Order who had belonged to the opposition group—were charged to examine the condition of the church in the country. The thirteen articles extracted from the *Landesordnung* served as a basis and were to be read out in public. The amount of property held by the secular clergy was to be investigated, instruction in ceremonial matters would be carried out in accordance with regulations which had meanwhile been issued, and the competence and conduct of the preachers had to be noted; at the same time, a detailed account was to be given of conditions among the peasants, particularly the amount of their labour service, in order to avoid excessive demands on the part of the *Ämter* or the landed nobility.[8]

The close connection between the secular order and the ecclesiastical order is remarkable. Even ecclesiastical law was determined by the laws of the land. And it is equally remarkable how the duke's own active personal commitment was matched by the unanimous assent of the Diet. The Protestant order was set up earlier here than in any other territory, including Saxony, and this found expression in the first church ordinance, the first visitation instruction and the first hymn-book [to be issued during the Reformation]. The great work of evangelization was added to piece by piece, and edicts were issued against un-Christian living, for instance against idleness; the facts brought to light by the first visitation were used as a basis for a fresh inspection of all incumbencies carried out in 1528. The new *Landesordnung* of 1529 contained another set of articles concerning religious matters. After the great plague of 1529, which included Bishop Queis of Pomesanien among its victims, there were further visitations in 1530, 1533, 1538 and 1541–3; in the last of these the duke himself took part. The conditions revealed led the duke to publish on February 1, 1543, his "mandate exhorting the people to the fear of God, attendance at church, taking of the holy sacraments, and other matters." Failure to attend church drew down sharp penalties, and no exception was made for the nobles. Every six weeks the minister was to test his parishioners' knowledge of the catechism by making them recite their prayers. . . . As early as 1528 Duke Albert had envisaged synods in the dioceses as well as a general territorial synod, though these were unable to convene until 1530. An official manual of instruction was drawn up by the synod for the Protestant ministers of Prussia, though it did not come into force because the acceptance of the Confession of Augsburg [of 1530] in Prussia rendered it superfluous. Not until 1567 did the general synod of Königsberg draw up and print a new manual of dogma.[9]

Since the practices of the territorial church in Prussia were

---

[8] Sehling, *op. cit.*, no. 4, pp. 41 ff.; Tschackert, *op. cit.*, Vol. II, nos. 459 ff.

[9] Sehling, *op. cit.*, p. 25.

developed so early on they retained many original Lutheran features. Duke Albert's avoidance of radical innovations was not governed merely by consideration for his feudal lord [the Catholic king of Poland], or by a cautious foreign policy. Thus the elevation [the raising of the chalice by the priest during the sacrifice of the Mass] was retained at first; the saints were invoked in the Reformation edict of July 1525, exactly as they were in the first prayer which Albert had written in his own hand for his consort during their wedding festivities. On the other hand, the use of German for the sermon and the administration of the sacraments had already been introduced before 1525. The Scriptures were now to be read out in such a way that the whole Gospel would be proclaimed in an unbroken series of consecutive passages Sunday by Sunday throughout the year. This *lectio continua*, the presentation of the pure Word, was intended to make the faithful thoroughly familiar with the foundation of their spiritual life, the Gospel. Here is yet another manifestation of the duke's conconcern to lead the people to righteousness in this world and eternal happiness in the next. It was only when church ordinances came to be drawn up in other German Protestant territories that a number of restrictions had to be imposed on the Prussian church for the sake of conformity. Thus the German introductory psalm came to replace the Latin introit, as in the electorate of Saxony. This change was not the least of the factors leading to the considerable development of church music in Prussia; and here again the active personal contribution of the duke played no small part. The ecclesiastical ordinances introduced in Württemberg and the Palatinate during the 1550's also necessitated further adaptations. The abolition of signs of the cross and of the elevation as symbols of the sacrifice of the Mass, the decreasing role of the parishioners in favour of a developing ecclesiastical organization, and finally the suppression of the *lectio continua* all marked the gradual disappearance of the features which distinguished the Prussian territorial church. When Bishop Polentz died in 1550, followed in 1551 by Speratus, who had succeeded Queis in Pomesanien, and when the duke had in vain sought suitable replacements, even the Prussian episcopal constitution was provisionally suspended, as in other Protestant territories, and their offices were administered by presidents. . . .

The duchy of Prussia covered an area about the same size as the duchy of Savoy, the republic of Venice, or the Swiss Confederation as it then was, being 300 kilometres at its longest and 200 kilometres at its widest; it was only slightly smaller than the kingdom of Bohemia and the electorate of Brandenburg, and was larger than the duchy of Bavaria and the electorate of Saxony. . . . It was divided into three *Kreise*, or regions, each corresponding to a natural geographical area. The northernmost of these, Samland, comprised the central East Prussian area between the lagoons, and also the area along the river Memel, the upper reaches of the Pregel and its tributaries, and the Rominter Heide; this was a largely flat, and in places marshy, region with useful agricultural potential which had not yet everywhere been fully exploited. The ports of the duchy were all on the coast of Samland; the province had nine *Hauptämter*, in addition to the city of Königsberg. . . . To the south was the *Kreis* of Natangen, which stretched from the flat country near the Frisches Haff [lagoon] in the west to the lakes and hills of Masuria and the "wilderness" zone along the south-east frontier; it comprised fifteen *Hauptämter*. . . . The third was the *Kreis* of Oberland, which comprised sixteen *Ämter* after the territorial possessions of the diocese of Pomesanien had been dissolved. . . . This was the most highly populated *Kreis* and had the most cities, though these were without exception very small; but it had also been the most seriously hit during the war. . . . In addition, in 1560 Prussia received in pawn the profitable *Amt* of Grobin with Libau in Courland.[10] This division into *Kreise* was, by and large, a clear

[10] In this section the international history of the duchy can be considered only in so far as it is important for an understanding of Duke Albert's life. A survey of the *Ämter* is given by M. Töppen, *Historisch-comparative Geographie von Preussen* (Gotha, 1858), pp. 260 ff. A still largely valid description of the country in the period of the Reformation is in L. Weber, *Preussen vor 500 Jahren in cultur-historischer, statistischer und militairischer Beziehung nebst Special-*

and rational arrangement, and it remained in force to good advantage until the partition of Samland under Duke Albert's successors. The regional capitals were Königsberg in Samland, Bartenstein or Rastenburg in Natangen, and Saalfeld or Osterode in Oberland; the deputies of the Estates would assemble there periodically for local diets. Despite the privileged private estates belonging either rent-free to noble families or to the rent-paying families [holding land] by Culmic law, and despite the numerous properties which had been pledged for debts or given away, the duke as hereditary ruler retained rights of usufruct in the principality, which he administered just like a landowner to the advantage of his dynasty for as long as the hereditary treaties of his family would permit. Thus the duke's administration extended in the first instance over the entire area of his territory; and since there was no regional administration immediately under the prince, it was based exclusively on the central government and the system of *Amtshauptleute*. Given the more or less equal resources of the individual *Ämter*, it was important to engage efficient *Amtshauptleute* in order to increase the revenues, which, with considerable fluctuations, amounted to an annual average of about 20,000 Prussian marks.[11]

Geographie (Danzig, 1878). A detailed description of the *Ämter* in the last years of Duke Albert's rule is in Kaspar von Nostitz, *Haushaltungsbuch des Fürstentums Preussen 1578*, ed. K. Lohmeyer (Leipzig, 1893). Contemporary descriptions of Prussia: Georg Joachimus Rheticus, "Encomium Borussiae (1539)," *Acta Borussica..*, Vol. II, pp. 413–25; Sebastian Münster, *Cosmographei oder Beschreibung aller Länder* (Basle, 1556 and later edns., pp. 915–28: "Von dem Preussenland"); Albert Krantz, *Wandalia... Adjecta est... Polonici regni et Prussiae, tum regiae, tum ducalis descriptio* (Frankfurt am Main, 1575); David Chytraeus, *Vandalia. Regionum ad mare Balthicum, Pomeraniae, Prussiae... principes et statum rei publicae et ecclesiae... exponens* (Rostock, 1589); Caspar Hennenberger, *Kurtze und warhafftige Beschreibung des Landes zu Preussen* (Königsberg, 1584): by far the best and most thorough and knowledgeable of these works.

[11] Nostitz, *op. cit.* A short account of the history of the *Ämter*, based on sources, is in H. Schweichler, "Das Domänenwesen unter Herzog Albrecht in Preussen (1525–1568)" (Ph.D. thesis, Königsberg, 1911; also in *Mitteilungen der Litterarischen Gesellschaft Masovia*, XVII (1912), 74–120); Töppen, *Geographie*; W. von Brünneck, *Zur Geschichte des Grundeigentums in Ost- und Westpreussen*, 2 vols. (Berlin, 1891–6).

But in this matter Duke Albert's hands were tied. When he renounced the Order he had no idea of making any fundamental change in the existing administration of the country. The decisive moves in the direction of a princely territorial state in the modern sense had already been introduced by Albert's predecessors, and for this reason no radical innovations were needed in administrative matters. The continuity of the state is here brought out most clearly; the institutions of the Teutonic Order in Prussia survived its secularization. Not merely administrative institutions, but even the administrators themselves were taken over from the state of the Teutonic Order into the new duchy. The registers of the *Ämter* continued to be kept by the same clerks in the same way as before. The new constitution of the state seems to have passed completely unnoticed in the sphere of practical administration, especially since administrative and judicial authority were exercised by the same persons (right up to the duke himself) and the castles of the Order continued to be the seats of local government. The obedience which the peasants had for centuries been brought up to pay the Order as its subjects was still expected and still rendered in the new territorial state; it took the form of submissiveness and the claim to protection. Economic and regional organization remained the same, with the castles as seats of administration and the towns as centres of trade and traffic; and the fact that the Commanders of the Order were now called *Amtshauptleute* would scarcely have had much effect on the habits of the peasant or his attitude towards the territorial ruler, especially when the administration was carried on by the same persons as before. The peasants' rights were based, just as before, on the privileges granted under the rule of the Order, and thus the ducal registers contained many copies of such dispositions whose validity was even now not disputed. Whatever opinions later generations might have about the Order, one thing is clear: the Teutonic Order was the political predecessor of the duchy, and it had been responsible for creating the country as Albert succeeded to it. The original political idea of the Teutonic Order continued to exert its influence along lines already laid down, and these ensured an unbroken transition into the new era. . . .[12]

At the head of each *Hauptamt* stood an *Amtshauptmann* appointed by the duke; he was responsible for implementing the prince's instructions, for which purpose he was supported by a castellan and a clerk. Some of the larger *Ämter* also employed a steward; but all the *Hauptämter* were subdivided into *Kammerämter*, just as they had been under the Order. The *Amtshauptleute* filled the roles of administrator and judge, presided over the district hospitals and supervised the exchequer for the ducal demesne in their area. All these offices remained filled in 1525, in most cases by the former officials of the Order, some of whom were given *Ämter* for life, or even in hereditary tenure, as a means of keeping them in the country. The people in the *Ämter*, as well as the landed nobles who did not owe any services directly to the duke, were obliged to perform military service as required; all the same, the military reviews in the first years of the duke's new levy revealed alarmingly low figures. These, however, simply reflected the general state of contributions from the *Ämter*, which fluctuated considerably during the period of reconstruction, and were later also often exploited for the private gain of the *Amtshauptleute*. The administrative system was not yet sufficiently developed to put a check on embezzlement, let alone prevent it. It was to be quite some time before the duke was able, in the words of a contemporary proverb, "to draw water from the well instead of having to carry it there. . . ."[13] All the same, it would have been

[12] On the question of continuity, W. Hubatsch, "Kreuzritterstaat und Hohenzollernmonarchie. Zur Frage der Fortdauer des Deutschen Ordens in Preussen," *Festschrift Hans Rothfels* (Düsseldorf, 1951); *idem*, "Deutscher Orden und Preussentum," *Zeitschrift für Ostforschung*, 1 (1952), also in *Eckpfeiler Europas: Probleme des Preussenlandes in geschichtlicher Sicht* (Heidelberg, 1953). On the commanderies and *Kammerämter* under the Order, see now P. Thielen (ed.), *Das grosse Zinsbuch des Deutschen Ordens* (Marburg, 1958); [*idem*, *Die Verwaltung des Ordensstaates Preussen vornehmlich im 15. Jahrhundert* (Cologne, 1965).]

[13] On the role of the *Amtshauptleute*, cf. A. Horn, *Die Verwaltung Ostpreussens seit der Säkularisation 1525–1875* (Königsberg, 1890), pp. 230–40; Duke Albert to Achatius Zehmen, Insterburg, January 25, 1548, Staatsarchiv Königsberg, Ostpreussische Folianten 81, pp. 206 ff. Estimates of the approximate yield of the *Ämter* in Prussia, 1554–5, with older notes, are in the former

possible to increase the yields considerably; even as late as 1555 there were 129 ravaged and deserted hides in the *Amt* of Osterode. The numerous *Ämter* granted as fiefs and pledged for debts or to raise money reduced the income of the state appreciably; by 1527 no less than twelve *Hauptämter* and three *Kammerämter* had been conferred upon the nobles, and the number increased in the next few years. By 1556 fourteen *Ämter* and *Kammerämter* were mortgaged ... thirty *Ämter*, however, were still in the duke's possession and in that year brought in 38,700 Prussian marks. Not until the time of Margrave George Frederick at the end of the century were the alienated estates returned to the state. Under Duke Albert the yield from the individual *Hauptämter* mainly took the form of natural produce, the net value of which amounted to an annual average of 300 Prussian marks each. ... Given good management, this figure could, and not infrequently did, amount to more than 2,000 Prussian marks a year, as can be seen from the accounts of Neidenburg, Rhein, Lötzen, Lyck, Brandenburg, Balga, Schaaken, Labiau, Georgenburg, Insterburg, Tilsit and in particular Ragnit, which in 1567 brought in 11,446 Prussian marks, the highest figure for any of the *Ämter* during Albert's reign. A second important source of revenue remained the regular payment of ground-rent, which was due from all owners of rentable hides in both town and country. Further yields accrued from the ducal prerogative over mills, from fishing in ducal ponds (the layout of which was to the considerable credit of the duke's counsellor in the treasury, von Nostitz, by origin a Silesian), and from the forests, even though the increased demands for the production of pitch and charcoal led to a good deal of uncontrolled felling. The exercise of petty jurisdiction by *Amtshauptleute* and village magistrates was a further source of revenue for the duke; on the other hand, the rights over the extraction of amber, which, as is well known, had been so profitable under the Order, brought in comparatively little during the Reformation

---

Preussisches Geheimes Staatsarchiv, Berlin-Dahlem, now Deutsches Zentralarchiv II Merseburg, Rep. 88 A Tit. II B 1, no. 22, fo. 47, concerning Osterode.

period, and it was not until leases were extended to Danzig merchants that the annual revenue amounted to about 30,000 Prussian marks—more than the average yield of all the *Ämter* put together.

The economy of the duchy of Prussia was based, as before, on agricultural produce: the bulk of all exports was provided by grain, fodder and flour. Next in importance came wood and wood-processing, in particular timber for shipbuilding and other specialized requirements, as well as the production of tar, pitch and potash. The villages in the honey-producing areas of the southeast delivered honey and wax, and the yield from salt and freshwater fishing was equally high; the forging of iron, however, only covered domestic requirements. Prussia was favourably situated for the carrying trade, which provided a constantly increasing source of revenue; of major importance here were Silesian textiles, and Prussia also imported saltpetre from Breslau and copperware from Posen. The three cities of Königsberg (which Albert tried in vain to merge together into a single economic and administrative unit) made the highest profits, since they belonged to the Hanse and enjoyed the right of staple by charter. Although Königsberg at that time had only an insignificant share in the shipping trade and left this to the Dutch and the English, the whole of Lithuania's exports passed through her harbours. . . . The other cities of the duchy were a long way behind Königsberg in importance; a considerable cloth industry had grown up in Bartenstein, though the sharp competition of Livonia presented at that time an obstacle to the growth of Memel as a harbour. Between 1540 and 1554 the cities of Memel, Prussian Holland, Mühlhausen, Labiau, Friedland and Garnsee were devastated by fire; and in 1553 Neudorf on the Nehrung was swallowed up by quicksands. The duke was interested in Livonia's coastal cities, to which he hoped to gain access through his brother, the archbishop of Riga, but he was even more interested in Danzig, with which he was keen to preserve active commercial relations. Time and again he occupied himself with a plan to set up a foundry in Danzig for the purpose of smelting

Swedish metals for his own requirements. Ever since his years as grand master of the Order he had been in contact with the Fuggers, who were later to be of assistance to him in the papal Curia in securing for Margrave William the administration of the archbishopric of Riga and the bishopric of Ösel. For his own part, Albert backed up the Fuggers' claims against his brother-in-law Christian III of Denmark from 1537 to 1539, among other things sending his councillor, Johann Pein, as a special envoy to Denmark. As against this, he was unsuccessful during the 1540's in his efforts to obtain silver through the Fuggers for his mint. As a result of the Turkish occupation Hungary dried up as a source of precious metals, though the Fuggers presented Albert with a number of decorative cannon. Even by then, however, the Fuggers were beginning to withdraw from the Baltic trade.[14]

Albert furthered the economic recovery of his duchy by renewing cultivation of deserted farms and settling peasants on the land. Although the allocation of land to religious refugees from the Netherlands proved unsuccessful at first, the formerly uncultivated zones in the north-east and south-east of the country were increasingly colonized by Protestant exiles from Poland and Lithuania. The *Amtshauptleute* of Insterburg and Angerburg, Johann Pein and Hans von Pusch, founded over twenty parishes

[14] A thesis by H. Kempas on Prussia's maritime trade in the sixteenth century is in progress. No adequate economic history of the duchy exists. For individual towns, see *Hanserezesse*, Vol. IV (i) (1531–5), ed. G. Wentz (Weimar, 1941); H. Rachel, "Handel und Handelsrecht von Königsberg in Preussen im 16.–18. Jahrhundert," *Forschungen zur brandenburgischen und preussischen Geschichte*, XXII (1903), 95–134; T. Wotschke, "Herzog Albrecht von Preussen und Posener Kaufleute," *Historische Monatsblätter für die Provinz Posen*, IV (1903), 37 ff.; M. Hein, *Bartenstein, 1332–1932* (Bartenstein, 1932); G. von Pölnitz, *Fugger und Hanse* (Tübingen, 1953). The largest Königsberg ship, *Der Auerochs*, was 102 feet long, 29 feet wide, and 20 feet deep (when laden), carried seven sails, and had a capacity of 120 *Last* [about 240 tons]: Preussisches Geheimes Staatsarchiv, Rep. 42, 1 Fränk. Abt. C., no. 1 (1545). On May 5, 1561, the duke gave power of attorney to Horatio Curio to negotiate with the Venetians for the building in Venice of ten ships with a capacity of between 100 and 150 *Last* [between about 200 and 300 tons] (HBA). For Hans Nimptsch on the encouragement of shipbuilding, see Staatsarchiv Königsberg, Etats-Ministerium 127 d (n.d.); April 30, 1546, HBA J 1, 936.

and many other villages. The most important new centres of traffic and administration in this part of the country were also granted the status of cities: Tilsit (1552), Marggrabowa (Markgrafenstadt, 1560) and Goldap (1567). These were German foundations despite the influx of foreigners; several written complaints and petitions addressed to the duke by the burghers of Tilsit, among others, protested against the plan to grant immigration rights to non-Germans. In every case, however, immigrants to the duchy submitted to the laws of the land and its religion, which means that they fitted themselves voluntarily into the established structure of the state. Those who, in consequence of the Reformation, decided to emigrate to Prussia and assimilate into the Prussian state, were *ipso facto* abandoning their Polish or Lithuanian nationality in favour of German nationality, together with German law and culture. Those who came directly under the territorial ruler enjoyed the terms of Culmic law, whereas those who settled in lands belonging to the nobles received only the same rights as the peasants, which were at that time very considerably diminished.[15] Colonization, however, required capital in the sixteenth century just as much as it had under the Order; and since very little capital was available it proved impossible to bring in greater numbers of German peasants, who in any case were in short supply and could be attracted only by good conditions. The increase of population could not be expected to show any useful economic results for a long time after the end of the war. The

[15] W. Kuhn, *Geschichte der deutschen Ostsiedlung in der Neuzeit*, Vol. II (Cologne and Graz, 1957), pp. 1–36; O. Barkowski, "Die Besiedlung des Hauptamtes Insterburg unter Herzog Albrecht und Markgraf Georg Friedrich von Ansbach, 1525–1603," *Prussia*, XXVIII (1928) and XXX (1930); *idem*, "Beiträge zur Siedlungs- und Ortsgeschichte des Hauptamtes Rhein," *Altpreussische Forschungen*, XI (1934), 197–224; *idem*, "Quellenbeiträge zur Siedlungs- und Ortsgeschichte des Hauptamtes Stradaunen-Oletzko," *ibid.*, XIII (1936), 183–233; R. Seeberg-Elverfeldt, "Der Verlauf der Besiedlung des ostpreussischen Amtes Johannisburg bis 1818," *ibid.*, XI (1934), 41 ff.; F. Gause, *Geschichte des Amtes und der Stadt Soldau* (Marburg, 1959); H. and G. Mortensen, *Die Besiedlung des nordöstlichen Ostpreussen*, 2 vols. (Leipzig, 1935); O. Natau, *Mundart und Siedlung im nordöstlichen Ostpreussen* (Königsberg, 1937); P. Karge, *Die Litauerfrage in Altpreussen in geschichtlicher Beleuchtung* (Königsberg, 1925).

requirements of the court and its embassies still loomed very large, since it was necessary to ensure the survival of the state among its neighbours. Albert was not especially inclined to economy by nature and was always tempted to spend above his income. Nonetheless, there can be no denying his achievements in economic reconstruction; the arbitrary rule in the *Ämter* belonged to the very last years of his reign.

The duke's regular revenues went straight to the Revenue Chamber, an institution which had already displaced the older Exchequer during the last years of the Order. The Revenue Chamber was administered by councillors of the Chamber... whose activities extended to the supervision of receipts and expenditure, the settlement of accounts and the inspection of the *Ämter*; the latter function gave them influence over the removal and appointment of the *Amtshauptleute*. The Revenue Chamber rapidly became the most important branch of administration in the conciliar central government, the ducal Supreme Council, the composition and duties of which corresponded to some extent to those of the Council of Commanders under the Order. With its up-to-date reorganization on the lines of a privy council, the Supreme Council, together with the revenue and chamber administration which formed part of it, was the most modern administrative institution possible at that time. The central territorial government which came to assist the duke was comprised of the majordomo, chief castellan, chief marshal, and chancellor. It was later laid down that these high officials should all be of native noble families of Prussia and of German origin. The duke was also served at his residence by six to eight additional councillors, after whom came the *Hauptleute* of the immediately adjacent *Ämter* of Fischhausen, Schaaken, Tapiau and Brandenburg; those who held these *Ämter* would be next in line to fill any vacancy in the Supreme Council. In the Supreme Council itself, the office of chancellor had always to be filled by a trained lawyer; the requirement that only natives might be eligible had to give way to professional qualifications so long as Prussia had no university of her own. Except for foreign affairs, which the duke reserved for his own attention, and ecclesiastical matters, which remained the concern of the bishops, the responsibilities of the Supreme Council were to deal with all matters of justice and administration, including buildings and roads, land and water transport, and, not least, the ducal household.[16] The earlier combination of central and household government in one body was still reflected in the fact that the chancellor, the Council, the chief marshal and the major-domo had sole responsibility for local administration in the capital. . . .

At all events, the setting up of the Supreme Council was a process which took place over a relatively lengthy period extending into the 1530's. The activities of its members were laid down in the ordinances for the household—a practice common in Prussia as in all princely territories in the sixteenth century. The chief marshal was to supervise the servants of the royal household, the ducal table and the heating. The chief castellan was commandant of the castle of the residence, inspector of mills and public works, and guardian of public morality. The major-domo was a sort of aide-de-camp and master of ceremonies, and was also responsible for the ladies' chamber. The chancellor headed the central administration and conducted official correspondence with foreign courts, in which he was assisted by twelve councillors and a subordinate staff of about the same number; the work of this subordinate staff was laid down in the chancery regulations, and all the councillors had fixed working hours. . . .

In setting up his administration Duke Albert was assisted by no less an authority in this field than Johann Freiherr von Schwarzenberg und Hohenlandsberg, who has been described as the "greatest German legislator of the Reformation era."[17] As chancellor to the

[16] Horn, op. cit., yields little; more detailed is F. Arndt, "Die Oberräte in Preussen, 1525–1640," Altpreussische Monatsschrift, XLIX (1912), 1–64; in general, see W. Ohnesorge, "Zum Problem Fürst und Verwaltung um die Wende des 16. Jahrhunderts," Blätter für deutsche Landesgeschichte, LXXXVIII (1951), 150–74; for officials, cf. Altpreussiche Biographie, ed. C. Krollmann, 5 parts (Königsberg, 1936–8); T. Muther, in Neue preussische Provinzialblätter, VII (1861); H. Freytag, "Zur Lebensgeschichte des Hans Nimptsch," Altpreussische Monatsschrift, XXXV (1898), 456–62, and Altpreussische Biographie, Pt. II, pp. 472 ff.

[17] E. Wolf, Grosse Rechtsdenker der deutschen Geistesgeschichte (3rd edn., Tübingen, 1951), p. 101.

bishop of Bamberg he had drafted the ordinance for criminal procedure issued [for Bamberg] in 1507, which provided a direct model for the subsequent similar legislation issued by the Emperor Charles V; he had been an early convert to the Lutheran faith and had entered the service of Brandenburg-Ansbach. . . . Duke Albert invited him to Prussia at the end of 1525, "because we also desire to rule in a Christian manner and because a work of Christian order is to be undertaken, and since we have recognized your person to be endowed more than others with a profound and Christian understanding, we therefore promise you that we wish to retain you not as a servant but as our brother." Schwarzenberg was willing to go immediately, but he was prevented at first by an operation for the stone . . . but was able at last to appear in time for Albert's marriage to Dorothea [princess of Denmark and Holstein, in July 1526], and remained in Königsberg until the spring of 1527. No detailed accounts have survived of his activities there or the scope of his advice, which was given mainly by word of mouth, but it would be difficult to overestimate their importance, as can be seen from the sheer quantity of documents on governmental and legal procedure of which he left behind copies in Königsberg. Schwarzenberg engaged in a lively exchange of ideas with his fellow-countryman Dr. Fischer, who was chancellor, and with the Prussian reformers; the revised procedure for the high court of justice, which convened every quarter, has been attributed to him, and he endeavoured to get the *Carolina* [the criminal code later issued for the Empire] accepted as a penal code and trial procedure in Prussia as well. He used the Ansbach household ordinance as a model in drawing up regulations for the duchess's household. In 1526 he wrote and had printed in Königsberg a defence of clerical marriage; and it is certain that the duke's printed edict against vagrants was prompted by Schwarzenberg. He certainly worked on the draft of the Prussian *Landesordnung* of 1528; his rigorous ordinances against the competitive drinking of pledges clearly had their origin in a work of popular education he had written in 1512. From the very start Schwarzenberg was anxious to make the principles of the *Landesordnung* apply also to the bishopric of Ermland and West Prussia. One of the main concerns which he was constantly urging on Albert was the need to moderate all religious and social conflicts: the government should act with mildness and consideration towards the poor misguided people. . . .[18] In the spring of 1527 he left Prussia without having quite completed his work of reconstructing the state.

Among the Prussian councillors in the sixteenth century there emerged ever more clearly a distinct group of men who were particularly well qualified by training and ability to represent their master's interests at foreign courts. This was of considerable importance to Albert in view of the difficulty of the general situation, his own personal position, and the claim to independent action in foreign policy which he was so anxious to secure. He still had no permanent representation abroad, apart from a number of merchant agents in important centres such as Nuremberg. The envoys were usually councillors in the Supreme Council, occasionally *Amtshauptleute* or the district presidents; at all events they were familiar with current administrative affairs and were called upon to carry out special missions as the need arose. Much the same system had prevailed towards the end of the Order's rule. Nevertheless, distinct spheres of diplomatic activity began to emerge: Johann Pein, for instance, was preferred for missions to the Danish court, where he was well known, as also were Claus von Gadendorf and Joachim von Borcke; the latter also travelled frequently to Pomerania, where he was able to count on the support of distant relatives and his brother, the Pomeranian chancellor. . . . Among the envoys of Albert who possessed

[18] R. Philippi, "Freiherr Johann von Schwarzenberg in Preussen," *Zeitschrift des Westpreussischen Geschichtsvereins*, I (1880), 45–69, using Ostpreussische Folianten 78, fos. 38–46; letter of invitation to Schwarzenberg, November 29, 1525, *ibid.*, fos. 3–5; Tschackert, *op. cit.*, Vol. II, nos. 509–10, 519, 522, 605a. On December 2, 1525, Duke Albert had asked Margrave Casimir for Schwarzenberg, "who will be most useful to us all in this matter, and with whom we intend to make an arrangement on more favourable terms than with any ordinary councillor," Ostpreussische Folianten 56, fo. 46. Margrave Casimir reported Schwarzenberg's return to Franconia, Plassenburg, May 5, 1527, *ibid.*, 78, fos. 38 ff.

sufficient skill and dignity to appear before the imperial court the most important was Georg Klingenbeck the Elder, who was sent to the courts of Spain, Scandinavia, Moscow, Livonia and Poland, to the foremost princes of the Empire, and to the Diets of Speyer (1529) and Augsburg (1530). Most versatile of all was Asverus von Brandt, who served Albert as councillor and ambassador for twenty years in France, Hungary, Poland and Livonia, and at the Diets of Nuremberg (1543), Speyer (1544), Worms (1545) and Augsburg (1559). He was very hard-working and reliable, and his reports were clear and detailed, showing independence of mind; from 1548 onwards he was *Amtshauptmann* of Tapiau, though this did not exempt him from his work as ambassador. Although no particular elite came into being as yet, this branch of service was certainly a further example of important state business being centralized within the duke's own personal sphere of activity and influence; the result was to make diplomacy an expression of the duke's sovereignty.[19]

As early as 1526—and certainly with the assistance of Schwarzenberg—an ordinance had been issued for procedure in the local courts in the duchy; according to this a regional tribunal, consisting of a clerk of the court and a number of jurors and presided over by a local judge appointed and paid by the duke, met once a year in Saalfeld, Brandenburg, Bartenstein, Gilgenburg, Hohenstein and Johannisburg for the purpose of judging any suits which might be presented. Twenty years later a revised court procedure was issued for Bartenstein, Rastenburg, Mohrunge, Hohenstein and Riesenburg. The judicial centres had changed and even diminished in number, despite the rising number of cases. As a result the larger cities complained at the diets about the increasing tendency for the ducal supreme court to draw in work which really belonged in the local courts. They were told in reply

[19] E.-T. Thiele, *Das Gesandschaftswesen in Preussen im 16. Jahrhundert* (Göttingen, 1954); *Die Berichte und Briefe des Rats und Gesandten Herzog Albrechts von Preussen Asverus von Brandt, nebst den an ihn ergangenen Schreiben in dem Kgl. Staatsarchiv zu Königsberg*, Pts. I–IV, ed. A. Bezzenberger (Königsberg, 1904–21); Pt. V (conclusion and index), ed. E. Sprengel (Hameln, 1953).

that in rural areas disputes had often been passed undecided from one court to another, that the defendants had frequently refused to comply with the verdicts of the courts, and that there had occasionally been intervention by third parties in the execution of sentence. Whereas the ducal supreme court in this way gradually suppressed the regional courts and older quarterly courts in favour of centralized jurisdiction, the duke did not succeed in excluding appeals to the Polish supreme court. . . .[20]

Duke Albert was, however, able to assert his claims to sovereignty in another matter, the monetary system. It had been decreed in [the Treaty of] Cracow that Prussia was provisionally to suspend her own coining. Poland's aim was to secure a single currency with West Prussia and the duchy and to reserve for herself the right to issue coins and decide on the standard. Albert was determined from the outset to assert and exercise his right to mint coins; he had otherwise every reason to fear that an alteration in the value of the coinage would lead to a fall in the purchasing power of money and the value of land. In 1526 he did manage to persuade the Polish king in Danzig to agree in principle to his right to mint coinage, though Sigismund continued with his usual tenacity to pursue his economic policy and later even let the duke know that he wished him to have his coins struck in Poland. . . . Even as late as the years 1546 to 1554, during the Schmalkaldic War [between Charles V and the Protestants] and its after-effects, when Poland was intent on prohibiting the circulation of Prussian coins in the kingdom altogether, the minting of coins at Königsberg continued only on a small scale. . . .[21] During the reign of King Sigismund Augustus [1548-

[20] F. S. Bock, *Leben und Thaten des Durchlauchtigen Fürsten und Herrn, Herrn Albrechts des ältern, Markgrafen zu Brandenburg und Ersten Herzoges in Preussen* (2nd edn., Königsberg and Leipzig, 1750), pp. 155 ff.; Horn, *op. cit.*, pp. 89 ff.; L. Von Poblocki, "Die Zeit der grössten Abhängigkeit des Herzogtums Preussen von Polen in den Jahren 1566-1568," *Zeitschrift für Preussische Geschichte und Landeskunde*, xx (1883), 245-70; on the question of appeals, see Ostpreussische Folianten 475, fo. 332.

[21] W. Schwinkowski, "Das Geldwesen in Preussen unter Herzog Albrecht (1525-1569)" (Ph.D. thesis, Königsberg, 1909; also in *Zeitschrift für Numismatik*, XXVII (1909), 185-377, pp. 69 ff.).

1572] Poland no longer disputed Prussia's monetary sovereignty, though the considerable quantity of inferior coins struck in Lithuania threatened to undermine the Prussian currency, since they made their way in large numbers to the northern districts of East Prussia. . . .

While Duke Albert had been able to model his administration on the German territorial states and emerge as dynastic ruler and sovereign despite the formal feudal relationship [with Poland], he had the further task of finding a constitutional structure which fitted in with the modern aspirations of a princely state, yet at the same time corresponded to his ideal of a Protestant territory and took into account the particular domestic and foreign problems of his duchy. The constitution was still purely dynastic in form, being dependent not only on the ruler's own person but on the guarantee of successors. The "house of Brandenburg" as a constituent part of the "German nation" provided the framework of Albert's view of the state, and within this context he conceived his own role as that of the supreme magistrate and authority "by God's grace," divinely installed to render service in the world. He therefore entered upon his responsibilities with definite intentions and obligations, and sought advisers who would support him in this course. Albert had ruled in this way as sovereign prince during his years as grand master and had called upon the country's resources without hesitation. Those who had sustained this burden now wished to evade it in the future. They considered their interests to have been secured through the guarantee of their privileges contained in the Treaty of Cracow, and they treated with great distrust any sign of an independent foreign policy on the part of the duke because they were constantly expecting the threat of war. Thus the nobles and the cities found themselves naturally and inevitably in opposition to the aspirations of the duke, who was trying to throw his country's resources into the scales of high politics as he himself saw fit.

At first, however, the interests of duke and Estates appeared to coincide. The peasant disturbances, with their unmistakably dangerous tones of social revolution, had rallied nobles and cities to the side of authority. The duke was unable to turn this unique moment of goodwill to any permanent advantage because social peace was vitally necessary for his work of reconstruction. He was, moreover, dependent on the financial co-operation of the Estates. The once disciplined and obedient Knights of the Teutonic Order had become independent nobles with land of their own, and the duke had afforded both them and the oligarchic city councillors his protection without imposing any obligations in return. From then on an extremely skilful advocate of the duke's interests with the Estates emerged in the figure of Hans von Besenrade, whom Albert had brought back with him to Prussia in 1525 and who had a good deal of economic and administrative experience. By bringing about a division among the Estates at the diets of 1526 and 1528, where he appeared as chief castellan and plenipotentiary of the duke, he succeeded in gaining consent for an excise on drink which was to remain in force in the country during the reign of Duke Albert and his immediate successors; this brought in an annual yield of about 40,000 Prussian marks. The cities immediately affected, however, started a move to reassert long-standing privileges; Besenrade promised the duke that "he intended, through the power of the Holy Gospel and in the shortest possible time, to secure for his prince a loyal people who would not be able to make use of special rights or privileges."[22] The chief castellan set up a permanent ducal garrison in the castle and the burghers' houses; he hoped that if the refractory cities of Königsberg could be made more compliant with the aid of military force, it would be easy to subdue the provincial cities.

[22] M. Töppen, *Zur Geschichte der ständischen Verhältnisse in Preussen* (Raumers historisches Taschenbuch, Neue Folge VIII, Leipzig, 1847), p. 311. The introduction by K. Breysig to Vol. XV of *Urkunden und Aktenstücke zur Geschichte des Kurfürsten Friedrich Wilhelm von Brandenburg* (Berlin, 1894) deals with the Estates under Duke Albert on pp. 19–53, but is based only on secondary material (principally Töppen, the extreme advocate of the policy of the Estates) and contains many crude and inaccurate opinions, for instance on what the ecclesiastical ordinance of 1558 has to say about exorcism at baptism. B. Schumacher, *Geschichte Ost- und Westpreussens* (2nd edn., Würzburg, 1957) and F. L. Carsten, *The Origins of Prussia* (Oxford, 1954), pp. 150 ff., are still based on Breysig.

But in the spring of 1529 the plague carried off this resolute man of action, whom the hostile chroniclers of the Estates described abusively as the "evil councillor." The dispute over governmental power took second place to the more immediately perceptible distress wrought among the population, which had been terribly hit by the plague. But the differences had come out fully into the open for the first time and were not to disappear again: the particularist interests of the Estates could not be reconciled with personal government for the benefit of the country as a whole. Occasionally a compromise seemed possible, but time and again the Hohenzollern duke set about trying to check the irksome and, to his mind, unacceptable influence of the Estates. It was the same struggle as was going on at that time in all the German territorial states; the princes, whose power was growing enormously, strove for absolute rule, though none of them managed to overcome the established powers of the Estates at the first attempt. Even the most energetic and ruthless of Albert's fellow rulers, the Elector Maurice of Saxony, was unable to break the rule of the Estates. Throughout the sixteenth century the struggle remained undecided. Furthermore, the central power of the emperor was still too strong for the full development of the sovereign territorial state, which did not come about until the imperial dignity had been reduced to a mere adornment and the Habsburgs had turned aside to pursue the interests of their dynasty. Charles V, on the other hand, was still perfectly able to assert his own will in the Schmalkaldic War: it may have caused a considerable stir for princes of the Empire to be taken prisoner and sentenced to death, but at that time it was still completely within the realms of the possible, even though it was never to be repeated.

The representative system made it easier for the duke to bring his centralizing authority to bear on the individual Estates within the diet or to play them off against one another. The assembly of the Prussian Estates consisted of the prelates and twelve district presidents, who were generally elected from among the ducal *Amtleute*. This, the first Estate, was followed by the Estate of landowners in the strict sense, consisting of nobles and gentry with their own powers of taxation; and the third Estate was made up of the cities, though only Königsberg was of any significance. Difficult questions were thoroughly aired in advance at provincial diets and dealt with by committees [of the Estates]; here, too, the central government of the duke had its trusted agents everywhere and could count on their influence. When, in 1539, the diet debated the tax for the war against the Turks and the Estates were assessed for the unusually high tax of 60,000 Prussian marks, the ground was prepared by the *Amtshauptmann* of Bartenstein, Georg von Kunheim, who, as the city chronicler complained, "helped contrive many new taxes and burdens for this poor land."[23] For their willingness to help the duke out of his immediate financial embarrassments, the nobles insisted on compensation in the form of privileges. In the *Landesordnung* the ordinance fixing the price of grain included the injunction that the grain was to be offered for sale in nearby towns. It was not long before the nobles were conceded the right to sell wherever they wanted, and the law itself was so frequently circumvented that it failed altogether in its purpose of guaranteeing parity of living costs with Ermland and West Prussia. For [voting] the tax for the war against the Turks, the Prussian nobility received the privilege that all properties held in fee were to revert to the duke only when the whole family had died out in both the male and female line.

The Estates secured their most important concession in the Memorandum on the Regency Government, which was presented to them on July 31, 1542. This had been preceded by additional heavy taxes which had been made necessary by the dangerous advance of the Turks and the defeat of the imperial army under King Ferdinand before Ofen at the end of August 1541; partial mobilization had already been carried out in Prussia itself. Since Duke Albert had been called on to lead in person a section of the fighting forces under the command of the elector of Brandenburg, it became necessary to draw up the prince's personal testament and to make other general arrangements for the whole of the duke's

[23] *Freibergs Chronik*, ed. Meckelburg, p. 239; Töppen, *Zur Geschichte der ständischen Verhältnisse*, p. 337.

absence by installing a regency. It was laid down first that the achievements of the Reformation must be protected and the ecclesiastical activity of the bishops guaranteed without any hindrance; the ecclesiastical ordinance was ratified. Four supreme councillors were appointed as regents and would be assisted by six to eight other councillors and judges. As further advisers were named the *Amtshauptleute* of the neighbouring *Ämter* of Brandenburg, Fischhausen, Schaaken and Tapiau, who had often been called in for consultations with the government, and three deputies of the cities of Königsberg. The duke's consort and daughter were to be provided "with a fitting princely sustenance"; the guardians for his descendants were to be supplied by the Estates and to be expressly named in his will. The decisions of the regency council were to be made by majority vote and the appointed regents to be paid out of the revenues of the principality. The castle of Tapiau or Brandenburg would be placed at the disposal of the Estates as a firm guarantee of their privileges. Nevertheless, this arrangement gave the duke's officials complete predominance, and even the concession to the landed nobility that all these posts were to be reserved in future for native nobles lost a good deal of its strength through the system of appointing administrators with legal training: for these posts burghers or specialists from abroad were readily admitted, and especially so in the case of the important office of chancellor. The nobles may certainly have considered this administrative statute as furthering their interests, though there can be no doubt that the duke would always be able to find men he could trust from among the large numbers of the Prussian nobility. The duke himself chose his own advisers and the Estates had no influence whatever on their appointment. But in that very same year, 1542, the first step was taken to set up a high school in Königsberg, with a view to developing it in the near future into a university; this gave rise to the hope that the native population could be drawn on for the future supply of well-trained administrators to ensure the best possible services to the country. In this way the dynasty became less dependent on foreign councillors. Under these circumstances, when Duke Albert officially promulgated the Memorandum on the Regency Government on November 18, 1542, he was able to look forward to satisfactory collaboration with the Estates. He was sure of the prelates and the district presidents, and had won over the lower nobility; the cities, which in any case enjoyed the smallest financial resources, had no option but to comply. When, later, the nobles approved a further grant of money made necessary on the eve of the Schmalkaldic War, the duke issued a "Little Privilege of Grace"; it was backdated to November 14, 1542, and its principal import was that the four *Amtshauptleute* of the regency were also to be resident nobles and that the native nobility were in general to enjoy priority over foreigners in nominations to official appointments.[24] The Memorandum on the Regency Government was never ratified by the Polish court, yet it remained in force for over twenty years without its validity being disputed, a sure sign of how independently Prussia arranged its internal affairs. Nevertheless, the duke was not prepared to grant the nobles any further privileges beyond the concessions already made, since these could easily have altered the favourable balance within the ducal system of government to his disadvantage. . . . Altogether, foreign affairs only came before the diet when they could be introduced as evidence of the general emergency [which required taxation]. . . .

Duke Albert attended most of the diets in person. In 1544 there were thirty-three persons present, including the supreme councillors and the nine representatives of the cities of Königsberg; two nobles were absent on account of illness. Out of this number a committee of nine was formed. It would be wrong, therefore, to think that these assemblies were of any great size. The duke's personal interventions were concerned in the main with raising

---

[24] Staatsarchiv Königsberg, Urkunden auf Pergament, including a draft that was not executed; the "privileges" printed in *Privilegia der Stände des Herzogtums Preussen* (Braunsberg, 1616), fos. 50 ff.; copy of the privileges of November 14, 1542, Ostpreussische Folianten 80, fos. 125–8; Albert's will, *ibid.*, 79, fos. 802 ff. (July 2, 1541); for the diets from 1543 to 1559, cf. *ibid.*, 475, 477, 480, 483; Etats-Ministerium, 87 e. I have to thank Herr Norbert Ommler for the use of an extensive collection of excerpts from the Königsberg state archives, made at my instigation.

the general moral standards of the population; in 1549, for instance, he demanded severer prosecution of sexual crimes and infanticide. Conditions in ale-houses were to be reviewed; and he went on to recommend that granaries be built in the regions and *Ämter* in order to ensure low-priced grain for the poor in the event of harvest failure. He also promised to see that fishing rights in the lagoons and in coastal waters were respected, since fishing was often leased out to merchants and exploited on a large scale. By and large, many good and just proposals were made, though a considerable number of projects were frustrated by the cumbersomeness of government in council and the complicated business of raising the necessary resources.

The duke was indefatigable in his efforts to obtain cash on security at between 5 and 8 per cent. interest, appealing in turn to his subjects, his neighbours in Ermland, the princes of the Empire and many other sources. In many cases villages or *Ämter* were pledged, a highly questionable system which gradually became a permanent condition. But the lack of ready money was a universal phenomenon among the princes of the time, and the great banking houses were to grow even more in importance as providers of credit to the princes throughout the century of the Reformation. What the Fuggers meant to the Habsburgs was represented on a reduced scale for the house of Brandenburg by the Danzig banking house of Loitz. Albert tried in vain to make good his shortage of ready money by tightening up his own administration; and the visitations of the *Ämter* which he undertook in 1546 and even as late as 1560 achieved very little, since his financial requirements were constantly growing.

8 Financial Policy and the Evolution of the Demesne in the Netherlands under Charles V and Philip II (1530–1560)

MICHEL BAELDE

THE financial history of the Netherlands in the sixteenth century has hardly been studied. Some recent articles, however, reveal the importance of this new topic.[1] The present contribution is by no means intended to give a full exposition of all financial questions. It is merely a preliminary survey of the most important decisions taken in the financial sphere. Budgetary matters and the evolution of the demesne are singled out for special attention.[2]

Our research has been chiefly concerned with the period 1530–1560. 1530 marks the beginning of the second half of the reign of Charles V, and the year 1560 can serve as the finishing point because, although Charles V abdicated in 1555, the influence of his financial policies made itself felt for five years after the end of his reign, and it was in 1560 that Philip II's sojourn in the Netherlands came to an end. The wealth of archive material obviously requires the imposition of some sort of limitation.[3]

In 1531 the financial condition of the Netherlands was subjected to scrutiny by the conciliar bodies responsible for finances.

[1] F. Braudel, "Les emprunts de Charles-Quint sur la place d'Anvers," *Charles-Quint et son temps* (Paris, 1959), pp. 191–200; R. Carande, "Maria de Hungria en el mercado de Amberes," *Karl V. Der Kaiser und seine Zeit*, ed. P. Rassow and F. Schalk (Cologne, 1960), pp. 38–50.

[2] No monograph treating of the princely demesne in the sixteenth-century Netherlands exists to date. Some interesting information is provided by A. Henne, *Histoire du règne de Charles-Quint en Belgique*, Vol. VII (1859), pp. 132–8; however, the figures given there are based on calculations in which not all expenses are itemized.

[3] The following abbreviations will be used: ARAB, Algemeen Rijksarchief, Brussels; Aud., Papiers d'État et de l'Audience; VSPA, Vienna, Haus- Hof- und Staatsarchiv, Politisches Archiv; SAG, Simancas, Archivo General; Estado, Secretaría de Estado; Sec. Pr., Secretarías Provinciales.

Charles V had come to Brussels on January 25 and did not leave for his territories in Germany until the beginning of the following year.[4] On March 13, 1531, the emperor met his sister Mary at Louvain; as the widowed queen of Hungary, she was to act as regent of the Netherlands until 1555. On October 1, 1531, three collateral councils were established: in this way the central administration of the Netherlands was thoroughly reorganized and became concentrated in the Council of State, the Privy Council, and the Council of Finance.[5]

The last of these councils, the Council of Finance, changed its membership in 1531. The institutions now existed to tackle financial problems more vigorously. Yet the new administrative machinery could not of itself immediately bring about a change in the far from rosy financial situation. The accounts for the year 1531 suggested a rather gloomy prospect. The revenues amounted to £1,229,292, while expenditure ran to £1,645,270, so that the accounts were closed with a deficit of £415,878.[6] How was this deficit for 1531 to be explained? The excess of expenditure was

[4] G. de Boom, Les voyages de Charles-Quint (Collection Lebègue et Nationale No. 121, 1957), pp. 68–9; M. Gachard, Collection des Voyages des Souverains des Pays-Bas, Vol. II (1874), pp. 98–101.

[5] E. Strubbe, "Staatsinrichting en Krijgswezen," Algemene Geschiedenis der Nederlanden, Vol. IV (1952), p. 137. For a more detailed treatment of the subject, see [M. Baelde, De Collaterale Raden onder Karel V en Filips II (1531–1578). Bijdrage tot de geschiedenis van de centrale instellingen in de zestiende eeuw (Brussels, 1965). The Council of State was the main advisory council of the ruler and his regent in the Netherlands; the Privy Council was responsible for drafting legislation and administering justice.]

[6] All figures are given in Flemish pounds (livres) of 40 groats each, sometimes also called florins. This was the standard governmental monetary unit for accounting purposes in the sixteenth century. The figures here cited are based on accounts for 1531, entitled "Statement of the revenues of the emperor our lord for the year beginning on the first day of January 1531 and ending the last day of December 1531 for the surplus accounted for by the receiver-general over and above the charges for fiefs, alms, rents, the salaries of officials . . . assigned to the demesne lands and ordinary revenues," ARAB, Aud., no. 875, fo. 2. The size of the deficit is borne out by the introduction to a decree dated May 4, 1536, confirming the accounts. The relevant passage reads ". . . our finances have ever since then been heavily burdened and in arrears, so that the state of our finances of the year ending in December 1531 was a deficit of more than four hundred thousand florins . . .," SAG, Sec. Pr., no. 2561, fo. 101.

chiefly due to the recent war against France.[7] But Charles V's conquests in the northern Netherlands had also demanded great financial exertions.[8] Furthermore, in 1530 the coastal regions had been ravaged by floods, so that revenues were reduced.

The emperor took note of the unsound financial situation, but did not undertake the required measures of reform.[9] It is hardly surprising, then, that the financial problems of the Netherlands came up for discussion as soon as Charles V had departed for Germany. The Regent Mary, together with the Council of Finance, repeatedly investigated the precarious condition of the treasury. In this connection, she soon came to carry on a busy correspondence with Charles V. On February 2, 1532, she writes from Brussels, "... we have had so much trouble with your finances, which are in a state you well know, that we have been able to accomplish little...."[10] On April 5 the reply comes "... and as for the state of the finances, I know in truth that this is no easy task for you, considering how little comes in, and if I remember rightly, at my departure it was decided that it was necessary to take and consume one year with the other, or as one says in financial administration, to overlap; moreover, I see no great willingness on anyone's part to delay payment of their

[7] This war began in 1522–3, reached its zenith in 1525–7, and was concluded in 1529 at the Peace of Cambrai.

[8] The decree of May 4, 1536, describes them as follows: "... for having contributed to the burdens and expenses of past wars, the conquest of Friesland, Tournai, the county of Tournai, Utrecht, and Overysel...," SAG, Sec. Pr., no. 2561, fo. 101. See also W. Formsma, "De Onderwerping van Friesland,' *Algemene Geschiedenis der Nederlanden*, Vol. IV, pp. 72 ff.

[9] Thus at the end of the accounts for 1531 there stands the following note: "This account and the five following ones, together with the summary and extracts written at the end of each account, were several times seen and inspected by the emperor in his council in the presence of the queen and of the chief officials, the treasurer and commissioners for his demesne lands and finances; and because expenditure exceeds receipts and changes could still occur any day in the entries of these accounts, even in the expenditure, the advice was given to leave the accounts as they stand without completing or closing them; and His Majesty ordered that expenditure should be regulated and controlled for the greater profit and lesser expense of His said Majesty as far as was possible," ARAB, Aud., no. 875, fo. 38[v].

[10] ARAB, Aud., no. 47, fo. 39[v].

pensions. . . ."[11] Clearly the regent started out with a handful of financial troubles.

The next year only added to these difficulties: in November 1532 Flanders, Zeeland, and Holland were again ravaged by tremendous floods. One direct consequence was the extremely low yield from the demesne lands [belonging to the ruler] in these regions, and the rather dim prospect for income from subsidies [a property tax voted by the Estates]. It was in fact because of these floods that loans in excess of £600,000 were contracted in the city of Antwerp.[12] In order to reverse this lamentable development, two influential members of the Council of Finance were sent to Charles V in the spring of 1533. They were Philip of Croy, duke of Aarschot, first director of finance; and Hughes de Grammez, lord of Wingene, a member of the Council of State and the Council of Finance.[13] A detailed analysis of receipts and expenditures until the end of 1533 was submitted by these emissaries; at the same time, the fearful rise in loans was pointed out to the emperor.

After this mission, resolutions for reform were soon forthcoming. To begin with, certain economies were proposed so as to reduce expenditure; in particular, it was intended to delay payment of certain salaries and pensions, and perhaps disband some units of the army. Next, measures were taken to raise

[11] *Ibid.*, no. 47, fo. 64. An extremely important collection of letters of Charles V and Mary of Hungary has been preserved in Vienna, VSPA, nos. 20–90.

[12] According to the decree of February 1, 1535, SAG, Sec. Pr., no. 2596, fo. 116. For further information concerning the flood years 1530 and 1532, see M. Gottschalk, *Historische geografie van Westelijk Zeeuws-Vlaanderen*, Vol. II, *Van het begin der 15e eeuw tot de inundaties tijdens de Tachtigjarige oorlog* (Assen 1958), pp. 168–75.

[13] Philip of Croy was born in 1496; in 1516 he became a knight of the Golden Fleece; on October 1, 1531, he was appointed ordinary member of the new Council of State; on August 26, 1532, he succeeded Jaak of Luxemburg, lord of Fiennes, as director of the Council of Finance. As duke of Aarschot he was also governor of Hainault, and in 1521 had inherited all the titles of nobility of his uncle William, the famous lord of Chièvres. He died in 1549. Hughes de Grammez, lord of Wingene, was appointed a member of the Council of Finance on October 1, 1531. He was also a commissioner at the codification of legal customs in Flanders. He remained in office until *c.* 1548.

receipts: the regent was given instructions to sell some demesne lands or else a perpetual annuity guaranteed on them; at the same time, the central authorities in the Netherlands were given complete freedom to sell annuities [equivalent to negotiable and redeemable bearer bonds] guaranteed on revenues from the demesne or the subsidies; the principal cities were to be induced to issue similar annuities; and finally, loans were now to be negotiated in exchange for appointment to offices and "to be repaid by annual instalments or on a fixed date, resignation, or death."[14] Were all these proposed measures carried out in the Netherlands? The delicacy of the problem confronting the regent and the Council of Finance must be borne in mind. The instructions of October 1, 1531 contained serious restrictions on the freedom of action of both regent and Council in financial matters.[15] Thus the sale or alienation of demesne lands was forbidden.[16] Each of the many such "extraordinary" transactions which were recommended consequently required the emperor's express confirmation.

Discussion as to what steps should be taken to implement the emperor's resolutions was somewhat delayed, because the lord of Wingene was taken ill and his return to the Netherlands delayed. On June 3, 1533, the regent was able to report to the emperor:

Your Royal Highness, my cousin Aarschot on his arrival asked me to postpone his explaining and reporting on the decision of Your Majesty concerning the orders and instructions which you gave to him and the lord of Wingene, until the latter's arrival, which was twelve days after that of the duke of Aarschot, in order the better to understand your good resolve. I was happy with this arrangement, knowing that the delay was only for the good. Your Royal Highness, on the return of the lord of Wingene, my cousin Aarschot came with him to see me together with your financial councillors whom I had summoned.

[14] May 4, 1536, SAG, Sec. Pr., no. 2561, fos. 161–2.
[15] *Recueil des Ordonnances des Pays-Bas*, 2nd Series, Vol. IV, pp. 244–54, 260–2.
[16] "The emperor issues this prohibition and expressly orders his financial officials that during his absence they confirm none of his letters by which his demesne might be sold or alienated by hereditary descent, for life, or otherwise . . .," *ibid.*, p. 252.

Having heard their report on all items and articles concerning your finances and other affairs for which they had been sent to Your Majesty, I made them give a similar report on matters they knew about to your Council of State, which they also did.

By these reports, I and your councillors of state and of the finances knew for sure that Your Majesty had well understood, weighed and considered everything put to you by my cousin and Wingene concerning the disposition of your affairs in the Netherlands. . . .[17]

Reforming the financial situation proved far from easy. Despite the good intentions of the central government, new pecuniary resources had to be found again and again. In place of the existing short-term loans, new loans amounting to £300,000 had to be taken up. This sum was used for payments of the utmost urgency, so that action on the emperor's instructions had to be postponed.[18] Shortly after, however, Mary proceeded to carry out his directives. A decree of the emperor's of February 1, 1535, ratified all decisions made in this sphere. From this decree we learn that many annuities had been issued and that there had been offered for sale out of the demesne "none of our ancient houses and inheritances . . . except our mill-houses at Antwerp, Ypres, Wervik, Tenremonde, Namur, Oostvoorne, and others."[19]

From all these transactions for the years 1533–5 Jan Micault, the receiver-general, obtained £434,214. This money was used "to discharge the said debts, charges, expenses and finances, payment of our soldiers, fortifications at the frontiers, and other affairs of our country, as appears in the accounts presented by him at our audit office at Lille."[20] It should not be concluded that the financial problems were now solved. Soon new political developments

[17] VSPA, no. 29, fo. 87.

[18] According to Mary of Hungary's letter to Charles V, Brussels, July 14, 1533, ibid., fos. 95–6.

[19] SAG, Sec. Pr., no. 2596, fos. 116–20.

[20] Excerpt from the ratification of May 4, 1536. For a copy of this decree, see ibid., no. 2561, fos. 101–8. In 1535, Jan Micault had been receiver-general for nearly thirty years; he was also treasurer of the Order of the Golden Fleece; on August 1 of that year, 1535, he resigned as receiver-general; Hendrik Stercke was his successor. Micault died in Brussels in 1539.

called for fresh financial exertions. The Danish question [Charles V's support of the dynastic claims of his family to the throne of Denmark provoked conflict also with the free city of Lübeck] and the imminent threat of war with France rendered altogether insufficient the sum of over £400,000 which had been raised over and above the regular revenues.[21] The war with France broke out at the beginning of 1536.[22] On March 2 the emperor wrote to the regent from Naples:

> . . . although the financial officials, acting truly as good servants, have always prevented and avoided selling lands, nevertheless, if necessity requires it and there is no other remedy, it would be far better to pledge lands than to lose them. Whatever the finance officers may say or protest, if you see such irremediable necessity, you should sell and pledge any piece of land to meet it, since once the war is over, we shall consider means to recover these lost territories, which may prove a lesser evil than to take up such excessively usurious loans as I have done in Spain in a hard decision. . . .[23]

In confirmation of this letter, a new decree concerning the pledging of demesne lands and the sale of annuities was sent by Charles to the Regent Mary from Florence, on May 4, 1536.[24] At the same time, a fresh subsidy was requested, although the

[21] ". . . and it happens that subsequently other important events have occurred in our territories in the Netherlands, such as the war with the city of Lübeck, against which we were forced to defend ourselves, both for our reputation and to protect and preserve our provinces of Holland, Zeeland and Friesland, which would have been conspicuously ruined, had not provision been made for them; similarly, news and reports were current that certain neighbouring princes of our lands were mustering cavalry and infantry and making other signs and preparations of war; likewise the king of France demonstrated his desire to attack us aggressively, both by sending out envoys and ambassadors and by certain indications of extremely large musters of troops . . .," SAG, Sec. Pr., no. 2561, fo. 103.

[22] For a good survey of these wars, consult J. Craeybeckx, "Maria van Hongarije, landvoogdes. De oorlogen tegen Frankrijk (1531–1555)," *Algemene Geschiedenis der Nederlanden*, Vol. IV, pp. 97–122.

[23] VSPA, no. 33, fos. 120–1. The original letter, in code, was deciphered in the margin; a copy is kept at Brussels, ARAB, Aud., no. 49, fo. 23.

[24] SAG. Sec. Pr., no. 2561, fos. 101–8.

provincial Estates had already granted substantial sums in 1531 and 1534. In conjunction with this new subsidy, many annuities were also sold.[25] The war with France lasted until the truce of July 30, 1537, and called for many sacrifices. The correspondence between regent and emperor discloses the financial difficulties in no uncertain terms. On January 8, 1537, Mary writes from Brussels:

> Your Royal Highness, your finances and revenue are so burdened, sold up and in arrears because of past wars that all revenues until 1539 are eaten up and consumed in advance; Moreover, expenses and outgoings standing to your charge run to more than four or five hundred thousand florins, for which your financial officials and several other lords of your Order of the Golden Fleece, the Council of State, and the Privy Council are committed in their own names; in addition, the same nobles were recently again obliged to assume responsibility for a sum of eighty thousand florins, and each did the best he could. . . .[26]

Even after the settlement with France on June 18, 1538, financial problems remained, in which Ghent's refusal to pay its quota of the subsidy played no small part. On January 21, 1540, Charles V arrived once again in the Netherlands.[27]

Let us now consider how the financial policy described above affected the budgets for the period 1530–40. That a budget bodes well for the future if receipts exceed expenditure is a notorious truism. A few preliminary observations concerning sixteenth-century budgets may, all the same, prove instructive:[28] a favourable balance in the accounts did not always signify a sound cash

[25] See Charles V's interesting letter to Mary from Naples, dated March 2, 1536, and Mary's to Charles V of May 24 and July 25, ARAB, Aud., no. 52, fo. 167^v; no. 49, fos. 52–3, 82^v–84^v.

[26] Ibid., no. 49, fos. 161–2. In April 1538 Mary is still writing about the dire financial situation, and the following slips from her: "It displeases me, Your Royal Highness, that I always have to sing a most tiresome note, but what I do is in order to give your Majesty the full facts . . .," ibid., no. 50, fo. 65^v.

[27] De Boom, op. cit., p. 81; Gachard, op. cit., p. 159.

[28] Further information, both general and specific, concerning taxation, loans and annuities, may be found in M. Arnould, "L'impôt sur le capital en Belgique au XVIe siècle," Le Hainaut économique, I (1946), 17–45; P. Brouwers, Les aides et subsides dans la comté de Namur au XVIe siècle (Namur, 1924); J. Craeybeckx,

position in the treasury. Revenues in the Netherlands were divided into three categories in the sixteenth century.[29] Firstly there were the receipts from the demesne. This income was chiefly drawn from the sale of agricultural products such as grain, cattle, and fowl, and also from the numerous seigneurial rights, especially the rights to enforce use of the lord's mill or to levy tolls.[30] The yield from the demesne could vary sharply from year to year, depending on how favourable or unfavourable weather conditions were; the same held for proceeds from seigneurial rights. In drawing up the accounts the average for normal fiscal years was taken as the yield from the demesne, while the expected expenditure of the budget year itself was taken into account.[31]

"Aperçu sur l'histoire des impôts en Flandre et au Brabant au cours du XVIe siècle," *Revue du Nord*, XXIX (1947), 87–108; J. Dhondt, "Bijdrage tot de kennis van het financiewezen der Staten in Vlaanderen," *Nederlandsche Historiebladen*, III (1942), 149–81; H. Longchay, "Étude sur les emprunts des souverains belges au XVIe et au XVIIe siècle," *Bull. Acad. roy. de Belg., Cl. des Lettres*, XII (1907), 923–1,013; see also B. Hermesdorf, "Andere Aspecten van stedelijke lijfrenten," *Numaga*, VIII (1961), 169–75; and J. H. Kernkamp et al., "Vijftiende-eeuwse rentebrieven van Noordnederlandse steden," *Fontes Minores Medii aevi*, XIII (1961).

[29] This assertion is based on a passage in the accounts for 1534, ARAB, no. 868, fos. 19–46. The final sentence of this document has the interesting dating "So made and concluded by the queen or the emperor's council at Malines, the seventeenth day of July 1534." It is signed by Willam Pensart, who had been since 1532 financial secretary and also secretary to the Council of State. In 1538 he was succeeded as financial secretary by Pieter Verreycken, and Nicolai was appointed secretary to the Council of State.

[30] The relevant passage in the accounts for 1534 runs ". . . And equally it is necessary to understand that the revenue of His Majesty in his territories is divided into three parts. The first is the demesne, the nature of which has already been described . . . derived from revenue largely 'in the air and at risk,' as the saying goes," *ibid.*, fo. 45. M. Martens, *L'Administration du domaine ducal en Brabant au Moyen Âge (1250–1406)* (Brussels, 1954), p. 3, has the interesting definition: "A princely 'demesne' is in itself a multiplicity of diverse rights having only a tenuous connection with a territorial unit, but forming the basis of power of him who is master of it."

[31] E.g. in the accounts for 1531 we read: "This revenue from the demesne is changeable and varies from year to year according to how much the crops, woods, meadows and farms yield, for which the receivers render account every year. In any case, the yield amounts to the sums set down here in ordinary years; the receivers present accounts annually in the audit office which show

The budget figures were therefore approximate but quite reliable. The revenues given below for purposes of illustration are drawn from such accounts.

Table 1 below shows the yield from the demesne by province for the years 1539, 1548, and 1551, in Flemish pounds:[32]

TABLE I

Province	1539	1548	1551
Brabant	69,736	44,812	70,392
Limburg-Overmaas	3,500	1,525	3,939
Luxemburg	8,589	4,660	5,453
Guelders-Zutfen	—	8,114	6,622
Flanders	86,000	82,633	52,625
Artois	19,813	7,442	13,401
Hainault	33,043	15,166	19,088
Holland	80,300	64,457	55,299
Zeeland	38,100	30,512	—
Friesland-Utrecht} Drente }	79,280	82,825*	84,237†
Namur	11,793	15,840	10,724

* Including Overysel.

† Including Overysel and Groningen.

Nevertheless, the most important source of revenue was the subsidies. These funds were voted and raised by the provincial Estates "according to the circumstances and according to the wealth of each province."[33]

the true and accurate figures, so that the emperor cannot suffer any loss or diminution of his income," ARAB, Aud., no. 875, fo. 2.

[32] Based on the accounts for the years 1539, 1548, and 1551, *ibid.*, no. 868, fos. 116–17ᵛ, 227, 232–40.

[33] In 1534 the comment was made on the subsidies that ". . . they are at present considerably exhausted, reduced and weakened by the two floods of 1530 and 1532, which caused damage greater than can properly be estimated. It would be wrong to rely upon the present subsidies, which are quite large but expire in 1536; thereafter it will be a great mystery how to obtain fresh subsidies . . .," *ibid.*, no. 868, fo. 45.

Tables 2 and 3 below, which give the revenues by province from the demesne and the subsidies for the periods 1531–4 and 1535–8, show that the revenues from the demesne were much lower than those collected as subsidies:[34]

TABLE 2 (1531–4)

Province	Demesne	Subsidies
Brabant	112,178	946,733
Luxemburg-Limburg	8,972	21,800
Flanders	238,129	921,160
Artois	34,636	239,494
Hainault	55,927	150,189
Holland	220,098	413,208
Namur	31,713	61,825

TABLE 3 (1535–8)

Province	Demesne	Subsidies
Brabant	181,645	1,624,000
Flanders	68,717	1,350,000
Tournai	24,000	27,600
Artois	41,624	257,851
Hainault	147,073	307,000
Holland-The Brill	86,420	564,700
Zeeland	78,283	211,191
Namur	46,290	40,000

Yet since subsidies were granted at irregular intervals, it is difficult to establish a constant ratio between revenues from the demesne and from subsidies; each of them was also subject to considerable fluctuations.

[34] Table 2 is based on an "abbreviated" set of accounts combining the four years 1531–4 and "made for the emperor"; Table 3 is an extract "of the receipts and expenditure of the accounts for the years 1535, 1536, 1537 and 1538," *ibid.*, no. 868, fos. 4–10ᵛ and 105–6.

Table 4 below shows the total revenues drawn from the demesne and the subsidies for the years 1534, 1539, and 1545:[35]

TABLE 4

Year	Demesne	Subsidies
1534	260,572	591,466
1539	201,229	73,692
1545	78,078	204,576

Finally, there were the "extraordinary revenues," generally indicated in the sources as *l'extraordinaire*. These, by their very nature less important than the other two, stemmed mainly from confiscations and other judicial decisions. Though this income would likewise usually fluctuate from year to year, it was estimated at £16,000–£20,000 per annum.[36]

We turn now to expenditure. Revenues from the demesne as well as those from subsidies were earmarked for recurrent expenditure, e.g. salaries and pensions, but also for the maintenance and repair of all kinds of demesne buildings. These expenses were usually subtracted from the receipts, the accounts recording only the net receipts, marked *cler* [surplus]. Now when the annual accounts were drawn up, these ordinary, recurrent expenses were frequently the only ones considered, so that revenue often exceeded expenditure and in this way a favourable balance was obtained, showing a sum "which remains clear." Occasionally, of course, the accounts would nonetheless show a deficit; the formula then ran: "thus there remains a deficit of. . . ." In studying the budgets, one does well to check the heading, generally opening with the words "expenses against this surplus," which follows the final figure. This item can include both ordinary and extraordinary

[35] Based on the accounts for these years, ARAB, Aud., no. 868, fos. 24ᵛ–25, 117ᵛ–19, 170.

[36] The nature of these extraordinary revenues is more closely defined in article 9 of the decree for the Council of Finance of October 1, 1531, and in article 17 of a similar decree of February 27, 1546: *Recueil des Ordonnances des Pays-Bas*, 2nd Series, Vol. III, p. 245; Vol. V, p. 217.

expenditure met from the ordinary revenues. More than any others, these extraordinary expenses were chiefly responsible for the ever-increasing debts that weighed so heavily upon the overall financial situation of the Netherlands.

During the reign of Charles V accounts were drawn up regularly. According to the text of a decree of October 1, 1531, addressed to the Council of Finance, such accounts were to be made "whenever they see the need."[37] Obviously such documents, usually provided with a brief synopsis at the end, a summary "extract,"[38] could furnish a clear picture of the development of revenue and expenditure. Charles V himself set great store on regularly studying these accounts.

The figures in the accounts for the decade 1530–40 show that the year 1534 closed with a credit balance of £69,518, but a further sum of £400,202 had still to be paid from this "surplus," so that the accounts for that year were really charged with a deficit of £330,684. The analogous deficit for 1535 ran to £500,244.[39] 1538 actually produced a deficit in the accounts,

[37] *Ibid.*, Vol. III, p. 252; Vol. V, p. 226.

[38] For purposes of illustration there follows the "extract" for 1532:

Receipts:	demesne:	IIᶜXLIIIᵐVIᶜXLI £.XIS.	[£243,641	11s.	0d.]
	subsidies:	VᶜIIIIˣˣXIᵐIIIIᶜL £.XS.VIIId.	[£591,450	10s.	8d.]
	total:	VIIIᶜXXXVᵐIIIIˣˣXII £.IS.VIIId.	[£835,092	1s.	8d.]
Expenses:	total:	IXᶜLXVIᵐVIIᶜV £.VS.IId.	[£966,705	5s.	2d.]
Deficit:		VIˣˣXIᵐVIᶜXIII £.IIIS.VId.	[£131,613	3s.	6d.]

In addition the following pensions are paid. . . .

ARAB, Aud., no. 875, fos. 69–69ᵛ.

[39] For 1534, cf. ARAB, no. 868, fos. 40–1; for 1535, *ibid.*, fos. 62–104. The accounts for 1535 open with the following explanation: "In order that the emperor or the lords and members of his council with His Majesty inspecting the accounts of the revenue of the Netherlands for the years ending 1535 may enquire whether that revenue is not greater than the sums and items entered and declared in the accounts—which are only the 'surplus' coming to the disposition of the ruler and his financial officials through the hands of the receiver-general—and where, to whom and how the balance and remainder of the revenues, apart from the 'surplus,' are spent and distributed, the directors, treasurer and members of the Council of Finance have investigated the amount of the entire revenues of each province as accurately as is possible to estimate for normal years and for ordinary expenses which are charged to these revenues and which are itemized in the exact accounts rendered in the audit offices at the end of each year. This estimate now follows . . . ," *ibid.*, fo. 63.

since ordinary expenditure exceeded revenues by £207,555; other payments amounted to £1,148,826, so that the accounts were charged with a total deficit of £1,356,381. In 1539 this sum increased to £1,421,836.[40]

Understandably by 1540 this financial state of affairs had come to seriously alarm both the emperor and the regent. Charles V had meanwhile returned to the Netherlands, so that he was now able to join the central administration personally in a thorough investigation. On October 12 all previous financial commitments were ratified by the emperor, chiefly to relieve the collateral councils of responsibility. This document specifically mentions that, despite the intention "to relieve and discharge our revenues and demesne" [of debts], revenues were seriously lessened "by sales of many pieces of land and property and of hereditary and lifelong annuities in our provinces of Brabant, Flanders, Hainault, Lille, Groningen and Overysel, all with the right of redemption at eighteen or sixteen times the annual value of the pensions, or a similar sum; all these sales amount altogether to a total sum of nine hundred and sixty-three thousand, seven hundred and forty-one pounds, five shillings and three pence, at the rate of forty groats of our Flanders money to the pound. . . ."[41]

On the renewal of the ordinance for the Council of Finance, also on October 12, a radical change in financial policy was proposed.[42] The most important decision was "that every possible opportunity and occasion should be sought to regain and redeem parts of the demesne which are pledged at a low value." But this was easier said than done. In the preceding period many demesne lands had been acquired by a few powerful noblemen and cities. Since they were all anxious to continue enjoying the revenues from the demesne, it was by no means easy to recover these

[40] The accounts for 1538 are signed by the Regent Mary and by the secretary of finances, Pensart, Brussels, December 20, 1537, ibid., fos. 110–14ᵛ; for the accounts of 1539, see ibid., fos. 116–19.

[41] Pieter Verreycken, secretary of finances from 1538 to 1552, made a copy of this document, which in turn was copied by Pieter d'Overloepe, his successor until 1577. This second copy is in SAG, Sec. Pr., no. 2561, fos. 71–3.

[42] Recueil des Ordonnances des Pays-Bas, 2nd Series, Vol. IV, pp. 243–53.

possessions. The central government in Brussels requested the emperor in 1542 to publish the projected measures in a new edict, "so that all may know that the matter comes not from here, but from the full authority of your own commands, which would be most essential not only to expedite and further the matter but to avoid all murmuring and discontent."[43] This resolve shows how firm was the commitment to reform the state of the finances.

Once more many unanticipated financial difficulties had to be met in the ensuing years, for on July 20, 1542, a new war with France broke out, and in 1544 Guelders and Zutfen became permanently the property of Charles V. The financial repercussions of these events on the accounts are characteristic. The most noteworthy trait of this period is the standstill in the public debt —it went neither up nor down. Thus the accounts for 1545 show a deficit of £1,421,135.[44] The steady growth of the public debt was arrested, but not reversed. Table 5 below summarizes the development of the finances over the whole period 1531–45.[45]

During the second half of 1545 Charles V again remained in the Netherlands and therefore decided to negotiate new loans "at the least cost and for the shortest possible time." These funds were to serve ". . . for new mercenaries . . . for the defence of the Netherlands and for other expenses carried over from the recent war. . . ."[46] The measures taken shortly after Charles V's departure should also be seen in this context. On May 12, 1546, and with the advice of the Council of Finance, Mary of Hungary promulgated new regulations for co-ordinating the management of the numerous outstanding loans. Laurens Longin, a member of the Council of Finance, was appointed commissioner responsible

[43] Mary to Charles V, Brussels, April 2, 1542, VSPA, no. 49, fo. 135.

[44] Yet this deficit does not include all the financial burdens, for shortly after the last figures of the accounts there follows the marginal note: "excluding extraordinary defence works and the artillery; also excluding expenditure on the navy . . .," ARAB, Aud., no. 868, fo. 171ᵛ.

[45] Based on the sources already given, which are all gathered in one fascicle, *Ibid.*, no. 868, *passim*.

[46] According to the decree of July 13, 1554, SAG, Sec. Pr., no. 2596, fos. 41–3.

TABLE 5

Year	Revenue (demesne + subsidies + extraordinary receipts)	Expenditure (ordinary + extraordinary)	Total deficit
1531	1,229,292	1,645,270	415,978
1534	866,338	796,820	330,684
		+ 400,202	
1535	803,038	922,598	549,144
		+ 429,684	
1538	233,628	441,184	1,356,382
		+ 1,148,826	
1539	279,931	879,118	1,141,804
		+ 542,617	
1545	282,654	1,703,789	1,421,135

for all financial transactions concerned with these loans. This decree was unquestionably an attempt to bring the regional tax-collectors, who often acted independently, under the control of the central government.[47] Although the regent in her correspondence continually lamented the dire lack of funds, the financial situation did not worsen dramatically between 1546 and 1550:[48] great

[47] ARAB, Aud., no. 868, fos. 188–90.

[48] Consider, for example, the following passage from a letter from Mary to Charles V, Brussels, July 25, 1543: "Your Royal Highness, Your Majesty knows that I have never neglected to perform and accomplish everything which it has pleased you to command me, as I wish to do now more than ever and as, I do not doubt, the central financial officials also wish to do; but Your Majesty knows the state in which you left your finances and that nothing is left for the coming year, the subsidies for three years which began to come in on last St. John's Day are for the most part already collected and spent, and the receivers have discharged their obligations for whatever can be raised for these subsidies. If they were forced to collect more, I do not know how one could reassure them, and I have no hope of recovering such additional obligations from them. Your Majesty knows that when the central financial officials meet, they will have reason to make difficulties in approving this new burden, and even if they imposed it they would not know how to secure the contributions of the collectors within six months . . . ," ARAB, Aud., no. 57, fos. 230–230ᵛ.

burdens remained, but the deficit on the accounts around the year 1550 was just about the same as in 1540.[49]

In the autumn of 1551, however, the political sky of Europe became heavily overcast. France now went all out for spectacular war preparations. This compelled the central government of the Netherlands to negotiate a loan for £400,000 "to continue the defence works and fortifications of our cities and frontier posts and to finance the purchase of cannon, shells, food supplies and other provisions necessary for war, as also for equipping and maintaining a good number of warships. . . ."[50] Nor did this loan entirely meet the shortage of money. On February 1, 1552, an edict was sent to the Netherlands from Innsbruck with the object of encumbering the emperor's demesne by selling annuities for the not inconsiderable sum of £600,000. Shortly afterwards a loan of £300,000 was negotiated with Anton Fugger by selling annuities at a rate of 10 per cent. Moreover, on July 13, 1554, Charles V at Namur again signed a decree ordering the issue of hereditary annuities totalling £600,000.[51] At the same time as issuing this remarkable series of annuities, Charles V also resorted to new loans, which by July 1554 already added up to the very large sum of £3,071,000. These funds were allocated solely to the war effort. The incredible rise in the public debt was naturally the cause of great worry for the Regent Mary and the Council of Finance. At the repeated urging of the government in Brussels, Charles V ratified all their financial decisions on July 13, 1554. This decree also authorized the government to negotiate further loans for "all such sums, however large, which are recommended by the Council of State and the Council of Finances, as high and according to necessity; these and the monies already raised should be prolonged at as low a cost as possible, until we shall have the

[49] In 1551 the deficit ran to more than £1,300,000, a figure that is for all practical purposes the same as the deficit for 1538, viz. £1,356,382: cf. SAG, Sec. Pr., no. 2561, fo. 47ᵛ; ARAB, Aud., no. 868, fo. 114ᵛ.

[50] February 1, 1552, SAG, Sec. Pr., no. 2561: summarized in ARAB, Aud., no. 865/1 (unfoliated).

[51] SAG, Sec. Pr., no. 2561, fos. 37–8. [See also the quotation in note 62 below.]

means to discharge and acquit them. . . ."[52] It is by no means exaggerated to call the war with France which began in 1552 the "most exhausting and most destructive of the many wars conducted by the emperor."[53]

Do all the figures here cited agree with Braudel's results? Firstly, it should be noted that Braudel's study [see note 1] is chiefly concerned with Charles V's loans on the Antwerp money market; Braudel's attention is focused on Charles V's total debts, not on the deficits in the accounts for the Netherlands. Some of the loans negotiated by the emperor may not have been charged against revenues in the Netherlands. The final figures, however, are not in conflict. The accounts for the Netherlands were burdened with a deficit of £1,350,000 at the beginning of 1552; soon annuities were issued for a further £1,200,000; loans had by July 1554 climbed to £3,071,000. By adding these figures together, the public debt in mid-1554 turns out to be as high as £5,621,000. Taking account of the fact that new loans were negotiated immediately afterwards, one comes very close to the figure of £7,000,000 at which Braudel puts the public debt in 1555.[54]

One important question remains to be answered. What effect, if any, did the emperor's financial policy have on the revenues from the demesne? Charles V's financial transactions were based to a great extent on demesne revenues. Only on condition that certain demesne revenues were offered as guarantee could the policy of issuing annuities meet with success. A passage in the accounts for 1534 illustrates this point:

> To meet the sales [of annuities] made—since the return of my lord the duke [of Aarschot] and the lord of Wingene—in order to discharge some of the old debts contracted for the building of dykes and for other items which had to be paid and settled, the cities and castellanies [financial and administrative units in the countryside] of Brabant, Flanders, Hainault, Holland, Namur

---

[52] *Ibid.*, no. 2596, fos. 41–3.   [53] Craeybeckx, *loc. cit.*, p. 120.
[54] Braudel, *loc. cit.*, p. 195, where there is also a brief comparison with the results of the impressive study by R. Carande, *Carlos V y sus banqueros* (Madrid, 1943).

and others have with great difficulty agreed to sell annuities on behalf of the government and also to purchase annuities from it on their own account. As security and to indemnify themselves, they have taken into their hands as a special mortgage the finest demesne lands of His Majesty and those with the greatest surplus, even though there have been strict prohibitions of such purchases. It is undoubtedly true that the surplus from the demesne, which His Majesty enjoys today throughout his provinces, consists only of tolls, dues levied on the herring catch, the excise on beer, dues for safe conduct, and the profits of justice, which are all revenues in the air and at risk, neither sure nor certain, but rights subject to fluctuations on which, therefore, no one wishes to own or buy annuities. Moreover, most of the fixed demesne revenues are already assigned and mortgaged for many previous annuities, and the great tolls like those of Zeeland, Antwerp, Gravelines and others are pledged to lawyers in the cities of Antwerp and Malines and to several merchants for the pensions of a number of German princes and for the loans of these merchants, so that in no two places can the government rely on the same source of revenue. . . .[55]

Clearly the chief attraction of having a portion of the emperor's demesne as security was that certain revenues were, in effect, fixed and regular and that this income came directly to the ruler, who could dispose of it in any way he saw fit. Moreover, these revenues were quite different from the subsidies which were granted by the provincial Estates, often only after prolonged discussion, and which were usually assigned for an agreed and specific purpose. Still, it would be a mistake to suppose that the growth of the public debt was closely matched by an increase in the debts charged against revenues from the demesne. After periods in which large debts were contracted there had always to be periods of consolidation. Consequently, the curve depicting the development of the demesne shows periods in which the debts paid from it grew and others in which the revenues were in some measure relieved of this burden. But such relief was no longer available in the 1550's, so that one can speak of a genuine crisis of the demesne.

[55] ARAB, Aud., no. 868, fo. 44ᵛ.

Although much of the evidence is lacking that would enable us to survey this development in detail,[56] a few milestones can be noted.

In 1531 the demesne yielded £244,441; the total deficit on the accounts was £415,978.[57] In 1539 the yield from the demesne amounted to £201,229: expenditure set against this sum was £276,519; the demesne was therefore £75,290 in deficit; and the total deficit on the accounts was £1,141,804.[58] Between 1530 and 1540 both the revenue from the demesne and the total budget display an ever-rising deficit. The decade 1540–50 was probably a period of recovery.[59] Proceeds from the demesne rose to £383,598 in 1551; the net income after deduction of expenses was £173,502.[60] Oddly enough, the demesne could recover while the total deficit on the accounts remained practically as large as before.[61] Yet this turn for the better in the demesne did not last. Excessive burdens were placed on it from 1552 onwards and increased thereafter in a rising curve. This fatal development was chiefly attributable to the war with France.[62] In the period 1552–

[56] Many of the surviving accounts do not differentiate between expenditure charged against the demesne and that charged against the subsidies, but cite only the total.

[57] ARAB, Aud., no. 875, fos. 6–18.

[58] Ibid., no. 868, fos. 116ᵛ–19.

[59] During this period the Council of Finance made every effort to restore the demesne; many sources would bear closer study in this connection, e.g. an interesting series of recommendations from the various audit offices entitled: "Advice of the audit offices on the redemption of pledged lands," ARAB, Manuscrits Divers, no. 5062, fos. 232–60ᵛ.

[60] The figures are based on an exceedingly important register, the title of which begins: "Accounts to explain and show how the demesne lands of the Netherlands since the year ending the last day of December 1531 have not only been greatly reduced in size but heavily burdened with debts . . .," SAG, Estado, Libros, no. 1423, fos. 169, 178.

[61] On February 1, 1552, Charles V ratified the sale of annuities for a sum of £384,000 which was "used to repurchase several large and substantial portions of our demesne previously pledged by ourselves and our predecessors at a very low price . . .," SAG, Sec. Pr., no. 2561, fo. 49.

[62] The Regent Mary to Charles V, July 12, 1554: "Your Royal Highness, I remind Your Majesty of the sales of annuities guaranteed here in your Netherlands on the demesnes of Your Majesty to make provision for your urgent affairs and amounting to large sums of money. Your Majesty was

1559 the demesne was charged with over £70,000 because of increases in salary and pension payments; the annual charges on the demesne arising from annuities which had been sold amounted to exactly £443,667 in 1559; to this must be added another sum of nearly £65,000, as Philip II had taken over [responsibility for] all the annuities which had been sold in anticipation of a six-year subsidy which came to a premature end in 1558.[63] Taking account of the usual yield from the demesne of about £173,000, and the total expenses of £588,652, the annual deficit on the demesne amounted to precisely £415,149 in 1559; in addition a debt of more than £1,000,000 was charged against these same demesne lands.[64] In short, compared to the already bad year of 1539, the burdens imposed on the demesne were over five times as high in 1559. Since the policy of selling numerous portions of the demesne was revived during the next period, the upward trend of the deficit was by no means reversed. Apart from the debts on the demesne, there were war debts in 1559 "exceeding eight million florins. . . ."[65]

pleased to send me from Germany your letters patent confirming and ratifying six hundred thousand pounds of this capital sum. However, annuities of thirty thousand florins at 10 per cent. have meanwhile been granted to the Fuggers to avoid even greater rates of interest. I have also found it necessary in council to continue similar sales of annuities at 8½ per cent. totalling a further six hundred thousand pounds, of which I have already received a goodly proportion. Moreover, in order to meet the present dire necessity and to obtain ready money until the Estates produce the sums arising out of the subsidies which it will be necessary to demand shortly, I have asked several of the principal cities of this country to commit their corporate bodies and revenues for the sale of annuities on your account. This can be achieved as long as portions of the demesne are placed in their hand, so that they may make the payments due on these annuities . . .," VSPA, no. 85, fo. 2. See also A. Louant, "Charles de Lalaing et les remonstrances d'Emmanuel Philibert de Savoie (juillet et novembre 1556)," *Bulletin de la Commission royale d'histoire*, XCVII (1933), 255–67; *ibid.*, XCIX (1935), 223–55.

[63] SAG, Estado, Libros, no. 1423, fos. 201, 195, 220.

[64] *Ibid.*, fos. 221–3.

[65] *Ibid.*, fo. 223. See also ARAB, Rekenkamer, no. 434, fo. 228. In the years 1558–60 the lordships of Ranst, Zomergem, Sijsele, and Male were sold, among others: ARAB, Aud., nos. 865/1, 865/2. Many annuities were also issued on the demesne. In order to avoid having to make out numerous "letters establishing an annuity," the Council of Finance occasionally combined several

Finally, a few brief conclusions may be in place. The financial difficulties in 1530–1 called for radical measures. The directives which Charles V sent to the Netherlands in 1533 were the foundation of all subsequent attempts to cure the financial ills of the Netherlands. Yet because of the constantly recurring money shortage, the deficit lingered on. Remittances from abroad, especially Spain,[66] should of course be sharply distinguished from the actual revenues of the Netherlands. The revenues of the Netherlands provinces—the demesne, the subsidies, and the extraordinary revenues—were totally inadequate to meet expenditure. Above all, preparations for war and the waging of war raised the public debt tremendously in certain periods.

Many statistics required for a minute description of the development of the finances have yet to be compiled. It has been possible, however, to establish that the budget for the Netherlands was ever more heavily encumbered except for a brief period of stabilization in 1540–5, that the yield from the demesne shows a [precipitous downward] trend of its own, and that after a period of recovery in the 1540's the demesne was catastrophically overburdened between 1552 and 1559. From all this we may well conclude that Charles V's excessively risky financial policy and the too prolonged unfavourable balance of the budget played their part in the great crisis that occurred during the first years of the reign of Phillip II.[67] Finally, it is apparent that Charles V had an outstanding assistant in the regent, Mary of Hungary. Together with the Council of Finance, they tried all possible means to solve the financial problems of the Netherlands.

such grants such in one document. See *ibid.*, no. 865/2 for a document of this kind for Hainault, November 14, 1559. See also M. Arnould, "Les rentes d'État en Hainaut aux 16e et 17e siècle," *Ann. du cercle arch. du canton de Soignies*, VIII (1942), 164–82.

[66] See O. Decombele, "De Financiering van de Spaanse politiek in de Nederlanden onder Filips II" (unpublished licentiate thesis, Ghent, 1956).

[67] The economic causes of the crisis of 1557 are discussed by A. Friis, "The Two Crises in the Netherlands in 1557," *Scandinavian Economic History Review*, I (1953), 193–217. See also C. Verlinden and J. Craeybeckx, *Prijzen- en Lonenpolitiek in de Nederlanden in 1567 en 1588–1589* (Brussels, 1962), pp. 17–22.

9 Royal Administration before the Intendants: *Parlements* and Governors

GASTON ZELLER

CERTAINLY no one today would be tempted to take credit for this sentence by a scholar of the last century: "Before the establishment of the intendants, there was, strictly speaking, no administration in the provinces."[1] Since this statement was written, the history of our early institutions has made some progress. We should not, however, labour under a delusion. The problem which the statement implicitly raises has not yet found its solution. Only a short time ago Georges Pagès believed himself justified in recording that we do not know how France was administered during the long period which extends from the reign of Francis I to the ministry of Mazarin.[2]

Does our ignorance actually reach such proportions? Have its limits not been exaggeratedly drawn by a too exacting and scrupulous historian? We propose to show here that, without having recourse to unpublished sources, it is already possible to reconstruct in one's mind with sufficient precision the administrative practices of the *ancien régime* before the institution of the intendants. . . .

The sense evoked by the [sixteenth-century French] word *police* very often overlapped with our modern notion of administration . . . although its meaning remained vague and changeable. . . . The fundamental problem of administrative institutions in

[1] M. Cohendy, *Mémoire historique sur les modes successifs de l'administration dans la province d'Auvergne* (1856), p. 6.
[2] G. Pagès, "Essai sur l'évolution des institutions administratives en France, du commencement du XVIe siècle à la fin du XVIIe," *Revue d'histoire moderne* (1932), 8. When in this article Pagès sought to determine who were the principal agents of the royal administration in the sixteenth century, it is remarkable that he did not stop to consider either the *parlements* or the governors.

sixteenth-century France was that of who held the powers of *police*, in the widest sense of the word. The question prompts the initial, very general reply that *police* and the exercise of justice were found in the same hands. *Police*, although clearly distinct from justice and in large measure contrasting with it, was also readily considered to be dependent on justice, or at least an indispensable complement to it. It comprised a power of execution, and at need of coercion, without which justice is powerless. All those who, under whatever title, exercised powers of justice at the same time enjoyed the powers of *police*. All judges were simultaneously administrators. Consequently the hierarchy of command was exactly the same in the two sectors. At the lowest level were the ancient seigneurial or municipal authorities. City magistrates and lords of the manor holding rights of justice were equally capable of tackling all matters relevant to *police*, in every sense of the word. For instance, jurisdiction over crafts, the regulation of markets, and the taxation of consumables were matters of *police* within the competence of all exercising justice at a subordinate level.[3]

The representatives of royal authority also performed the two kinds of function at once. Bailiffs and seneschals, as well as their subordinates who were called "ordinary" judges (provosts or castellans) not only passed sentences, but had the right to issue commands and the means to make themselves obeyed. From the middle of the century onwards they were exclusively chosen from the ranks of the hereditary nobles, nobles "of the short robe." Thereafter there were no longer to be jurists among them. They would also no longer have the right of judging, but would have to be content with bearing the honorific title of president of the court of the bailiwick or seneschalsy.

Currently there is talk of "government by bailiwick." The phrase should not be condemned, but is bound to lead to confusion. M. Dupont-Ferrier has suggested a comparison which

[3] Cf. H. Hauser, *Travailleurs et marchands dans l'ancienne France* (1929 edn.), pp. 132 ff.; F. Olivier-Martin, *L'organisation corporative de la France d'Ancien Régime* (1938), pp. 198–200.

seems dangerous to us. "The bailiwicks and seneschalsies," he says, "were the units of royal administration at that time, just as the departments are the administrative units of our time."[4] Undoubtedly the number of bailiwicks and seneschalsies at the beginning of the century was approximately equal to that of our departments. Thus the province of a bailiff was nearly equivalent to that of one of our modern prefects, but there is otherwise no comparison between the two. The prefect of the nineteenth and twentieth centuries is the linch-pin of the whole administration. He is directly subordinate to the central government and therefore placed on a higher level than the rest of the administrative structure. By contrast the bailiff only played a secondary role as administrator. Interposed between him and the central government, two kinds of authorities kept him under strict control and used him as a simple executive agent—the governor of the province on the one hand, and the *parlement* on the other.[5]

It was essentially the *parlements* and governors who exercised administrative authority in the sixteenth century. They shared it, or rather disputed it. They engaged in permanent rivalry over spheres of competence. Sometimes the monarchy intervened directly over their heads. This royal intervention was exercised through the Council, called a Privy Council until the time of Henry III, and then the Council of State. It is from the Council, according to the Estates of Languedoc in their complaints to the

[4] *Les officiers royaux des bailliages et sénéschaussées et les institutions monarchiques locales en France à la fin du moyen âge* (1902), p. 1.
[5] This double subordination has been clearly established, but insufficiently emphasized, by Dupont-Ferrier, *op. cit.* See further, on the role of the *parlement* in nominating the officials, in the inquiry prior to their appointment, and in their taking of an oath before the full assembly, F. Aubert, *Le Parlement de Paris au XVIe siècle* (offprint from *Nouvelle Revue historique de droit*, 1905). On the bailiffs and seneschals of the sixteenth century we have few monographs. Among the best are P. Dupieux, *Les institutions royales au pays d'Étampes (1478–1598)* (1931); E. Maugis, *Essai sur le recrutement et les attributions des principaux offices du bailliage d'Amiens de 1300 à 1600* (1906); P. de la Bussière, *Le bailliage de Mâcon: Étude sur l'organisation judiciaire du Mâconnais sous l'Ancien Régime* (1914); J. Malmezat, *Le bailli des Montagnes d'Auvergne et le présidial d'Aurillac comme agents de l'administration royale* (1941).

king, that "the first initiative in the administration and direction of this kingdom stems, as from its principal fount and source."[6] But the Council was a court of supreme instance, called upon to give advice only in difficult questions, when there were court cases to be settled. It was more concerned with contested administrative matters than with administration *per se*.[7] This will exempt us from discussing the Council any longer, in order to concentrate on the role played by the *parlements* and the governors. . . .

The right of *police*, upon analysis, can be split up into several elements. Side by side with the power of restraint, the most apparent, should be placed the right to issue regulations. All those who held the right of *police*—lords of the manor, municipal magistrates, "ordinary" judges, bailiffs or seneschals, and finally *parlements*—all exercised it, each in their own sphere of authority. All could validly issue regulations which, through being wrongly grouped with legislative acts, are sometimes designated as ordinances, but which differed radically from royal ordinances in that on the one hand they were enforceable only within the limits of the jurisdiction from which they emanated, and on the other they could always be changed or annulled by a superior authority.[8] The regulatory powers of the *parlements* were not specifically different from those of the lower jurisdictions, but were exercised over a much wider field. Certain scholars have read into the exercise of this power participation by the *parlement* in legislative power, and have assumed that the monarchy had delegated to it special authority to this effect. This seems entirely pointless. The *parlement* issued administrative decrees on its own authority, and these decrees had exactly the same validity as all other acts of the sovereign courts. They did not enter into

[6] P. Dognon, *Les institutions politiques et administratives du pays de Languedoc du XIIIe siècle aux guerres de religion* (1896), p. 431.

[7] N. Valois, *Inventaire des Arrêts du Conseil d'État: Règne de Henri IV* (1886), introduction, pp. cxxiv-vi.

[8] Cf. C. Loyseau, *Des seigneuries* (1608), Ch. III, section 12 and Ch. IX, sections 3 and 7; B. de La Roche-Flavin, *Treize livres des Parlements de France* (1621), Bk. XIII, Ch. XXIII, sections 2 ff.

competition with the enactments of the monarchy. An administrative decree would never prevail against a royal ordinance. Its object was to fill a gap in legislation, or, better still, to provide guidance for the application of some legislative clause: in this it assumed the role of what we term today an "edict outlining practical measures for the application of a law." Just like judicial decisions delivered by the *parlements*, administrative decrees could be broken and annulled by decrees of the Council. Several of them, moreover, contained a formula safeguarding the prerogatives of the monarchy along the following lines: "As a provisional measure and until it may otherwise be ordered by the king."[9]

Let us first consider the work of the *parlement* of Paris: an immense subject, which we shall not pretend to treat fully. It should suffice to collect a number of characteristic features, taken from the different spheres in which the court was active. We shall not raise the question of whether these interventions were legal or not. It was enough that the monarchy did not offer opposition for them to appear legitimate in the light of the public law of the time. A whole volume might be written just about the part taken by the *parlement* in the administration of ecclesiastical affairs. There was hardly a corner of this vast field which escaped its attention. It was scarcely deterred by the barrier which the fundamental distinction between spiritual and temporal power placed before usurpations by the secular authority. In the *parlement* church and state appeared to be closely linked. Besides, its original composition made it a half-lay and half-ecclesiastical body. Undoubtedly the clerical councillors constituted only a minority and little by little were supplanted by laymen, but their place

---

9 G. Saulnier de la Pinelais, *Le Barreau au Parlement de Bretagne* (1896), p. 31; cf., *idem, Les gens du roi au Parlement de Bretagne* (1902), pp. 295–341. Any attempt at an exhaustive study—and the present one makes no such claims for itself— would entail the collecting of the largest possible number of administrative decrees. Fragmentary collections have been published: references to them may be found in E. Glasson, *Histoire du droit et des institutions de la France*, Vol. VIII (1903), pp. 215–16, and in E. Chénon, *Histoire générale du droit français public et privé, des origines à 1815*, Vol. II (1929), p. 364.

nevertheless remained distinctive; their substitutes were officially designated "lay councillors taking the place of clerics."

The innumerable conflicts brought about by the possession of benefices were naturally within the jurisdiction of the *parlement*. Even if the parties involved did not have recourse to it, even if there was no formal lawsuit, it appropriated the right to settle their conflict. The same held true for disputes concerning tithes. At the time of the civil wars [at the end of the sixteenth century] those liable to tithes, in revolt against the severity of the tax, solicited arbitration by the *parlement*.[10] It reminded negligent or extravagant bishops of certain financial burdens which were traditionally imposed upon them and which they were not allowed to shirk. It saw to it that convents observed their rule, and was associated with all attempts at monastic reform. If necessary it would have an abbot transferred or recalcitrant monks confined.[11] Anticipating the decrees of the Council of Trent, it tried, in agreement with the monarchy, to impose upon the clergy the obligation of residence. It gave orders to bishops and it threatened those who would not obey with seizure of their temporalities.[12] So far, it is true, we have been dealing with questions which have to do with the general relations between church and state, an aspect of the activity of the *parlements* which we do not have to consider here. We shall limit ourselves to matters of a more strictly administrative nature.

Education and welfare had been concerns of the church for several centuries. Their history in the Middle Ages is a chapter of ecclesiastical history. In the fifteenth and sixteenth centuries the *parlement*, by its continuous and persevering action, tended to give

[10] P. Viard, *Histoire de la dîme ecclésiastique en France au XVIe siècle* (1914), *passim*; V. Carrière, "Les épreuves de l'Église de France au XVIe siècle," *Revue d'histoire de l'Église de France*, XII (1926), 172 ff.

[11] P. Imbart de la Tour, *Les origines de la Réforme*, Vol. I, (1905), pp. 117–21; Vol. II, *passim* (esp. pp. 486 ff.); F. Pasquier, *Les Grands Jours de Poitiers* (1874), pp. 75–80. For a slightly earlier period, one may refer to Glasson, *op. cit.*, Vol. VI (1895), pp. 265 ff.

[12] E. Maugis, *Histoire du Parlement de Paris de l'avènement des rois Valois à la mort d'Henri IV*, Vol. I (1913), p. 725.

them little by little the character of state services, administered under its supervision, that is to say, under the control of royal authority.

"The history of the University has been written several times," said L. de Laborde with indignation, "without introducing the *parlement* of Paris, which was so important to its development."[13] His viewpoint is hardly an exaggeration, as we are in a position to judge for ourselves, thanks to a chapter in the *Histoire du Parlement de Paris* by Edouard Maugis.[14] This discussed not only the judicial powers in which the *parlement* replaced the ecclesiastical tribunals, but the *parlement*'s right to issue general regulations for the university and to reform it, which it arrogated to itself without encountering any opposition. Its decrees concerned both discipline and teaching, "the content and length of courses, the distribution of subjects between the years of the academic cycle, and the rules for examinations (constantly broken), for the promotion of regents, and the election of rectors, deans of the faculties, principals of colleges . . . etc." All the universities within the jurisdiction [of the *parlement* of Paris]—Orléans, Angers, Bourges, and Poitiers, as well as Paris—came under the same authoritarian supervision. Another historian of the sixteenth century compares the action of the *Grand' Chambre* [the central court of the *parlement*] in this sphere to that of a veritable supreme council of public education.[15]

Hospital institutions, established by pious foundations and placed by their founders under the protection of a bishop or a chapter who appointed their administrators, had for the most part

[13] Preface to *Inventaire des Actes du Parlement de Paris* (1863), p. xlvii.

[14] "Du contrôle et de la réformation des Universités par le Parlement au XVIᵉ siècle," *op. cit.*, Vol. II (1914), pp. 352–87. This may be supplemented with Imbart de la Tour, *op. cit.*, Vol. II, pp. 531–4; F. Aubert, *Le Parlement et la ville de Paris au XVIᵉ siècle* (offprint from *Revue des Études historiques*, 1905), pp. 464–76; idem, *Histoire du Parlement, de l'origine à François 1ᵉʳ*, Vol. I (1894), pp. 311–15.

[15] Aubert, *Le Parlement et la ville de Paris . . .*, p. 467. The university founded at Issoire in 1518 by Thomas Duprat, bishop of Clermont, was forced by the *parlement* to close its doors, at the request of the University of Paris; cf. E. Jaloustre, *Les anciennes écoles de l'Auvergne* (1881), pp. 104–5.

come by the sixteenth century to acknowledge the superior authority of the *parlements*. The case of the Hôtel-Dieu in Paris allows one to see how this development came about. Here again it was by extending its powers of jurisdiction, by a slow movement from the sphere of justice to that of *police*, that the *parlement* made its conquests. The chapter of Notre-Dame exercised the powers of supervision over the Hôtel-Dieu. The official called the master of the Hôtel-Dieu, the head of the male personnel, was chosen by the chapter. In 1497 the *parlement* was called upon to settle a lawsuit between the chapter and the master, but its decision, which condemned the master to dismissal and imprisonment, was unfavourably received at the Hôtel-Dieu. Hostility towards the chapter increased, and its authority was flouted; insistent demands were made that the supervision should be taken away from the chapter and entrusted to laymen; for years no one was willing to accept the office of master. In 1505 the canons, discouraged, resigned themselves to asking the municipality of Paris to take over the administration of their secular affairs. The *parlement*, which had never ceased to take an interest in the question, sent representatives to an assembly which met at the Hôtel-de-Ville [the townhall] to discuss the matter. The statutes setting up the new regime were submitted to it for approval. Eight lay supervisors would henceforth be named by the city; they would be answerable for their accounts to a commission composed of delegates of the city council, the *parlement*, the *Chambre des Comptes* [another royal court], and the chapter. One can well imagine that the representatives of the *parlement* made their voices loudly heard. Not only by their intervention, but by delivering judgements in favour of the supervisors in their continuous lawsuits with the chapter, the *parlement* obtained a preponderant influence in the administration of the Hôtel-Dieu.[16]

Other welfare institutions both in Paris and throughout the kingdom successively experienced a reform of the same kind. Everywhere the church had to give up to the cities its powers of

[16] E. Coyecque, *L'Hôtel-Dieu de Paris au moyen âge: Histoire et documents*, 2 vols. (1891), Vol. I, pp. 178 ff.

administration, and everywhere the control of the *parlements* was superimposed on that of the municipal bodies. At Amiens, for example, the *parlement* intervened for the first time in 1530 in its capacity as a court of justice, because the bishop had had the imprudence to refer to it a decision made by the lieutenant-general of the bailiwick, which enjoined the Brotherhood of the Hôtel-Dieu to present to him its accounts for the last ten years. Then, since its decree had not been sufficient to calm everyone down, the *parlement* decided that the administration would have to be reorganized. This reorganization was put into the hands of an official nominated by the *parlement* in agreement with the bailiff and the city, and it resulted, here as elsewhere, in the virtually total elimination of ecclesiastical authority.[17]

The censorship of printed works, from the moment when printed works began to appear, was first exercised by the faculty of theology [of the University of Paris]. But the church was very soon swamped by the magnitude of the task and was compelled to solicit the assistance of the secular arm. The *parlement* made no show of reluctance. Introduced to this role at the time of the controversies provoked by Luther's first writings, it soon assumed complete control. Its intervention seemed all the more natural because authors had been applying to it for the last ten years for the grant, under the name of "privileges," of a sort of guarantee of their copyright. From year to year its powers increased: it no longer limited itself to granting or refusing the authorization to print, but published lists of banned books and appointed councillors to visit booksellers' shops and to provide for the seizure of works of which the sale was prohibited.[18]

[17] E. Maugis, *Recherches sur les transformations politiques et sociales d'Amiens* (1906), pp. 457 ff. For Dijon, see J. Garnier and E. Champeaux, *Introduction aux chartes de franchise de la Bourgogne* (1918), pp. 787 ff. Extremely numerous interventions by the *parlement* are reported in Lyons, Dijon, Orléans, Rouen, and Grenoble by Fosseyeaux, "Les premiers budgets municipaux d'assistance: La taxe des pauvres au XVIe siècle," *Revue d'histoire de l'Église de France*, XX (1934).

[18] E. Maugis, "L'histoire de la censure des livres et de l'imprimerie par le Parlement au XVIe siècle," an appendix to Vol. II of his *Histoire du Parlement de Paris...*, pp. 310–51. From 1563 onwards the powers of the *parlement* in authorizing publications devolved upon the chancellor.

Of its own accord, under the pretence of maintaining public order, the *parlement* assumed the supervision of the theatre. From 1541 onwards it is to be seen intervening in the activities of the *Confrères de la Passion*, a privileged company which produced mystery plays in Paris. It allowed the confraternity to carry on its performances only on certain conditions. A few years later, by a famous decree of November 17, 1548, it forbade it to perform the *Mystère de la Passion* and other plays drawn from Holy Scripture: it would have to limit itself to "secular, proper, and licit mystery plays."[19] On that condition, moreover, the *parlement* was disposed to protect the company: it defended it against the *Châtelet* [the royal administration of Paris, equivalent to a bailiwick], which, at the request of the parish priest of Saint-Eustache, had invited it not to begin its Sunday performances before the end of Vespers.[20] In 1571 and again in 1577 and 1588 it found fault with the companies of Italian comedians which the king had called to his court; it forbade them to give performances, either public or private. On the first occasion, Charles IX did not interfere; on the second, Henry III reacted by conveying an order to the *parlement* that it should leave his protégés alone. The third time, the king was at Blois, at odds with the Estates—in other words unable to intervene; the *parlement* had the last word.[21]

On the subject of the *parlement* and the city of Paris, L. de Laborde again says, "Nothing was done in Paris relating to the administration of justice, *police*, or the maintenance of public highways, without the *parlement* intervening or at least being associated with it; the evidence of this is recorded in its registers. Now in reading Félibien, Lebeuf, de la Mare and other historians of Paris, it is impossible to suspect the continual intervention of the *parlement*, or even to have an idea of the multiple action of this active mainspring of government, the most important one of

---

[19] L. Petit de Julleville, *Histoire du théâtre en France: Les Mystères*, Vol. 1 (1880), pp. 412 ff.

[20] E. Pasquier, *Un curé de Paris pendant les guerres de religion: René Benoist, le pape des Halles (1551–1608)* (1913), p. 156.

[21] A. Baschet, *Les comédiens italiens à la cour de France sous Charles IX, Henry III, Henri IV et Louis XIII* (1882), pp. 19–26.

all."[22] Since these words were written, Paris has fortunately found other historians who have given the *parlement* the place which it deserves. Of the various chapters which should be included in a complete study of the role assumed by the *parlement* in administrative matters, this is indubitably the one for which most evidence is already available in digested form.

One of the most characteristic episodes in this history took place just before the beginning of the sixteenth century. A catastrophe plunged the Paris of 1499 into mourning. The Pont Notre-Dame, one of the three bridges which connected the *Cité* with the right bank, collapsed into the Seine with numerous houses which it had supported and some of their occupants. In order to give initial satisfaction to public opinion, the *parlement*, without waiting for the results of the investigation which was immediately opened, ordered the imprisonment of the provost of the merchants, the four aldermen, the magistrates of the preceding year, and the city treasurer and attorney, all of whom it appeared might have had some responsibility in the matter. It also provisionally appointed "to the administration and government" of the city five persons of its choice, whom one of its own members installed at the Hôtel-de-Ville. This municipal commission would remain in office for several months, as long as the criminal proceedings brought against the imprisoned magistrates were still in progress, and even longer. A decree of January 9, 1500, proclaimed the latter to have forfeited their offices and to be incapable of filling similar positions in the future. Then, on the following August 1, the *parlement* ordered that elections should be held to replace the fallen municipality, in accordance with a special regulation which it issued for the occasion. It seems to have made profitable use of this long period during which it was in control at the Hôtel-de-Ville to become acquainted with all the details of the municipal administration. In any case, its authority was solidly established from this moment on, and the municipality would not attempt to escape from it.[23] Just like the

[22] *Op. cit.*, p. liv.
[23] P. Robiquet, *Histoire municipale de Paris*, Vol. 1 (1880), pp. 288–97.

provost of Paris, who acted as royal bailiff in the capital, the provost of the merchants, elected from among the Parisian population, considered himself henceforth the humblest subordinate of the *parlement*. He acknowledged himself responsible to it for a large part of his administration, and submitted without protest to the injunctions or interdictions which it conveyed to him. The chief magistrate of the city cut a sorry figure beside the gentlemen of the *parlement*. In 1571, during an incident to which we referred earlier, the Italian comedians exposed to the hostility of the *parlement* objected that the authorization to perform was given to them by the provost of the merchants. The provost, immediately questioned, replied that he did so upon the king's recommendation, and the *parlement* issued a decree "inhibiting and forbidding the said provost from granting such permissions any longer, or from issuing or causing to be drawn up any other documents, whether in his house or elsewhere," without first informing the civil and criminal lieutenant, that is to say, the *Châtelet*.[24] The city council seems to have accepted this subjugation without taking umbrage. As a matter of a fact there was no opposition of interests between its members and those of the *parlement*. Both categories of officials were recruited from the same circles, the commercial upper-middle classes. A number of members of the *parlement* also exercised the functions of city councillors or other municipal officers.[25] This resulted in a certain sense of solidarity against a government dominated by the influence of the nobility of the sword. This solidarity was manifested particularly clearly in the question of annuities guaranteed on the Hôtel-de-Ville. In 1587, after the king had decided to lay hands on the funds set aside for an outstanding quarterly payment, the city office appealed to the gentlemen of the *parlement* "to beg them to remonstrate with the king on their behalf," and the *parlement* intervened forcefully, as it had been requested to do. It would intervene similarly in 1604, in agreement with the *Chambre des Comptes*, against a contemplated reduction of the

24 Baschet, *op. cit.*, pp. 19–26.
25 Robiquet, *op. cit.*, Vol. I, pp. 297, 476.

annuities.[26] On other occasions, too, it can be seen transmitting to the king grievances which the municipality did not dare present directly. In 1581, addressing itself to its masters, the municipal administration humbly acknowledged its subordination and took pride in its own docility: "In this city of Paris, capital of this kingdom, three kinds of magistrates and political judges are established: the first and supreme category consists of yourselves, my lords, from whom the other two derive their authority, their splendour, and their glory; the second, of the provosts of Paris and other royal officials, and the third of the provosts of the merchants and councillors of this city, all of whom put the edicts and ordinances promulgated by you into action and have them executed with the greatest care, diligence and good will."[27]

The *parlement* kept a close check on municipal elections, at which it was always represented by several of its own councillors. It had, moreover, no less an interest than the municipal councillors in the free operation of the electoral system. On the eve of the elections of 1596, Henry IV informed the outgoing municipality that he would retain it until the following year. This amounted to suppressing the elections and violating the city's privileges. The city applied to the *parlement* for help, and with its approval, in spite of orders received, convoked the electors. Thanks to this agreement, the king could be blocked and was forced to accept the unwanted elections. Since the electors had the good sense to re-elect the provost in office, the king abstained from pursuing the matter any further.[28]

At times of crisis, when the municipality was invited by the central authorities to undertake the defence of the city and the maintenance of order—in 1512, for example, because of the English threat, and in 1525, folllowing the captivity of the king [after the Battle of Pavia]—it was the *parlement* which exerted the preponderant influence. It suggested indispensable measures to

[26] P. Robiquet, *Paris et la Ligue* (1866), pp. 269–70; *idem, Histoire municipale de Paris: Règne de Henri IV* (1904), p. 445.

[27] Robiquet, *Paris et la Ligue,* p. 138.

[28] Robiquet, *Histoire municipale de Paris: Règne de Henri IV,* pp. 253–9.

be taken; and when necessary it gave orders and assumed the direction of the entire administration. In 1525, in the atmosphere of general confusion, it even took on a political role of the utmost importance. The episode has been recounted many times,[29] so we will not spend time on a matter which in any case lies outside the scope of our subject.

In normal times the *parlement* was concerned with problems of town planning. In 1508 it prescribed that the municipality, which was having the street leading from the Pont Notre-Dame to the Petit-Pont widened, should have all the demolished houses rebuilt to the same height and shape.[30] In 1533 it invited house-owners to have their houses conform to the general alignment by removing superfluous projections.[31] In 1558 it ordered that lanterns be placed at every street corner between ten o'clock at night and four in the morning; this innovation, about which the provost of the merchants felt called upon to declare certain reservations, did not in fact succeed in taking root at this date.[32] The sanitation of Paris concerned the *parlement* no less than its aesthetics. It intervened in matters of highway maintenance and, for example, issued a decree in 1578 compelling the city, the abbot of Saint-Germain, and the inhabitants of the suburb of Saint-Germain to contribute jointly to the removal of the slush and refuse which obstructed the rue de Tournon.[33] In cases of epidemic, it was in the name of the *parlement* that the necessary recommendations were brought to the attention of the public.[34] In 1522 it enjoined "all persons living in rooms, hovels, and other places in which there are no toilets,

[29] Cf., in addition to the works by Robiquet and Aubert already mentioned, R. Doucet, *Étude sur le gouvernement de François Ier dans ses rapports avec le Parlement de Paris (1525–1527)* (1926), pp. 36–46. In the sombre days of 1525, the authority of the *parlement* extended beyond the capital and its outskirts: the entire bailiwick of Amiens relied on it and turned to it (Maugis, *Essai sur le recrutement . . .*, p. 8).

[30] M. Poëte, *Une vie de cité*, Vol. II, *La cité de la Renaissance* (1927), p. 103.

[31] Aubert, *Le Parlement et la ville de Paris*, p. 340.

[32] Robiquet, *Histoire municipale de Paris*, Vol. I, p. 454; Poëte, *op. cit.*, p. 260.

[33] Robiquet, *Paris et la Ligue*, p. 173.

[34] Cf. A Chèreau, *Les ordonnances faictes et publiées à son de trompe par les carrefours de ceste ville de Paris pour éviter le dangier de peste, 1531* (Paris, 1873).

cesspools or drains to empty their garbage, to refrain from throwing such garbage from windows or otherwise into the middle of the streets."[35] Over the head of the municipality, the *parlement* was also concerned with the provisioning of the city. It authorized or forbade the movement of corn, imposed certain restrictions on merchants, and gave orders for stockpiling in times of shortage.[36] Nothing that affected Paris was alien to it. It will suffice to mention everything that is a *police* matter in the narrow sense of the word: control of foreigners, Jews, taverns and cabarets, fairs and markets, and prisons, measures against begging, vagrancy, demonstrations on public thoroughfares, masques and masquerades, blasphemies, games of chance, etc.

Paris was not the only city to come under the authority of the *parlement*, which was sometimes despotic. Throughout the extent of its jurisdiction, urban communities submitted to its decisions, even when they did not actually solicit them. At Troyes it was a decree of the *parlement* which put into operation in 1493 the control of municipal elections established by various proclamations of Louis XI and Charles VIII. In their turn the *Grands Jours* [an assize court] of Troyes, an offshoot of the *parlement*, issued an important decree concerning this matter in 1535. The reform which they had started was then completed by the *parlement* on April 9, 1538. The town made no difficulties about putting this decree into effect, whereas it ignored royal letters, received several days later, establishing a slightly different system.[37] At La Rochelle in 1505 the *parlement* intervened as arbitrator between the inhabitants and the council.[38] At Poitiers the municipal administration communicated to the *parlement*, for purposes of confirmation, the principal ordinances which it issued.[39]

[35] M. Félibien, *Histoire de la ville de Paris* (1725), "Preuves," Vol. II, p. 642.

[36] Aubert, *Le Parlement et la ville de Paris*, pp. 345–9. [On these and many other administrative activities of the *parlement* of Paris, see now J. H. Shennan, *The Parlement of Paris* (London, 1968), esp. pp. 87–96.]

[37] J. Paton, *Le corps de ville de Troyes (1470–1790)* (1939), pp. 36, 44.

[38] Aubert, *Histoire du Parlement . . .*, p. 310.

[39] P. Boissonnade, *Essai sur l'organisation du travail en Poitou*, Vol. II (1900), p. 379; *idem, Le socialisme d'État . . .* (1927), p. 81. It would be desirable to be

In the sphere of labour, it was first and foremost the municipal administrations which exercised control and wielded the powers of supervision, but it would be rather surprising if the *parlement* had not become involved in some way. It fought against the "assemblies and monopolies" of the masters and journeymen. It found fault with the confraternities, which very often duplicated the craft guilds; for example in 1498 it forbade all banquets among members of the confraternity.[40] When a serious conflict led to a dispute between the printing workers of Lyons and their employers, the *parlement*, ignoring the fact that the seneschal and the Privy Council had been appealed to, settled by decree one of the questions in dispute, that of apprenticeship.[41]

A few words about finances may be in order. If the *parlement* refrained from intervening in financial matters, this was above all in order to please the king. In fact it accepted, though with some uneasiness, that the supreme financial courts, the *Chambre des Comptes* and the *Cour des Aides*, were sovereign courts whose prerogatives matched its own. It was constantly at variance and in conflict with them. Apart from its own sovereignty, it did not wish to acknowledge any other except that of the king. The principle by which the division of competence should be made is nevertheless very simple: the *Chambre des Comptes* confirmed edicts concerning finances, and the *parlement* all the rest; the *Cour des Aides* dealt with disputed matters of taxation (formerly called "extraordinary finances"), and the *parlement* with those affecting the demesne (formerly called "ordinary finances"). But the *parlement* spared no pretext to overstep these limits. In its capacity as guardian of the "fundamental laws" of the kingdom, among which the principle of inalienability of the demesne figured prominently, it claimed that everything which appertained to the

---

able to multiply these examples. Let us draw to the attention of scholars the history of relations between *parlements* and the urban communities as a field of research which has hitherto been little explored. For the earlier period, cf. H. Sée, *Louis XI et les villes* (1891), pp. 68–70.

[40] H. Hauser, *Ouvriers du temps passé* (*XVe et XVIe siècles*) (5th edn., 1927), p. 166.

[41] *Ibid.*, pp. 192, 204, 220.

demesne fell within its competence. Now the notion of what constituted the demesne tended to become larger and larger. Many taxes, new or old, which by their nature should fall into the category of indirect taxes or subsidies, were classified as demesne revenues. The *parlement* took advantage of this to claim responsibility for numerous fiscal edicts.[42] Moreover, all annuities were issued by letters patent, confirmed and registered at the *parlement*. It therefore had a say in the matter of loans, and never failed to take advantage of that privilege. However, it did not give orders to financial officials as it did to administrative officials.

We are less well equipped to discuss the *parlements* of the provinces than the *parlement* of Paris. The literature of the subject does not abound in works of value. Among the seven other courts between which the kingdom was divided—they are, in order of seniority, Toulouse, Grenoble, Bordeaux, Dijon, Rouen, Aix, and Rennes—only three, Toulouse, Rouen and Aix, have had their histories written with sufficient care to enable information of use in the study of institutions to be obtained.

The *parlement* of Toulouse, almost as old as the *parlement* of Paris, came close to competing with it in prestige and authority. It had the same ambitions and arrogated to itself the same rights. In *police* matters, the activities in which these two important organizations engaged within their own jurisdictions ran completely parallel.[43] Just like the University of Paris, the University of Toulouse came under the increasing control of the *parlement*, which interpreted or modified its statutes, supervised the organization of the faculties, the order of studies, and the costs of tuition, and summoned the rector to appear before its bar to ask him for explanations in the event of disturbances, and to admonish him. In 1516 it issued a decree prescribing the foundation of six new

---

[42] Maugis, *Histoire du Parlement de Paris . . .*, pp. 605, 675.

[43] In the affairs of the church, the interventions of the *parlement* of Toulouse were continuous: it kept close watch on the reform of monastic orders; in 1518 it opposed the sale of indulgences; in 1588 it confirmed in their functions the canons of the chapter of Albi, whom a new bishop had dismissed because of their attachment to the League, etc.

schools for the teaching of civil and canon law.[44] At the same date as in Paris, the administration of the hospitals of Toulouse was the object of a far-reaching reform initiated by the *parlement*. And it was this institution which henceforth supervised the maintenance and good order of welfare establishments throughout the province.[45]

Toulouse was no more managed by its municipal magistrates than Paris by its provost of the merchants and its councillors. Here again the municipality no longer seemed to have any powers of its own. Everything happened as if it exercised them only by delegation from the *parlement*. Its subjugation was even more complete [than that of Paris]: since the end of the fifteenth century there had no longer been any elections by the inhabitants or any semblance of elections. By a ruling of 1504, the *parlement* determined the method of appointing the magistrates and appropriated a preponderant role in this for itself. Sometimes it even named and dismissed these officials on its own authority. At the beginning of the civil wars, in 1562, it dismissed the municipality in office, suspecting it of being sympathetic to the Huguenots. It addressed magistrates as if they were underlings, displaying arrogance and sometimes harshness. It spared them no accusation of negligence or even of peculation; in 1528 it had several of them thrown into prison. And again as in Paris, the *parlement* acted as a substitute for the municipal authorities in regulating all sorts of matters having to do with *policing* of the city, in the narrow sense of the word: street-cleaning, the struggle against epidemics, care of the poor, etc.[46] Throughout the province, the municipal administrations had to submit to control by the *parlement*. It ordered that the results of elections should be presented to it, declared them void if need be, decided to hold a new election, or else elected the consuls on its own. In the first half of the century alone, it reformed the municipal constitutions of Limoux, Moissac,

[44] Imbart de la Tour, *op. cit.*, Vol. ii, p. 532; J. B. Dubédat, *Histoire du Parlement de Toulouse* (1885), Vol. i, p. 132.

[45] Imbart de la Tour, *op. cit.*, Vol. ii, pp. 508, 510.

[46] Dubédat, *op. cit.*, Vol. i, p. 51; Dognon, *op. cit.*, pp. 479–80.

Montauban, and Béziers, not to mention that of Toulouse. . . .[47]

In financial matters the provincial *parlements* followed the example of non-intervention set by the *parlement* of the capital. Even so, it would be wrong to take at face value their declarations that the management of public funds was no concern of theirs. If they refrained from summoning the representatives of the financial administration before the bar, as they did in the case of bailiffs and municipal magistrates, finances were nevertheless not exempt from the supervision which they exercised over the administration of urban communities. In Toulouse, for example, no tax was levied without the authorization of the *parlement*, or distributed save in the presence of its delegates.[48]

The administrative activity of the governors is more difficult to define than that of the *parlements*. We do not have at our disposal any relevant, systematically preserved and relatively accessible documents, registers of deliberations, collections of ordinances, etc. The little that remains of the papers of the governors is scattered among many archival collections, both public and private. So far only a small part of them has been exploited.

I have recently tried to explain what the powers of the governors were, in theory and in practice.[49] They extended to all sectors of the administration. The "governor and lieutenant-general" re-

[47] Imbart de la Tour, *op. cit.*, Vol. II, p. 150; Dognon, *op. cit.*, p. 478. [Professor Zeller gives further similar instances of the activities of all the other provincial *parlements*.]

[48] Dognon, *op. cit.*, p. 479; Imbart de la Tour, *op. cit.*, Vol. II, p. 155. Sometimes conflicts also occurred between the monarchy and the *parlements* concerning fiscal matters. Thus in 1597 the *parlement* of Bordeaux refused to register the edict concerning the *parisis* [a tax levied in the higher value Paris currency instead of the usual Tournois money of account]. In the same year the *parlement* of Rouen forbade the agents of the salt-tax to compulsorily sell salt by way of taxes. But these conflicts relate to the political activity of the *parlements* rather than to their administrative activity. Thus it is not necessary to treat the matter here.

[49] "Gouverneurs de provinces au XVIe siècle," *Revue historique*, CLXXXV (1939) [reprinted in G. Zeller, *Aspects de la politique française sous l'Ancien Régime* (1964)].

presented the person of the king and held all the authority which appertained to the king when he was present. In other words, he aspired to omnipotence. Moreover, the non-judicial functions of the *parlements* could be exercised only to the detriment of his own: hence there was a latent antagonism between them, punctuated by frequent conflicts. The *parlements*, whose presumption knew no limits, would willingly have made the governors their subordinates. As recently as under Charles VIII, certain letters of appointment referred to the obedience which the governors owed them.[50] The phrase was no longer current in the sixteenth century, but the *parlements* continued to claim superiority of rank over the governors. In 1565 we observe the *parlement* of Paris refusing to register certain royal letters relating to the powers of the postmaster-general under the pretext that, in the enumeration of the authorities forbidden to deal with postal matters, the governors and lieutenants-general preceded the *parlements*. It was not enough that the king should apologise for his oversight; in order to put an end to the dispute, new letters had to be drafted to appease the sensitivity of the court.[51]

When a new governor presented his letters of appointment to have them registered in Paris, he was admitted "on condition that he will not undertake anything against the authority of the *parlement* or of ordinary justice."[52] This naturally led to rejoicing by theorists who were members of the *parlement*, such as Jean du Tillet, clerk of the *parlement* of Paris under Henry II, followed by du Haillan, and at the beginning of the seventeenth century by La Roche-Flavin,[53] but they cannot be trusted without reservation. It is true that the *parlements* occasionally set conditions for the registration of letters of appointment which the governors were bound to present to them. However, judging from the small

[50] Dupont-Ferrier, *op. cit.*, p. 237.

[51] E. Vaillé, "Les postes, relais et messageries de Louis XI à Louis XIII," *Bulletin d'informations, de documentation et de statistique du ministère des P.T.T.* (1935), 46–7.

[52] J. du Tillet, *Recueil des roys de France* . . . (1618 edn.), p. 426.

[53] *Ibid.*; B. du Haillan, *De l'estat et succez des affaires de France* . . . (1594 edn.), p. 329; La Roche-Flavin, *op. cit.*, p. 523.

number of examples cited or known,[54] this was far from being the rule. Generally speaking, governors did not acknowledge the superiority of the *parlements*, except in matters of justice.

Justice constituted a sphere from which the monarchy tended to exclude the governors completely. Ordinances dating from the end of the fifteenth century refused them any jurisdiction, even at the lower level, though it is true that the rule was broken by exceptions. In Languedoc and Guyenne, provinces distant from the capital, where the governors had long exercised the powers virtually of a viceroyship, the rule was several times put in question until the reign of Francis I. The letters of appointment given to Charles de Bourbon and to the constable of Montmorency, in charge of Languedoc in 1515 and 1527 respectively, conferred upon them the right to consider all judicial matters as a court of final instance.[55] And Lautrec, governor of Guyenne, received powers in 1513 and 1515 which were at least as extensive.[56]

If the governors had to renounce justice, no one contested the fact that the *police* or administration fell within their province. Although lacking precision, their letters of appointment occasionally assigned these powers to them in explicit terms: this is true of those which were given in 1547 to Montpezat, successor to the constable in the government of Languedoc; he must assume "total charge and administration" of the province.[57] In different terms, Francis I said the same thing when he wrote to the seneschal of Poitou in 1533 that the governor of the province was to enjoy fully and without hindrance the powers associated with his office, "especially in what concerns the government and superintendence of the *police*. . . .[58] The principal issue at stake which continually set the *parlements* and the governors against one another was therefore the *police*, and more particularly the *police* in the towns. The control of municipal administration constituted, as we have

---

[54] E.g. for Bordeaux in 1515, see E. Brives-Cazes, *Le Parlement de Bordeaux et la Cour des commissaires de 1549 (Actes de l'Academie de Bordeaux*, XXXI, 1869), p. 180; for Toulouse in 1542, Dubédat, *op. cit.*, Vol. I, p. 196.

[55] Dubédat, *op. cit.*, Vol. I, p. 130; Dognon, *op. cit.*, p. 446.

[56] Brives-Cazes, *op. cit.*, pp. 175–6, 179.

[57] Dognon, *op. cit.*, p. 447.   [58] Zeller, *loc. cit.*, p. 11.

seen, the essential core of the administrative powers exercised by the *parlements*. The problems presented by the administration of the countryside appeared by comparison to be of rather small importance. They continued to depend on seigneurial authority, to which the central government willingly surrendered its own authority. In the towns, on the other hand, especially in those where the governor and the *parlement* existed side by side, the temptation was equally great for either of them to assume the role of master and assert itself over the local authorities. One of the most remarkable episodes in the dispute between *parlements* and governors took place during the reign of Henry II in Guyenne, Normandy, and Provence, and concerned the *police* of the towns.

On November 10, 1548, the king issued letters by way of proclamation, in which he specified and apparently augmented the powers of the governors of provinces. We do not have the texts; their existence is known to us only from the secret registers of the *parlement* of Rouen, where they were discussed at length several months later in April 1549.[59] On this date a new governor, Admiral d'Annebaut, communicated them to the *parlement* at the same time as he handed over his letters of appointment for registration, and a discussion took place about them.[60] As far as we can tell from the objections raised at the publication of the document, the letters dealt mainly with questions of justice. Jurisdictional powers were again conferred upon governors in certain purely civil matters; moreover, "Cognizance of police

[59] Since we were unable, owing to the general circumstances [of wartime], to visit the Rouen archives, which have the original copy of the secret registers, we have used a manuscript from the Archives Nationales (U. 761) containing transcriptions of important extracts. The letters of November 10, 1548, do not figure either in the collection of royal acts registered in the *parlement* of Paris: Arch[ives] Nat[ionales], x[1a] 8616.

[60] The *parlement* of Rouen had already had occasion under Francis I to take offence at a newly appointed governor: in 1531 it was perturbed because the letters of appointment given to Admiral Chabot de Brion allowed him to "summon and call before him the court of *parlement* as he should see fit." It was necessary for Chabot to flood it with assurances of his goodwill to prevent it from raising an official protest: A. Floquet, *Histoire du Parlement de Normandie*, Vol. 1 (1840), pp. 481–7.

matters was assigned to them for the towns belonging to their government." "If they were published," it was pointed out, "the ordinary judges would have no authority in the *police* of the towns, such as over the making of bread, wine and common beverages, with the result that the towns in particular would remain without administrative order." While remonstrances were being prepared for the king, two councillors were sent to meet the governor, in order to warn him before he made his entrance. The admiral assumed an indignant attitude. He declared that he had no intention of "taking cognizance of these minor administrative issues in the towns." Moreover, according to him, the royal letters concerned "only matters of state, which fell within his competence." He would not allow his powers to be curtailed. The courts of *parlement* had enough to do in dispensing justice "however much they would like to have cognizance of all the affairs of the kingdom." As far as he was concerned, he would never consent, considering that he exercised command for the king in Normandy, to let "anyone else besides himself have control over the *police* of the town in which he happened to be." And he repeated that he made little of the "minor administrative matters," "although when he was present they belonged to no one else except him." His vehement tirade ended with menacing statements: he should certainly be able to force them to obey; "he held from the king the power to command them and to have everything he pleased done for the public interest and the position of his government."

In their remonstrances to the king, the members of the *parlement* complained that "the *police* of the towns and the place of their government should again be assigned to the governors; this involves not only the negotiation and observation of contracts between parties,[61] but also the definition and conservation of good customs and the correction and punishment of bad customs, crimes and misdemeanours. . . . Item the control of taxes, markets, and

[61] The fact that contracts could be classified under the rubric *police* seems indeed to indicate that the people of Rouen, for the purposes of their quarrel, gave the word an inordinately wide connotation.

the defences, and the assessments, sharing of responsibility, and restraints necessary for these purposes. . . . Item the authority is assigned [to the governors] to convoke the Estates in case of serious danger, to give them orders as to what they should do. . . . Item the authority is granted to punish transgressors who have not observed the interdiction on carrying arms, and to transport wheat outside the kingdom. . . ."[62] The attorney-general, who was instructed to take these remonstrances to Paris, saw the constable, was heard by the Council, and was finally sent back to the secretary of state, de Laubespine, who was to draft an answer. The latter expounded the reasons which the king had had for issuing his proclamation: some persons had contested the extent of the governors' powers, and it had seemed opportune to stop their mouths. "The said proclamation had been formulated not to increase the power of the governors nor to diminish the jurisdiction of the sovereign courts and the ordinary judges, but to preserve them." The remonstrances of the people of Rouen produced altogether no important results. The king, however, agreed to modify the wording of one of the articles objected to, and he eliminated the right previously conferred upon the governors to assemble the Estates on their own authority.[63]

In the course of his explanations, Laubespine had referred to "the case which recently occurred in Bordeaux, in the government of Guyenne," as being the occasion which had led the king to modify the legislation concerning governors. This information is valuable. It is therefore the troubles of Bordeaux—the salt tax revolt in 1548—that were the cause of the affair; the November proclamation can be explained as the product of circumstances. The *parlement* of Guyenne had been suspended for not having clearly taken a stand against the rebels. Now it had the upper

[62] Arch. Nat., U. 761, fos. 20–22.

[63] Floquet, *op. cit.*, Vol. III, p. 146, has therefore misread the secret registers when he asserts that the *parlement* had won its case. It is, moreover, not the only error that can be pointed out in the pages which he devotes to that episode: he assigns the dates November 1547 to the royal proclamation and April 1548 to the admiral's arrival at Rouen.

hand . . . in the administration of Bordeaux, even though royal letters of January 17, 1535, had forbidden it to intervene in matters concerning the *police* of the towns.[64] It must have looked most unfavourably on the nomination by the governor of the province of a commission charged with the administration of the town, to replace the dismissed municipal officials. And it was no doubt in the circles of the *parlement* that the governor's right to intervene in this sphere was contested.[65] Whatever the case may be, the *parlement* of Guyenne, re-established by the end of 1549, was able to obtain from the king a few years later a decision which invalidated in its essential clauses the edict of November 10, 1548. Some royal letters of December 29, 1554, which we do not have and of which we do not know even the general sense, once more dealt with the "powers and authority" of the governors.[66] In its "articles" on this subject the *parlement* requested, among other things, "that it might also be the king's pleasure to declare that the control and jurisdiction over the towns of Guyenne will be and will remain entirely (and without the governor being able to intervene) in the hands of the mayor, aldermen, councillors, and other administrators of the towns, and the bailiffs, seneschals, and court of *parlement*, according to the said ordinances and the privileges of these towns, which have always been kept and observed." In the session of the Privy Council of March 21, 1555, the king ordered "granted" to be written in the margin opposite this article.[67]

The *parlement* of Rouen, informed of the manner in which the question had been settled in Guyenne,[68] wanted in its turn to benefit from the more favourable disposition shown by the king

[64] Brives-Cazes, *op. cit.*, p. 182.

[65] The extent of the powers conferred in that same year of 1549 upon the count of Lude, governor of Poitou, lieutenant of the king of Navarre, governor of Guyenne (cf. Zeller, *loc. cit.*, pp. 12, 16) also bears witness to the king's wish to subordinate the courts of *parlement* to the governors.

[66] They are mentioned at the head of the "articles" considered below.

[67] Arch. Nat., U. 761, fos. 187–8.

[68] As is proved by the transcription into its secret registers of the articles together with the royal answers.

towards his sovereign courts. By means of a petition presented by its *procureur-général* [the chief royal official in the *parlement*], it obtained on May 8, 1555, new declaratory letters in a sense directly contrary to that of the letters of 1548. The jurisdiction of the governor was limited in both civil and criminal cases to matters concerning military personnel. On the other hand, "the control and jurisdiction over the *police* of the cities of Normandy shall be and will remain entirely in the hands of the mayor and the administrators of these towns, the bailiffs, seneschals, and courts of *parlement* . . . without the possibility that the governor and lieutenant may intervene in any way whatsoever."[69] This is an exact duplicate of the article granted to the people of Bordeaux. The governors were thus stripped of the advantage which they had acquired in 1548. Their victory had been of short duration, and the reverse suffered by the cause of the *parlements* was quickly redressed.[70]

At exactly the same time as in Normandy and Guyenne, the authority of the *parlement* of Provence went through a critical phase, from which it took hardly longer to recover. Here a particular aspect of the question presented itself, since the governor had inherited the title and functions of grand seneschal, and at the time when Provence had been independent the grand seneschal had been the head of both justice and administration: the *police* therefore did not constitute the principal object of the dispute over influence and authority which took place, here as elsewhere, between the two powers. However, an initial passage of arms over the *police* occurred at the beginning of the reign of Francis I. The *parlement* had intervened in the *police* of the town of Aix.

[69] Arch. Nat., U. 761, fos. 186–7. This document mentions royal letters of April 19, 1549, which are also unknown to us. The abundance of legislative measures on the subject in a matter of a few years proves that the government of Henry II was very much concerned with it. The few pieces of information which we have been able to gather are certainly a long way from exhausting the subject.

[70] According to Floquet (*op. cit.*, Vol. IV, p. 14), the *parlement* of Normandy in the course of the civil wars once again lost this "great and sovereign *police*" to which it was so closely attached, but was restored to it by Henry IV in 1596.

After a protest by the attorneys of the province, the king reminded it by a letter of May 28, 1515, that by virtue of the ordinances the grand seneschal had sole competence for "the state and rule and *police* of the cities and towns of Provence."[71] When the *parlement* refused to register this letter, the king turned to the *Chambre des Comptes* of Aix and ordered it to carry out the registration, reminding it that the privileges of the province forbade the court of *parlement* from interfering in affairs concerning the state and *police* of the towns.[72] Some twenty years later the *parlement* was compensated for this. The edict of Joinville (1535) freed it from all subordination the grand seneschal. Thus its independence and judicial supremacy would thereafter remain uncontested. Nothing was changed, however, regarding the powers of *police*. The governor believed that they would continue to be his exclusively. Besides, the edict assigned to him the same powers as the governors of Languedoc and other provinces of the kingdom.[73]

The edict of Joinville did not settle all the disputes which could arise between *parlements* and governors. In 1543 the governor, the count of Grignan, complained that the *parlement* denied him jurisdiction over conflicts between the inhabitants and military personnel concerning the provisioning of the army. He obtained express confirmation of his power by royal letters, which the *parlement* registered only with reluctance and after making remonstrances.[74] Then it was the turn of the count of Tende, a strong-minded governor, who took the offensive in 1549 on the issue of the *police* of the towns. He must have known about the royal letters of November 1548, and no doubt derived his arguments from them when persuading the king, at the same time as he once more confirmed the competence of the governor in everything affecting military administration, to add to the list of his attributions—without, moreover, appearing to attach any

---

[71] *Ordonnances de François 1ᵉʳ*, Vol. I (1902), p. 249.

[72] *Ibid.*, Vol. I, p. 313. Letters of May 19, 1517, contained a new but rather similar call to order directed to the *parlement, ibid.*, Vol. II (1916), p. 68.

[73] R. Busquet, *Histoire des institutions de la Provence de 1482 à 1790* (offprint from *Les Bouches-du-Rhône. Encyclopédie départementale*, Vol. III, Marseilles, 1920), p. 84.

[74] La Roche-Flavin, *op. cit.*, pp. 969–72.

special importance to it—"the care, conservation, and *police* of the towns." Better still, the document revived the jurisdictional powers of the governor: "if lawsuits should arise within the sphere of his competence, he will have the right to pass judgement on them by calling on a tribunal composed of magistrates appointed by him from within the *parlement* or outside it."[75] One can well imagine the *parlement* struggling against this innovation. It had to wait some ten years before the monarchy reconsidered its decision. According to new letters patent of September 21, 1560, the *police* of the towns rested theoretically with the municipal magistrates and consuls alone. It also fell to them alone to judge cases which arose from the exercise of these rights. In case of appeal, the matter should be referred to the lieutenants of the main towns of the seneschalsies, and in the last instance to the *parlement*. Mention is no longer made of the governor.[76] The governor was thus finally beaten. In fact this was not the end of his disputes with the *parlement*, which were prolonged throughout the period of the civil wars. But the question of the *police* was not to be brought up again before the time of Richelieu.[77]

When the government of Henry II, in a moment of irritation with the *parlements*, refused to allow them any competence over *police* in the towns, the gesture was—it must indeed be acknowledged—of no far-reaching consequence. It was not within the king's power to undo what had been done by the *parlements* with the complicity of a large section of public opinion. Whether or not the *police* was assigned to them by ordinances, they intervened in it neither more nor less than before. The governors for their part were hardly tempted to make use of the powers which they were acknowledged to possess and of which they made themselves appear to be so jealous. They had a taste for authority, not for

[75] Busquet, *op. cit.*, pp. 86–7; cf. *idem*, "La jurisdiction du grand sénéchal gouverneur de Provence après l'édit de Joinville," *Études sur l'ancienne Provence* (1930).
[76] Busquet, *Histoire des Institutions . . .*, p. 87.
[77] *Ibid.*, pp. 99 ff.; P. Cabasse, *Essais historiques sur le Parlement de Provence depuis son origine jusqu'à sa suppression, 1501–1770*, Vol. 1 (1826), pp. 259 ff.; Vol. 11, pp. 26–30, 48 ff., 147 ff.

administration. They were noblemen of the short robe, who had no legal training; they had very limited knowledge of legislation, jurisprudence, and precedents. It was gratifying to them to claim that they had the right to intervene, but they did not intervene except in fits and starts, when their prestige seemed to them to be at stake. In ordinary times they considered it to their advantage to leave action to the magistrates, the gentlemen of the long robe. Paul Dognon has made a remark in the context of Languedoc which seems to us to be of very general application: from the middle of the century onwards, "the powers of the governor became no longer valid, for want of use; the limits set for his activity by his letter of appointment end up by being much greater than those within which he operates."[78]

This explains why, at the time of the civil wars, a period of unquestionable power for the provincial governors, the administrative role of the *parlements* remained as important as formerly, even if it did not acquire any new importance. The governors were more than ever diverted from administration by politics. They took on a role, and often a role of the utmost importance, in the struggle of the various factions: they either opposed the Huguenots or favoured them; they levied troops, led them to [join] the armies, and participated actively in military operations. When such great interests are at stake—those of religion and those of the state—how could they become enthusiastic about small municipal rivalries, questions of supplies, sanitation, or public roads?

It should be granted the two adversaries, moreover, that the harshness with which they asserted their rights did not stifle in them the sense of their common interests. When it was warranted by circumstances, when great danger threatened, they seemed to experience no difficulty in becoming reconciled and co-ordinating their efforts for the sake of public safety. They often had such opportunities in the period of the civil wars.[79] But even as early as

[78] *Op. cit.*, p. 451.
[79] E.g. for the *parlement* of Normandy, see Floquet, *op. cit.*, Vol. IV, pp. 54 ff., III ff.

the first half of the century, this sort of sacred union had formed spontaneously on several occasions under the menace of foreign invasion. At Dijon and Toulouse in 1512,[80] at Rouen in 1544,[81] and at Bordeaux in 1557,[82] the defence of the country was organized by the *parlements* and the governors in close collaboration. Their action in such cases was that of a veritable local council of government. As in Paris in 1525, it took the place of the government of the king's Council, which was prevented from acting effectively owing either to its remoteness or to an excess of other preoccupations. And the monarchy did not fail to ratify everything that these combined forces of goodwill had done in its name.

When the monarchy had to choose between its *parlements* and its governors, it generally supported the former. It had too much to fear from the spirit of independence of certain governors for anything else to happen. When Henry II, at the beginning of his reign, withdrew from the *parlements* the *police* of the towns, he seemed to be breaking away from the policy which had hitherto been pursued. But he did not take long, as we have seen, to return to the previous position. Of course the governors did not yet enjoy the privilege of irremovability which the officers [of the *parlements*] had. Consequently it would seem that the central authorities should have been in a better position to impose obedience on them than on the sovereign courts. In fact it only appears that way. As time passed, and the governors became more settled in their posts, the more difficult it became to dislodge, transfer or dismiss them. Here as everywhere else, but a little more slowly because the central government tried to restrain the tendency, venality and inheritance of office were gradually introduced.[83] "Formerly," Étienne Pasquier wrote at the end of the century, "when vacancies occurred at death, our kings favoured

[80] Imbart de la Tour, *op. cit.*, Vol. II, pp. 127–8.

[81] Floquet, *op. cit.*, Vol. II, pp. 98 ff.

[82] C. Boscheron des Portes, *Histoire du Parlement de Bordeaux depuis sa création jusqu'à sa suppression (1451–1790)*, Vol. I (1877), p. 133; B. de Ruble, *Antoine de Bourbon et Jeanne d'Albret*, Vol. I (1881), p. 142.

[83] See Zeller, *loc. cit.*, p. 30.

with governorships whomsoever they pleased. Nowadays, if they do not pass them on from father to son, an appeal is made."[84] The battle was henceforth begun against this new type of feudalism and would be fought with especial vigour by Richelieu.

Whereas the monarchy had to be on its guard against those powerful nobles to whom it traditionally granted the most important governorships, it had on the other hand the utmost confidence in the loyalty of its *parlements*. Through them it kept itself informed about the expediency of this or that measure to be taken in their jurisdictions, or about the degree of attachment on the part of the inhabitants to particular customs of the provinces.[85] It knew that their answer would always be prompted by concern for the public interest. It had only to be resigned to the idea that, occasionally, they might rebuke it. One could well apply to all of them what one historian, already cited, tells us about the court of Languedoc: "In it the king possesses a devoted servant, but not a tractable or docile one. The *parlement* of Toulouse is ill-tempered by nature. Like the great court [the *parlement* of Paris] from which it originated, it obstinately maintains the rights of the king against the king himself."[86] However inconvenient or unpleasant it might be to negotiate with subjects so obstinate about their wisdom and their rights—both those which were acknowledged as theirs and those which they attributed to themselves—at least the monarchy escaped the risk of finding malcontents or rebels among them. And if for some reason or other the governor should default, the *parlement* would simply be substituted for him. In Dauphiné . . . the *parlement* lawfully became the head of the administration in the absence of the governor. In Provence, in similar cases, the king vested the powers of the governor in the *parlement* or its first president. . . .[87]

In the administrative history of the *ancien régime*, the era of the

[84] *Lettres*, Bk. XV, letter 18.

[85] Dognon, *op. cit.*, p. 383; A. Dussert, "Les États du Dauphiné de la guerre de Cent ans aux guerres de religion," *Bull. de l'Académie delphinale*, 5th Series, XIII (1922).

[86] Dognon, *op. cit.*, p. 383.

[87] Busquet, *Histoire des Institutions* . . ., p. 27; Cabasse, *op. cit.*, Vol. II, p. 65.

intendants opened up a new chapter, which is infinitely better known than the preceding one. We know that the institution was made a general one by Richelieu, primarily in order to play a trick on the provincial governors. The monarchy had had to abandon the expectation of obedience from these powerful officials who now owned their offices, but was assured of finding it among those new agents, ordinary commissioners, who were entrusted in principle with temporary missions, and who were always revocable. The governors saw themselves stripped of their powers of *police*. Since this was about all that was left of their past omnipotence, they were reduced to a purely decorative role. Thus their chronic disagreements with the *parlements* came to an end.

As far as the *parlements* were concerned, they were in no mood to let themselves be ousted. The intendants, who combined judicial powers with their powers of *police*, found in them born adversaries. The long struggle in which they were immediately engaged exactly followed the lines of the dispute between governors and *parlements*. The issue, however, was not the same. The *parlements*, all things considered, had got the better of the governors in the long run. At the beginning of the seventeenth century they were scarcely hampered in the exercise of their powers of *police*. The intendants also learned at first to feel the power of their rivals. During the Fronde [in 1648], the *parlement* of Paris, momentarily victorious over the monarchy, imposed the suppression of the intendants, but they did not take long to retaliate. They were re-established several years later, and from that moment their ascent was uninterrupted. In the presence of these new proconsuls, the *parlements* were very often forced to retreat. . . .

The Provincial Governors of the
Netherlands from the Minority of
Charles V to the Revolt

PAUL ROSENFELD

IT was, in fact, no mere coincidence that the stadholderate reached
its fullest development during the reign of Charles V and under
his immediate successor. The sixteenth century was, in every
respect, the golden age of the higher nobility in the Low
Countries. As the Middle Ages closed in the resplendent autumn
of the court of Burgundy, a number of lineages of widely uneven
extraction, ranging from old feudal stock to mere upstarts en-
nobled by Duke Philip the Good, had coalesced with a sprinkling
of his own illegitimate progeny into a single caste, cemented by
the ties of marriage and by the bond of interest, and united in a
common outlook on their position in society and in the emergent
territorial state. In the midst of his aristocracy the frail young
archduke had grown to manhood. Though soon emancipated
from their overweening influence during his early years, the
emperor retained until the end of his life an affectionate regard for
his erstwhile mentors. In the late 1520's the *Flamencos* [Flemings]
still filled half the seats in the imperial council, which determined
the Habsburg policy throughout Europe.[1] The esoteric and almost
mystical bond which had attached the aristocracy to the dukes of
Burgundy was revived at the court of Charles V in Spain. "If you
could be in two places [at one time]," the emperor wrote to
Charles de Lannoy, his viceroy in Naples, "it would be my wish
often to have you in my presence. . . ."[2]

[1] "Relazione di Gasparo Contarini (1525)," in E. Alberi (ed.), *Relazioni degli
ambasciatori veneti al Senato*, 15 vols. (Florence, 1839–63), 1st Series, Vol. II,
pp. 54–7; "Relazione di Nicolo Tiepolo (1532)," *ibid.*, 1st Series, Vol. I, pp.
62–4.
[2] K. Lanz (ed.), *Korrespondenz des Kaisers Karl V.*, 3 vols. (Leipzig, 1844–6),
Vol. I, p. 74.

In this formative period of central institutions, the council of grandees around Margaret of Austria gradually emerged from the upper layer of the Archduke Charles's household in the Low Countries, the chamberlains.[3] Their pre-eminence at the court, and their daily commerce with the sovereign singled them out to become the regent's closest advisers.[4] They had so influenced Charles during his early and most impressionable years that he strove throughout his reign to perpetuate the ascendancy of the higher nobility within the central government. In 1523, when grievances reached him in Spain that the regent slighted the aristocracy in conducting state policy, the emperor emphatically warned Margaret "at all times to summon the grandees . . . to the Council, when they are in her presence, to communicate all matters to them, and not to transact any business without their knowledge. . . ."[5] The first or grand chamberlain, invariably the scion of one of the great houses, possessed powers over the court, the government and the direction of policy as sweeping as those wielded by the constable of France.[6] In 1531 Charles V formally sanctioned the supremacy which the aristocracy had acquired within the central government, by establishing a Council of State in which the higher nobility held nearly undisputed sway.[7]

[3] A. Walther, *Die burgundischen Zentralbehörden unter Maximilian I. und Karl V.* (Leipzig, 1909), pp. 15, 19–22, 97, 99; *idem, Die Anfänge Karls V.* (Leipzig, 1911), p. 103.

[4] For that reason, the colllege of grandees charged with governing the Netherlands was officially designated as the Privy Council during the Archduchess Margaret's regency. It should not be confused with her personal council, recruited almost exclusively from the ranks of the nobility of the gown of Savoy and Franche-Comté, nor with the new Privy Council, established in 1531 and charged exclusively with matters of justice and of law: Walther, *Die burgundischen Zentralbehörden* . . ., pp. 84–5, 87, 89, 199–203; M. Bruchet, *Marguerite d'Autriche, duchesse de Savoie* (Lille, 1927), pp. 57–61.

[5] Charles V's instruction for the lord of Mouscron, sent to the Archduchess Margaret, Valladolid, April 30, 1523, in *Compte-rendu de la Comm. roy. d'Histoire*, 2nd Series, Vol. v (1853), pp. 53–4.

[6] Walther, *Die burgundischen Zentralbehörden* . . ., pp. 140–52.

[7] The membership of the Council of State, upon its establishment in 1531, consisted of two churchmen, nine grandees, of whom seven were knights of

And yet Margaret's successor in the regency, Queen Mary of Hungary, rarely convoked the Council of State, preferring informal consultations with a few grandees, drawn either from the membership of the Council, or from among the knights of the Golden Fleece.[8] Indeed, Mary always consulted the higher nobility in matters of general policy affecting the Netherlands, and in matters of warfare, and the weight of their opinion often swayed her decisions. In 1540 the united opposition of the grandees thwarted the marriage of Charles's daughter, the Infanta Mary, to the duke of Orléans, and the ceding of the Low Countries to that French prince on the emperor's death. . . . [9]

The ascendancy of the higher nobility was even more apparent in the standing army, for the class tradition embodied the common

---

the Golden Fleece, and two jurists: J. Lameere (ed.), *Recueil des Ordonnances des Pays-Bas*, 2nd Series (1506–1700), 6 Vols. (Brussels, 1893–1922), Vol. III, p. 239. Though the representation of the gown increased to four by 1555, the nobility of the sword, with eight seats, retained an undisputed predominance. Antoine Perrenot de Granvelle, the bishop of Arras, was the only churchman in the Council in 1555: K. W. J. Verhofstad, *De regering der Nederlanden in de jaren 1555–1559* (Nijmegen, 1937), p. 29.

[8] Mary's predilection for informal consultations with selected members of the Council of State and of the Order of the Golden Fleece seems to have been foreshadowed by the elder Granvelle, Charles V's secretary and one of his chief ministers, who stated in a memorandum on the Council of State, probably drawn up about 1531: "It seems that it would be good that, of the great nobles whom it shall please the emperor to appoint to the said Council of State, two or three should always reside continuously near the said queen to assist her. They should be persons most suitable for her service and be told the duration of their period of residence. That when matters of importance arise, all the knights of the Order [of the Golden Fleece] should be summoned," Brussels, Archives générales du Royaume, Papiers d'État et de l'Audience, no. 1546, fo. 30ʳ. However, from 1555 onwards the Council of State convened at regular intervals, and it functioned as the principal policy-making agency within the central government: Verhofstad, *op. cit.*, p. 31; H. Kervyn de Lettenhove (ed.), *Relations politiques des Pay Bas et de l'Angleterre sous Philippe II*, 11 vols. (Brussels, 1882–1900), Vol. I, pp. 69, 70–8, 80, 87, 96–103, 104–6, 108; J. Lefevre, "Les Notules du Conseil d'État," *Archives, Bibliothèques et Musées de Belgique*, XXIII (1952), 17. [But see p. 25 above for the exclusion of the grandees from policy-making.]

[9] L. P. Gachard, "Trois années de l'histoire de Charles-Quint (1543–1546) d'après les dépêches de l'ambassadeur vénitien Bernardo Navagero," *Bull. de l'Acad. roy. de Belgique*, 2nd Series, XIX (1865), 345 n.

experience that a military career was the straight path to advancement. Without proficiency in the art of war none could hope to
accede eventually to a provincial governorship. During the sixteenth century the command over the troops levied in the Low
Countries was entrusted almost invariably to the grandees. They
held the colonelcies of the regiments of Walloon and Low
German infantry, the superintendence of the artillery, the
captaincies of the fifteen *bandes d'ordonnance*—mixed companies
of light and heavy cavalry which formed the mainstay of the
standing army—as well as a majority of the higher battle commands and, until 1553, the captaincy-general over the entire
standing army.[10] The chivalric tradition of Burgundy lived on in
the sixteenth-century aristocracy. . . .

From the minority of Charles V to the Revolt, the great houses
of the nobility of the sword almost invariably occupied the eleven
provincial governorships of the Netherlands. Consequently, the
nature of the aristocracy's relationship to the Habsburg dynasty
largely determined the evolution of the stadholderate during that
period. That relationship was marked by the grandees' heartfelt
allegiance to the dynasty, and by their readiness to offer their
lives in order to enhance its fortunes. And yet the recollection by
this hardy race of fighting men of an erstwhile feudal independence, and the claim to supremacy within the central government
which they asserted throughout this period, often strained their
loyalty. Their ideal of service to the state was united to a keen
awareness of nationality, encompassing the whole of the Habsburg
Netherlands, and it was intensified by their ceaseless striving for
renown and social advancement. These mixed motives and
aspirations underlay the attitude of the provincial governors, and
the clash of these motives and aspirations helps to explain the
contradictions of their conduct.

   [10] A. Henne, *Histoire du règne de Charles-Quint en Belgique*, 10 vols. (Brussels,
1858–60), Vol. III, pp. 35–223; H. L. G. Guillaume, *Histoire des bandes d'ordonnance des Pays-Bas* (Mémoires de l'Académie royale des Sciences, des Lettres et
des Beaux-Arts de Belgique, XL, Brussels, 1873), *passim*; *idem, Histoire de
l'infanterie wallonne sous la Maison d'Espagne (1500–1800)* (Mémoires de
l'Académie royale . . . de Belgique, XLII, Brussels, 1878), pp. 5–16.

All the stadholders clung with tenacity to the powers with which their instructions endowed them, and they usually succeeded in thwarting renewed efforts by the central government, and by the councils of justice of their own provinces, to curtail these powers. The governors especially guarded the right which they often possessed to nominate town magistrates, to confer church benefices, and to appoint to civil offices, and they were particularly susceptible to any encroachments on their prerogative of undivided command over all troops stationed within the region of their jurisdiction. They were wont to interpret any ambiguities in the instructions to their own advantage, and they seized on any sign of vacillation in Brussels as an auspicious moment for extending their own authority beyond legal limitations. The stadholders' jealous defence of their prerogatives, and their unwavering effort to augment these prerogatives seem the most distinctive common traits of their conduct.

The regents could, moreover, scarcely hope to restrain the stadholders within the bounds of a strict obedience to themselves, without simultaneously granting the aristocracy the preponderant influence within the central government. Indeed the Archduchess Margaret of Austria discovered, during her term of office (1507–1530), that an almost exclusive reliance upon the nobility of the gown [officials with legal training] in expediting the business of state was fraught with grave dangers, for it offended the governors. The disruptive force of feudal independence soon reasserted itself in a number of provinces, as the stadholders of Flanders and Holland usurped attributes of sovereignty, such as the unilateral nomination of town magistrates and of civil officials. Conditions in the isolated governorship of Luxemburg took an even more critical turn, for the incumbent bade fair to convert his province into an independent principality. Charles V's customary deference to the grandees' wishes, which often enabled the governors to designate their successors, lessened the possibilities of reform. And yet, in 1528, the regent made a first hesitant gesture towards reform by drafting an instruction for the rebellious governor of Luxemburg. This earliest, and entirely restrictive, definition of a stadholder's powers laid the foundation for all subsequent instructions for the provincial governors.

Drawing the appropriate lesson from the Archduchess Margaret's predicament, Queen Mary of Hungary inaugurated her regency (1531–55) by enacting drastic changes in the stadholders. Her inability in 1532, to render the governorship of Flanders temporary did not prevent her, soon thereafter, from withdrawing from that office, as well as from the stadholderate of Holland, the unilateral right to nominate the town magistrates. Twice during her regency she left Flanders vacant, rather than acquiesce in a recurrence of abuses. Guided by her aim to forestall the emergence of independent feudatories in the provinces, Mary of Hungary ordered the drafting of instructions for a majority of the governors, thereby sharply curtailing the powers which they had assumed during the regency of Margaret of Austria. To prevent the stadholders from converting the administration of their provinces into a court of vassals, she meticulously defined the governors' prerogative of conferring offices and benefices, either in the instructions, or in separate rosters drawn up for that purpose by the Privy Council. To avert heredity of tenure, Mary forbade the resignation of any governorship to the advantage of some relative. And yet her success in bridling the stadholders until the closing years of her term of office owed as much to her willingness to govern with the assistance of the grandees as to the sternness of her rule.

The appointment of the vacillating duchess of Parma to the regency in 1559 was bound to bring a drastic change, for her slippery hold on the reins of power, as the shrewdest contemporaries realized, merely emboldened the provincial governors. Moreover, the eclipse of the aristocracy at the summit of the central government by Spanish counsellors and by native members of the nobility of the gown, which had followed in the wake of Philip II's accession to the throne in 1555, inevitably estranged the stadholders. Already in 1558 their disaffection had manifested itself in failure to reside. In the early 1560's the governors of Hainault and Luxemburg seemed no longer to recognize any authority above their own, and by 1564 the stadholders of Holland and Flanders acted like nearly independent dynasts. These grandees made a sport of the instructions by their wholesale usurpation of the royal patronage, and by their attempt to dominate the provincial estates as well as the royal administrative and judicial agencies of their governorships.

Throughout Margaret's regency (1559–68), Philip II's statesmen in the Low Countries groped for some means to arrest the ominous drift towards autonomy in the provincial governorships. Old expedients were revived and new alternatives were suggested in order to loosen the higher nobility's grip on the stadholderates. Cardinal Granvelle repeatedly urged the king to vacate governor-ships whenever incumbents died. When the astute churchman perceived that his proposal could only palliate difficulties, he dreamed of dividing the larger stadholderates, and thus striking a decisive blow against the strongest governors. Philip II even tried to resuscitate Queen Mary's plan of temporary nominations. But all these schemes foundered on the rock of the grandees' defiant resistance to any reduction of their political power, and on the shoals of the government's inability to impose its authority and its policies on the provinces, except through the intermediary of noblemen of the sword.[11] Even the inflexible duke of Alba was forced to abandon his design of reform, though his iron hand bridled all the provincial governors.

The connection between the aristocracy's ability to exert the preponderant influence within the central government, the regents' resolute assertion of the authority which the Habsburg sovereign vested in them, and the governors' readiness to acknowledge their

[11] Thus when the duke of Alba sought to despatch troops through Luxem-burg in the summer of 1567, he observed: ". . . It can be imagined what in-convenience there will be, when both the said count of Mansfeld and his deputy are absent from his province, so that I shall have to address myself to a president and a councillor, regarding whom I do not know, since they are men of the long gown, whether they will understand or have the authority on which this passage [of troops] depends," Duque de Alba (ed.), *Epistolario del III Duque de Alba, Don Fernando Alvarez de Toledo*, 3 vols. (Madrid, 1952), Vol. 1, p. 656.

subordination to that authority seems so close that we may well regard it as the main feature of the stadholderate's evolution from the minority of Charles V to the Revolt. Moreover, it will now be seen that the issue raised by Edmond Poullet, concerning the extent of the provincial governors' powers, cannot be resolved in narrowly legal terms. If the stadholders were sometimes mighty viceroys, wielding almost undisputed sway over their provinces and answering to none but themselves, they did not, as Poullet maintained,[12] derive that ascendancy from their instructions, which, in reality, left them little independent authority. On the contrary, they could, and often did, achieve power, but only by flouting the many restrictions to their authority which these instructions contained.

[12] E. Poullet, "Les gouverneurs de province dans les anciens Pays-Bas catholiques," *Bull de l'Acad. roy. de Belgique*, 2nd Series, XXXV (1873), 387, 389, 427.

11 The Codification of Customary Law in France in the Fifteenth and Sixteenth Centuries

RENÉ FILHOL

ALTHOUGH this study is concerned specifically with the codification of French customary law during the fifteenth and sixteenth centuries, it may perhaps be useful to begin with a few purely general remarks. It may be observed, in the first place, that codifications mark a distinct phase in the development of customary law—a phase of maturity or (in some cases) of sclerosis. They take place at a moment when customs have almost become fixed already; the intention behind them is to fix them more securely; and the desired effect is duly produced. They appear as a sort of biological phase in the development of customary law.

More generally speaking, codification is a sign that the underlying elements of a civilization are undergoing change: it takes place when a civilization progresses from the spoken word to the written word, with all the consequences this entails at every level, e.g. modes of communication, the development of mental faculties, such as the change from auditory to visual memory. This certainly does not mean that the Middle Ages never committed acts to writing; on the contrary, abundant use was made of the written word, sometimes even to the point of investing it with a magical character. But looking at the broad sweep of history, it is possible to maintain that medieval civilization revolved round the spoken word, and that the transition to the written word did not take place till the fifteenth and sixteenth centuries.

Finally, a distinction should be drawn between private and official codifications. The former can take place during any epoch. The latter, however, presuppose that the structures of authority and administration have reached a developed stage, as was the case in France during the fifteenth and sixteenth centuries with the growth of administrative monarchy.

A general history has been drawn up by Klimrath in his *Études sur les coutumes*, which, though published long ago, remains a useful work of reference for the chronology of events.[1] Earlier collections of sources were abundant and variegated: private compilations had been made ever since the thirteenth century for various territorial areas and enjoyed a greater or lesser degree of authority; some, like the *Summa de legibus Normaniae* and the *Très ancienne coutume de Bretagne*, even came to be accorded official or quasi-official status.[2]

But with the ordinance of Montil-les-Tours of 1454 (new style), which concerned the reformation of justice, it was prescribed that the customs, usages and rules—collections of procedural practices—of all provinces of the kingdom should be codified and set down in writing in order to shorten the interminable lawsuits which resulted from the uncertain state of customary law and to

[1] H. Klimrath, *Travaux sur l'histoire du droit français*, ed. M. L. A. Warnkoenig (1843), Vol. II, pp. 133 ff. For his work Klimrath used almost exclusively the *procès-verbaux* (minutes) of codified customs contained in the *Coutumier Général* of Bourdot de Richebourg, which is still essential for any study of French customs (4 folio vols., Paris, 1724). An alternative to this, though less complete, is the *Coutumier Général* of Charles Dumoulin (2 folio vols. [1567 and later editions]). While these collections contain those customs which were officially codified, there are many texts of ancient customs which either have been set out in separate publications or have never been published at all. For the codification of customary law, see also J. P. Dawson, "The codification of the French customs," *Michigan Law Review*, XXXVIII (1940), 765–800; F. Olivier-Martin, "Les intérêts collectifs et leur organisation dans l'ancien Droit français" (lecture course for doctorate, 1937–8 (cyclostyled)); *idem*, "Les Lois du Roi" (lecture course for doctorate 1946–7 (cyclostyled)); R. Filhol, *Le Premier Président Christofle de Thou et la réformation des coutumes* (1937).

[2] *Summa de legibus Normaniae* (thirteenth-century), ed. E. J. Tardif, 3 vols. (1881–1903); *Très ancienne coutume de Bretagne* (fourteenth-century), ed. M. Planiol (1896).

relieve subjects of the costs which these involved.[3] The ordinance made provision for the procedure of codification: legal practitioners and representatives of all social classes of the various provinces were to come to an agreement about their customs and codify them. This codification was then to be submitted to the king, who would have it inspected and studied by the members of his *Grand Conseil* or the *parlement* [of Paris] for their assent and approval. The texts agreed on in this way were to enjoy official status: judges would have to conform to them, and advocates would be

[3] *Ordonnances des rois de France de la troisième race*, ed. L. G. O. F. de Bréquigny, Vol. xiv (1790), pp. 312–13, article 125 of the ordinance: "Item, whereas the parties to lawsuits, both in our court of the *parlement* and before the other judges of our kingdom, whether our own or others, plead and cite several usages, rules and customs which vary from province to province in our kingdom and which oblige them to provide proof of them, in consequence of which trials are often much prolonged and the parties put to great cost and expense; and whereas, if the customs, usages and rules of the provinces of our said kingdom were codified in writing, lawsuits would be much shorter and the parties relieved of expenses and costs, and the judges would be able to pass better judgements and with greater certainty (for it often happens that the parties cite contradictory customs in one and the same province, and sometimes the customs change and vary at their whim, from which our subjects are exposed to great loss and inconvenience). Therefore, being desirous of shortening lawsuits and litigations among our subjects and to save them expense and put certainty into judgements so far as is possible and to remove all manner of variations and contradictions, we ordain and decree, declare and resolve, that the customs, usages and rules of all the provinces of our kingdom should be codified, set down in writing, and brought into harmony by the customary lawyers, practitioners and people of each of the said provinces in our kingdom; and the customs, usages and rules thus resolved shall be set down in writing in books which shall be brought before us in order to be seen and examined by the members of our *Grand Conseil* or our *parlement*, and to be decreed and confirmed by ourselves. And these usages, customs and rules thus decreed and confirmed shall be observed and kept in the provinces for which they are intended, and likewise in our court of *parlement* in the lawsuits and proceedings of those provinces; and the judges of our said kingdom, both those in our *parlement* and our bailiffs, seneschals and other judges, shall pass judgement in accordance with the usages, customs and rules in the provinces for which they are intended, without adducing any other proof than that which shall be written in the said book; and it is our wish that the customs, rules and usages thus written, agreed and confirmed as has been said, shall be kept and observed both in the passing of judgement and otherwise."

permitted to cite no customs other than those which had been agreed.

This intention, however, was not realized all at once. The delays were due particularly to matters of procedure: according to letters patent of 1495, the texts codified in the local assemblies were to be examined by two commissions made up of members of the *parlement*.[4] Thus everything could remain in abeyance even though many of the proposed articles came up against no difficulties. The right procedure was hit upon in 1497. In place of the two commissions assembled in Paris, it was decided that commissioners should go out into the various localities to smooth out any difficulties which might arise among the inhabitants there. They were to proclaim immediately the articles which had been agreed, reserving only the disputed ones to send to the king or his *parlement* for a final verdict.[5] With this new and simpler procedure things moved much more quickly. By the middle of the sixteenth century the majority of all customs in the kingdom had been submitted to the processes of codification.[6] On the other hand, procedural rules were gradually eliminated from the codifications: questions of procedure came increasingly to be considered as coming under the competence of royal legislation. With the ordinance of Villers-Cotterets of 1539 the codification of particular procedural rules came to an end.[7]

From 1555 onwards a new wave of codifications can be discerned: the earlier codifications were taken up once more and became the object of new codifications or "reformations." The principal driving force behind this campaign was the first president

[4] Letters patent of January 19, 1495, confirmed in letters patent of March 15, 1497, concerning the *procès-verbal* of the customs of Touraine: Bourdot de Richebourg, *op. cit.*, Vol. IV, p. 639.

[5] *Ibid.*, Vol. IV, pp. 637–40.

[6] Many of the early codifications, particularly in the west of France, were carried out under the auspices of the president of the *parlement*, Thibault Baillet. The customs of Paris were codified in 1510; the work was presided over by Thibault Baillet and the king's advocate, Roger Barme: F. Olivier-Martin, *Histoire de la coutume de la Prévôté et vicomté de Paris*, 3 vols. (1922–30).

[7] It is noteworthy that the letters patent of Francis I of 1539 prescribing the codification of the customs and procedural rules of Berry were the last to order the codification of such rules: Bourdot de Richebourg, *op. cit.*, Vol. III pp. 972–3.

of the *parlement* of Paris, Christophe de Thou.[8] The era of the reformations finished at the end of the sixteenth century. It might have been thought that there would have been a periodical reformation of customs in the seventeenth and eighteenth centuries. In fact codifications now came to be quite the exception, and the texts codified in the sixteenth century remained in force until the *code civil* was drawn up in 1804.

THE AIM OF THE CODIFICATIONS

The primary intention behind the codifications was to secure clarity and certainty in legal matters: "We wish to shorten lawsuits and litigations among our subjects and to relieve them of expense and put certainty into judgements so far as is possible and to remove all manner of variations and contradictions. . . ." This was the declared aim of the ordinance of Montil-les-Tours, and the letters patent of the various commissions all came back to this formula. From 1497 onwards the letters patent also laid down that the commissioners, after consultation with the Estates, were to advise on what seemed to them to need correcting, expanding, abridging or interpreting. This formula had its roots in an ancient practice, dating from the Middle Ages, of reserving to the king the right to alter "hard, iniquitous and unreasonable" customs.[9] Nonetheless, there was a new element here in the very notion of custom and its development. No longer was custom to be merely a set of laws exercised in accordance with immemorial practice; henceforward it could contain new provisions, introduced in their entirety without prior assimilation into local usage.

These general aims of codification apply equally to the reformations of the second half of the sixteenth century, though these also had other ends in view, viz. to adapt customary law to the extremely rapid transformations which took place in both language and the law during the sixteenth century and to develop

[8] Filhol, *op. cit.*

[9] Letters patent cited in note 4 above; cf. F. Olivier-Martin, "Le Roi de France et les mauvaises coutumes," *Zeitschrift der Savigny-Stiftung* (G.A.), LVIII (1938), 108–37.

it in such a way that it could take precedence over Roman law.[10] The Renaissance in France was, indeed, an epoch which saw an extremely rapid rhythm of development in every sphere, and texts which had been codified in the early years of the sixteenth century as a rule very quickly became obsolete in both form and legal substance. The rhythm of development in traditional customary law was slow and quite unable to keep up with the rapid pace at which the law was changing. The reformations were carried out to a large extent in order to make allowance for these changes which customary law, with its slow process of formulation, could not follow. There was also a desire to enrich and perfect customary law. There is a very close parallel here between the movement to reform customary law and the movement to defend and give lustre to the French language. Just as Joachim du Bellay sought to enrich the French language so that it might become a single language for the whole country, so the reformers of the customs sought to enrich customary law so that it might become a common law for the whole country. The parallel is no mere coincidence.

Finally, some people—consciously or unconsciously—came to think of the reformations as a preliminary task leading slowly towards an overall codification of customary law and to a unification of the legal system.[11]

TERRITORIAL LIMITS OF THE CODIFICATIONS

In places where provincial autonomy had remained alive and well organized, as in Brittany and Normandy, it was the provincial boundaries which were adopted.[12] The framework of the

---

[10] Filhol, op. cit., pp. 136 ff.

[11] For the efforts at codification in France, see the incomplete accounts in J. Van Kan, Les efforts de codification en France (1929); idem, "L'unification du droit et les résistances des jurisconsultes sous l'ancien régime," Mélanges Paul Fournier (1929), 363–74.

[12] Normandy offers an example of a provincial administration's resistance to the dismantling of customs into bailiwicks; cf. the abortive attempt to draw up customs for the county and bailiwick of Eu in 1579: R. Filhol, "Le projet de rédaction de la coutume d'Eu en 1579," 31ᵉ Semaine de Droit normand (1960).

provincial governments was adopted only in exceptional instances.[13] The usual choice was the bailiwick, which was in a very special way the vehicle of royal administration; on top of this, it was also the judicial framework of common law. The adoption of the territorial limits of the bailiwick, however, had unfortunate results in so far as it led ultimately to the division into bailiwicks of units of customary law which had once been much more extensive, such as Champagne or the Paris region. The latter instance is notable in that the customs of Montfort l'Amaury, Mantes, Dourdan and Étampes were all codified separately, although they could easily have been put together to form a single set of customs for the Paris region as a whole.[14]

Within these boundaries, the codified customs applied to all persons without any distinction of social standing; those subject to the jurisdiction had to attend the assemblies summoned for the purposes of codification, where they were grouped within the traditional and functional framework of the three Estates of the clergy, nobles and Third Estate. As long as procedural rules were codified, only officials and practitioners of the law seem to have been consulted, and the revised rules referred to them alone; but, as has already been said, there ceased to be any codifications of such rules during the sixteenth century, and procedure was regulated by royal legislation.

THE AGENTS

The codification of French customary law resulted from the wishes of the interested parties coinciding more or less with those of royal authority. Many of the king's laws had come into being through his subjects' petitions rather than at his own behest; and in the same way the requests for codification came frequently from the interested parties and were favourably received by royal

[13] As in the cases of Péronne, Montdidier and Roye, which formed a government in place of a bailiwick: Bourdot de Richebourg, *op. cit.*, Vol. II, p. 627.

[14] Olivier-Martin, *Histoire de la Coutume de . . . Paris*, Vol. I, pp. 60 ff.

authority. But the king always reserved to himself the prerogative of ordering a codification or reformation through his appointment of the commissioners. At the Estates General of Orléans in 1560 the Estate of the nobles drew up a memorandum requesting that customs should be codified by "worthy and competent" persons *elected by the Estates*. In his reply the king made the distinction that "commissioners will be *delegated* in all places where need arises to reform and establish customs."[15]

Several kinds of people took part in the work of codification, each with a particular function to perform. It would be well at this point to single out the assembly of the three Estates, the officers of the law, the royal officials and the commissioners.

I. The assembly of the three Estates

This was the functional framework of society under the *ancien régime*, consisting of the clergy, nobles and the Third Estate. This assembly had a double role. The more important one was to examine customs, an extension on a larger scale of the traditional inquisitions by popular local assemblies, "seeing that there is no examination of customs more clear and evident than one made with the common accord and consent of the three Estates."[16] The assembly also had the purpose of creating law, in conformity with the notion of customary law propounded by jurists ever since the Middle Ages; this notion was based on Roman law, according to which customs took their binding force from popular consent. In accordance with a formula constantly reiterated during the sixteenth century, customary law emerged as a sort of agreement between the Estates, and all its provisions were to be drawn up "through the harmony of the three Estates."[17]

Before opening the discussions, the commissioners usually made

[15] Bibliothèque Nationale, Ms. Français 4815, 2ᵉ cahier de la Noblesse, fo. 176, Vol. 177.

[16] R. Filhol, "La preuve de la coutume dans l'Ancien Droit français," *Recueils de la Société Jean Bodin*, XVII, "La Preuve," Pt. II (1965); letters patent of March 15, 1497, Bourdot de Richebourg, *op. cit.*, Vol. IV, p. 639.

[17] Pleading by the advocate Robert, Archives Nationales, X Ia 4965, fo. 22ᵛ, May 15, 1556.

the three Estates take an oath: "That in their loyalty and conscience they will render to us an account of such ancient customs as they had seen to be kept and observed in the said bailiwick and of all they knew of them, putting aside all private and particular interest and having regard for the public good alone; that they will tell us also of their views and opinions about all that they found harsh, rigorous and unreasonable in the ancient customs formerly observed, in order that these might be tempered, moderated, corrected, repealed and annulled by us in accordance with the mandate of our commission."[18] In an age when meetings of the Estates General were frequent, it is quite natural to find that these assemblies drew inspiration from certain of the practices employed in meetings of the Estates General, such as that of appointing a spokesman for each Order: at Nogent le Rotrou in 1558 the commissioners laid down that "a councillor should be provided in each of the Estates of the church, the nobility and the Third Estate, so that everything which each of the said Estates had advised should be reported or objected to might be proposed through him."[19] Often the towns played an important role in the preliminary proceedings or the work of preparation, but they formed part of the Third Estate.[20] Rural parishes were not represented separately at these assemblies any more than they were at the Estates General. Seigneuries were normally represented by the lords of the manor.

II. The officers of the law

By the very nature of things, the officers of the law played a large part in the codifications and reformations of customs.

---

[18] Bourdot de Richebourg, op. cit., Vol. IV, pp. 823–4 (for the reformation of customs of Poitou in 1559).

[19] Ibid., Vol. III, p. 662.

[20] The procès-verbaux mention them under the heading of Third Estate, as in the case of Touraine in 1559: "And for the Third Estate, the summons was answered by the dwellers and inhabitants of the city of Tours in the persons of Laurant le Blanc, esquire, lord of the manor of La Vallière, the mayor, and the said masters René Gardete, Guillaume Ruzé and Guillot Mandat, aldermen of that city," ibid., Vol. IV, p. 681.

Knowing more than anyone else about the customs of the courts to which they were attached, they had always been chosen in preference to all others for the inquisitions by popular assemblies appointed to substantiate local customs; they were, moreover, the councillors of the major lay and ecclesiastical powers in whose interests they acted and as whose attorneys they were often to figure in the assemblies of codification. In most of the minutes of the proceedings of codifications in the sixteenth century they appear under the separate rubric of "officials and practitioners." This reflects a movement among the officers of the law to detach themselves from the Third Estate and form an independent Order; it was an aim very dear to their hearts, which Montaigne had in mind when he referred derisively to "this fourth Estate of people with the business of lawsuits completely in their hands."[21] The pretensions of the officers of the law never received official blessing, though it is worth noting that in 1600, when a partial attempt was being made to reform the customs of Normandy, the royal commissioners mentioned that the summons was answered by "deputies of every bailiwick and of particular viscounties, on behalf both of the clergy and of the nobles and the Third Estate, and even some deputies of the law."[22]

III. The commissioners

The commissioners were the representatives of the king in these matters. They were appointed by letters of commission which could be revoked at any time; there were mostly two or three of them, sometimes more, with the particular provision that in the event of one of them being impeded the others might act alone. The commissioners were normally members of the parlement, either a president and two councillors, or a president, an advocate of the king and a councillor.[23] Their function was to

[21] Michel de Montaigne, Essais, Vol. i, no. 23.
[22] Dumoulin, op. cit., Vol. ii, p. 1,089.
[23] At the time of the reformation of the customs of Paris in 1580 the commissioners appointed were Christophe de Thou (first president), Claude Anjorrant, Mathieu Chartier, Jacques Viole and Pierre de Longueil (councillors); Bourdot de Richebourg, op. cit., Vol. iii, p. 56.

control the task of codification in the name of the king by presid-
ing over the general assemblies, to arbitrate between the Estates,
and to obtain agreement on the articles under discussion. They
had no direct power over the substance of the law, but their
position and personal influence enabled them to play an important
role, though this was sometimes contested and criticized.[24]

IV. The royal officials

The royal officials appointed to every court also intervened in
the discussions to defend the sovereign's rights against the pretensions of the Estates; interventions of this nature were made
constantly during the sixteenth century on such thorny issues as
rights of jurisdiction and the confiscation of property. When, in
spite of this first line of defence, articles contrary to the sovereign's
rights had passed into the text of a custom, the attorneys and
advocates of the king could use this circumstance as an argument
before the sovereign courts in order to oppose the registration of
customs already codified.[25]

The various parts of this machinery normally worked well
enough to produce satisfactory results. It would be well, however,
to add a few comments. The most usual practice among these
general assemblies was for codification to be preceded by preparatory working sessions to codify a text in cases where no
previous codifications had been attempted, or to revise older
texts in cases where an earlier codification had been carried out.
There seems to have been no fixed rule governing the composition of these preparatory assemblies. Sometimes they consisted
of practitioners; occasionally representatives of each of the three
Estates gave their opinions in order, though the choice of representatives seems to have followed no hard and fast rule.[26]

Before their departure the commissioners immediately published

[24] Cf. the complaints of the nobles of Poitou after the codification of customs
in 1514: R. Filhol, *Le vieux coustumier de Poictou* (1956), p. 287, Appendix IV.

[25] E.g. opposition to the confirmation of the customs of Senlis, Archives
Nationales, X 1a 1574, fo. 36ᵛ, November 29, 1552.

[26] Cf., for example, the way in which the representatives of the Estates at Eu
were appointed in 1579: Bourdot de Richebourg, *op. cit.*, Vol. IV, pp. 170–1.

the articles agreed upon; they declared defaulters guilty of non-appearance and prohibited all future attempts to propose customs other than those which had just been proclaimed.[27] It was possible, however, for disputed articles to become the object of an appeal; within the jurisdiction of the *parlement* of Paris it was normally the *parlement* itself which resolved these questions.[28] An entire Estate, a corporation, a municipality, or even a single individual might raise objections to an article.[29] It seems, however, that most of the objections made at the time of the assemblies were never followed up. Once the new custom had been set down in writing by the commissioners it was sent to the competent *parlement* for confirmation or registration. The intention behind this confirmation—which was sometimes omitted—was to give binding force and sanction to the custom.[30]

THE SUBSTANCE OF THE CODIFICATIONS

The codifications of the fifteenth and sixteenth centuries in France contained customary law in the strictest sense, i.e. private law. The dividing line between public and private law, however, was always fairly fluid. On the other hand, the distinction between questions regulated by royal ordinance and those regulated by local customs was perpetuated right up to the end of the *ancien régime*, since the royal ordinances applied only to public law and the general preservation of law and order in the kingdom. When Chancellor d'Aguesseau later conceived a project to regulate deeds of gift, testaments and entails, he presented his ordinances in a document which set out to elucidate public law: the declared intention was to remedy the diversities of judicial interpretation

[27] This was the closing formula of all the *procès-verbaux* for both codifications and reformations; for the customs of Paris, cf. Bourdot de Richebourg, *op. cit.*, Vol. III, p. 85.

[28] As with the ruling made on the objection raised in 1556 to articles 58–61 of the old customs of Paris: Filhol, *Coustumier de Poictou*, pp. 260 ff.

[29] A reading of any *procès-verbal* will suffice to show the whole gamut of objections.

[30] It was normal practice to append a copy of the confirmation at the end of the *procès-verbal*; e.g. for Paris, Bourdot de Richebourg, *op. cit.*, Vol. III, p. 85.

concerning one and the same question which were evident in the different courts of the kingdom. In fact the ordinance concerning deeds of gift had the following title: "Ordinance to establish judicial practice concerning the nature, the forms, the charges or conditions of deeds of gift, given at Versailles in the month of February, 1731."

Traditionally, however, certain matters of private law like contracts and obligations were regulated by Roman law, even in provinces where customary law held sway; in these cases customary law remained silent, or at best laconic. Similarly, certain questions such as marriage and adoption continued to be the domain of canon law; and questions of procedure were gradually eliminated from customary texts.

Even those regulations which were incorporated into the texts of customals were of varying origins, and this characteristic of the codifications does not distinguish them in any way from the earlier customary law of the Middle Ages. Customary law had always drawn on a variety of different sources in the course of its development: contracts between individual parties becoming more and more like one another, the generalized application of the practices of the leading families, or borrowings from doctrine, learned law or judicial practice.

For the reformations of the second half of the sixteenth century, all that needs to be emphasized is the importance of the new elements of doctrine and judicial interpretation. One historian after another has pointed out, and quite rightly, how much the reformations owed to the influence of the jurisconsult Charles Dumoulin. On the subject of judicial interpretation, Guy Coquille, referring, in the preface to the customs of Nivernais, to the customs of Paris which had been reformed in 1580, declared: "The said articles of the new customs contain for the most part the verdicts arrived at concerning several difficulties and diversities of opinion among French jurisconsults, and even such as had been decided by solemn judgements." Speaking of the reformations which had gone before, he referred to the authority of the commissioners, "who were important personages and upright men, well versed in French law and in the best decisions reached in the judgements of the court."[31]

THE FORM OF THE CODIFICATIONS

The official codifications of customary law consisted of two essential elements: the text, and the *procès-verbal* (or minutes of the proceedings).

The text: no absolute norm was laid down for the presentation of the text. Normally the contents were grouped under a variable number of headings, which followed no fixed order. Their articles might be numbered in tens or hundreds: there were 362 articles in the reformed customs of Paris, 685 in the new customs of Brittany, and 623 in the new customs of Normandy.

The *procès-verbal* was considered an essential constituent of the customs. The jurisconsult Choppin described it as "the soul of customary law"; and a treatise preserved in manuscript at the Bibliothèque Sainte Geneviève, entitled *Treatise on the Law of the Customs of France, their Reformation, the Authority of the King over Customs, and the Validity of Customs*, expresses the matter in the following terms: "let minutes be drawn up of the codification or reformation, for this is the soul of customary law, and in it is contained the clauses of the public contract to which peoples submit."[32] This *procès-verbal*, drawn up by the commissioners, listed the persons who assisted in the work of codification and gave a report of the discussions or objections which arose in connection with each of the articles during the course of the sessions.

THE CONSEQUENCES OF CODIFICATION

The results of these codifications were numerous and complex:

1. It is certain that customary law, once codified and sanctioned

[31] Guy Coquille, *Œuvres*, Vol. II, p. 3.

[32] "Traité du droit des coutumes de France, de leur réformation, de l'autorité du Roi sur les coutumes et du pouvoir des coutumes," Bibliothèque Sainte Geneviève, ms. 404. The same manuscript text can be found in the Bibliothèque de l'Arsenal, ms. 671.

by the authority of the king, approximated very closely to statute law. But authors on customary law were at all times careful to highlight the difference, as did the author of the *Treatise on the Law of the Customs of France* cited above, when he declared: "From what has been said, it is possible to form two principal notions concerning this matter. The first is that, for the form and public authority of the codification and reformation of customs, it is necessary to recognize the authority of the king as the principal feature determining the custom and visible form of law, since it is from the king alone that the principle of legislation proceeds, as from the sovereign lord appointed by the power of God and recognized by peoples: this is an essential element of his royal and sovereign power, as also of the submission and obedience of the people. The other notion is that, because the determining form is reserved to the king and his power, it is necessary to leave the choice and disposition of the substance to the people themselves, for, since it is here a question solely of codifying or reforming their ancient custom and of elaborating what they have themselves established through the public consent which they have given to the execution of this law, it is only just that they should interpret, supplement, amend and mitigate the law which they themselves have devised and which is law only because they have so willed it through the use that they have made of it. . . ."[33]

2. In such circumstances customary law would be likely to approximate more to the published legislation of those provinces where written law prevailed. And indeed at the beginning of the sixteenth century, after the first codifications had been made, customary law was freely aligned with the legislation of provinces with written law by jurists influenced by the teachings of their counterparts south of the Alps. But according to these teachings, statutes had to be considered as legal provisions in the narrow sense, with restricted possibilities of interpretation; since Roman law was considered to be common law, they might not violate it in any way. It was against this doctrine that a reaction set in among the jurisconsults of customary law during the second half of the

[33] *Ibid.*, fo. 353.

sixteenth century and the reformers of customary law like the President de Thou. The doctrine defended by Charles Dumoulin and all those who championed the notion of a customary common law[34] was that customary law was the true common law of provinces where customary law prevailed, and Roman law was held to be nothing more than "written reason." It might be said that this doctrine had the effect of preventing any reception of Roman law in customary law provinces, as was in fact the case elsewhere.

3. The texts drawn up at the official codifications had the advantage of being easy to consult. Whereas previously the authors of works on customary law had inevitably had their field of investigation limited to a particular region, henceforth they could easily engage in comparative studies. It is no coincidence that collections of customs, general customaries, and compilations of comparative texts of customs made their appearance from the beginning of the sixteenth century onwards.[35] Large-scale comparative studies were made possible, and these were carried out largely by the champions of customary common law. These labours prepared the ground for the unification of the law. It is, however, certain that the customs compiled in the sixteenth

[34] Charles Dumoulin, *Opera*, Vol. 1, pp. 22–3, preface to the *Commentaire de la coutume de Paris*, which might be translated as follows: "There is nothing more stupid than what has been said by a number of inexperienced young people, fresh from the schools and churning out the arguments of the Italian doctors: that all statutes must be subject to a restrictive and literal interpretation in order to avoid any violation of the common [Roman] law, to which recourse must always be had and according to which all interpretations must be made. That may be true for Italy, where Roman law constitutes a common law overriding statutes, but it is certainly not true for France, where we do not recognize this common law. Our customs are our own true common law."

[35] These publications have never been made the object of serious study, though the results might well prove important. The oldest general customaries which we ourselves have discovered in the course of fragmentary research go back to the beginning of the sixteenth century: in 1512 there was published at Hesdin a collection of customs containing the customs of Montreuil, Boulenois, Guisnes, Saint-Paul, Saint-Omer, Hesdin, Aize, Thérouanne and Artois; in 1532 a more comprehensive general customary was published containing, in particular, the customs of Touraine, Poitou, Maine, Anjou, and Upper and Lower Auvergne.

century remained unchanged right to the end of the *ancien régime*, despite a number of ineffectual half-attempts at reform.[36]

While this fixing of customary law was proceeding, there developed an exception to this trend which resulted in greater scope being accorded to the will of individuals. This phenomenon was particularly noticeable in the question of succession in noble families. The amount of primogeniture established by customary law appeared insufficient to ensure the maintenance and splendour of noble houses. Rather than ask for the customary texts to be modified, the nobles preferred to have recourse to the extra-customary practices of entails and contractual appointment of heirs: the independence of individual choice supplemented established texts which did not seem to ensure adequate protection. The preamble to d'Aguesseau's ordinance concerning fidei-commissary entails makes definite reference to this: "In this way a new kind of succession has grown up, in which the will of man has replaced the law and has been the occasion of establishing a new order of judicial interpretation which has been received all the more favourably in that it has been regarded as tending towards the preservation of family patrimonies. . . ."[37]

4. Although it is undeniable that customary law in the strict sense did undergo a process of fixing, it is important that this should not be exaggerated. Legal doctrine and judicial practice continued their work, while new customs made their appearance in the margins of the drafted texts. After all, it should not be forgotten that inquisitions by popular local assemblies were only abolished by the ordinance of 1667 on procedure, which permitted the continued existence of attestations of usage and attested affidavits.[38] As regards the workings of legal doctrine and judicial practice, it is to be noted that numerous provisions added during

[36] Such as the project in 1600 to reform the customs of Normandy, and that in 1670 of the first president, de Lamoignon, to reform the customs of Paris.

[37] For the ordinances of Chancellor d'Aguesseau, cf. H. Regnault, *Les ordonnances civiles du chancelier d'Aguesseau* (1928–9). If reformations had been carried out periodically it is perfectly conceivable that this juridical elaboration would have been integrated into the customary texts.

[38] Filhol, "La preuve de la coutume dans l'Ancien Droit français," *loc. cit.*

the course of the reformations were not the outcome of long-established earlier practice, but were simply the registering of solutions accepted by recent judicial interpretation and as yet not fully elaborated. It was subsequently the task of legal doctrine and judicial practice to construct complete theories around these terse and fragmentary provisions: such was the case with the theory of legitimate succession, as also with that of compensation in questions of community of marriage, which was elaborated in the courts on the basis of article 232 of the customs of Paris.[39]

5. On the other hand, the champions of customary common law speeded the completion of what amounted implicitly to a single customary law by borrowing from the provisions contained in the customs of neighbouring districts; as time went on, these borrowings came to be made from customs of wider scope, and ultimately from those of Paris and Orléans, since these were considered to be the most complete expression of customary common law. The effect of this was to diffuse customs and bring about their interpenetration, a process which gradually prepared the way for the unification of the law.

A BALANCE-SHEET OF THE CODIFICATIONS AND REFORMATIONS

At the end of the *ancien régime* there were still sixty-five general customary laws and about three hundred local ones. The latter had not been systematically abolished when the codifications were being made, but a large number had disappeared, either because they were not brought before the commissioners, or because the commissioners had turned them down or contented themselves with a cursory mention in the minutes. A severe pruning of local customs had taken place. On the whole, however, it can be claimed that the anticipated results were achieved,

[39] There is no reason to conclude from this, as certain modern authors have done (E. Lambert, *La fonction du droit civil comparé* (1903)), that there was a merging of custom and judicial precedents. Even during the era of royal absolutism customary law continued to draw upon many different sources.

in spite of all kinds of difficulties (political obstacles to the reformations arising, for example, from the Wars of Religion at their height, or territorial difficulties arising from problems in ascertaining the area of jurisdiction of each custom, such as enclaves and the line of frontiers).

CONCLUSIONS

The official codifications of French customary law may be seen as a happy reconciliation of royal authority with respect for individual liberties and local rights, and of the requirements of clarity with the modernization of such rights.

12 The 1550 *Sudebnik* as an Instrument of Reform

HORACE W. DEWEY

THE 1550 *Sudebnik* (law code) appeared early in the reign of Ivan IV, after two of the most chaotic decades Muscovite Russia had experienced since achieving its independence from the Tartars. Issued in a period of important reforms, the *Sudebnik* was designed to combat a number of administrative abuses and social evils which had beset Russia, and to regulate the society which was to be delivered from these ills. Ivan's lawmakers followed a deliberate, conservative approach to the problems facing them. About two-thirds of the *Sudebnik's* provisions can be traced to earlier sources, and most of the issues confronting its compilers were old ones. Ivan's grandfather. Ivan III, had dealt with similar problems in his own collection of laws, enacted in 1497, and the creators of the 1550 *Sudebnik* drew extensively from the 1497 code.[1] Genuine conservatism, however, recognizes the need for some change, and the *Sudebnik's* compilers showed meticulous care in revising earlier laws. They also included some important innovations. In more settled times their code might have found wide application over a period of many decades, but events which soon transpired destroyed much of what the *Sudebnik* had stood for, and the code's subsequent role was a curious one.

I

Judicial and administrative corruption had been familiar evils long before Ivan IV came to the throne. In the 1497 code, Ivan's

---

[1] *Akademiya nauk SSSR. Institut istorii. Sudebniki XV–XVI vekov*, Podgotovka ktestov R. B. Mjuller i L. V. Cherepnina, Pod. obshch. red. B. D. Grekova (Moscow and Leningrad, 1952), pp. 611–12. [The codes of 1497 and 1550 are translated in H. W. Dewey (ed.), *Moscovite Judicial Texts, 1488–1556* (Ann Arbor, 1966), pp. 9–21, 47–74.]

grandfather had sought to combat bribery and other abuses simply
by prohibiting them. No official was to accept bribes for judging
or performing other duties; no official was to use the court for
purposes of personal revenge or personal favors; clerks and
scribes were enjoined from falsifying records and issuing unauthorized documents; constables and bailiffs were prohibited
from taking bribes, selling prisoners into slavery and so on. But
these prohibitions were not implemented; as a rule the 1497 code
did not specify how violators would be punished, or even whether
they would be punished.

Ivan IV could hardly have ignored the resentment and de-
moralization which resulted from official corruption. A visitor
to sixteenth-century Russia tells of an official who had taken a
goose "ready drest full of money" as a bribe. When the tsar heard
of the case, he had the official brought to the market place in
Moscow. There he poured abuse on him and told the onlookers
that such corrupt officials "would eat you up like bread." The tsar
then inquired which of the executioners knew how to dress a
goose, and ordered one of them to cut off the offending official's
legs and arms, asking the victim "if goose fleshe were good
meate." Finally he ordered the official beheaded, "that he might
have the right fashion of a goose readie dressed."[2]

The 1550 *Sudebnik*, while containing nothing so drastic as this,
put sharp teeth into its clauses prohibiting corruption and other
official malfeasance. Violators were threatened with specific and,
frequently, severe reprisals. The lower the rank of the offending
official, the harsher seem to have been the physical penalties
meted out. Thus, judges discovered to have convicted a person
falsely in return for a bribe were fined the sum at issue in the
lawsuit plus all fees connected with the suit, thrice multiplied.
The offending judges were further condemned to "whatever
additional punishment the sovereign shall decree" (article 3).
A secretary who was found to have falsified court proceedings for
a bribe was fined half the sum in issue and was cast into prison

[2] Giles Fletcher, *Of the Russe Common Wealth* (in E. A. Bond (ed.), *Russia at
the Close of the Sixteenth Century* (London, 1856)), p. 55.

(article 4). A scribe who had committed the same offense was sentenced to be publicly flogged with the knout—a punishment which could result in death (article 5). The same penalty awaited a scribe who tampered with court records or removed them from their official depositories (article 28). A court bailiff who had taken bribes for himself or for higher ranking court officials was flogged, fined thrice the sum of the bribe and discharged (article 32). A bailiff's agent who was convicted of "giving any offense" or "levying unauthorized assessments" was publicly flogged, while his principal, the bailiff, was fined the sum at issue in the lawsuit (article 47). Bailiffs who had released thieves or brigands for a bribe were flogged, imprisoned and subjected to further penalty "as the judge shall decree." Bailiffs who released such criminals on bail without authorization, or who sold them into slavery, received the same punishment.[3]

The measures described above were directed against abuses in the central government court system. In its introductory article the *Sudebnik* also addressed itself to the city vicegerents (*namestniki*) and rural vicegerents (*volosteli*) and their agents in the provinces. The vicegerents served as governors, judges, tax collectors and military commanders in charge of local defense. Many were boyars who had been in the military service of Moscow, and whom the grand prince (later tsar) had appointed temporarily as vicegerents in reward for their services. While in office these local administrators received no salary from the central government but had the right to collect income and foodstuffs from the populace under their jurisdiction. Since most of them came from the outside and held office only a few years, they had few interests in common with the local populace, and some of them took advantage of their position to become as wealthy as possible at the expense of those they governed. Vigorous complaints had been heard against the misrule of certain vicegerents, particularly during the troubled years of Ivan's infancy.

The 1550 *Sudebnik*, while reconfirming the authority of the vicegerents in local administration and even vesting them with

3 Articles 53–4; see articles 41, 44 and 48 for similar offenses and penalties.

important new responsibilities[4] also provided for a tightening of central government control over them and spelled out methods for rendering the vicegerents more directly accountable to it. Procedures were improved for persons who had suffered injustice at the hands of vicegerents and their agents to bring suit against them in central government courts (articles 62, 68 and 100). Signed and sealed copies of the court proceedings were given to the personal agent of the Muscovite grand prince (tsar) if the agent had been present, and also to elected representatives of the local populace (article 62). When the trial record was challenged by one of the litigants in a higher court, the grand prince's personal agent and the local representatives were summoned and the copies of the trial proceedings were compared. If discrepancies or forgeries came to light, the vicegerent (or his agent) who had sat as a trial judge was compelled to pay damages to the injured litigant, and was further subject to such punishment "as the sovereign may decree" (article 69). Vicegerents' agents who took a person into custody were obliged to present that person before the grand prince's personal agent and the elected representatives of the local populace. The latter could, in the case of irregularities, compel the release of the prisoner, who in turn had the right to sue the offending officials for damages to his honor (article 70).

In some respects the *Sudebnik's* tone was less severe when addressing the vicegerents than when dealing with the central government officials. Thus, the populace of a particular district could expect no legal redress against a corrupt or oppressive vicegerent unless it kept the central government in Moscow furnished with up-to-date tax rolls for the district (article 72), and the code's articles which prohibited vicegerents and their agents from taking bribes failed to spell out any penalties for violation of this injunction (articles 62, 68). This may have been

[4] The Moscow government entrusted them with the conduct of inquests to ascertain the value of local residents' property and to furnish information on trade conducted by city dwellers under their jurisdiction. They were to scrutinize the tax shares for which city dwellers were registered on tax rolls (article 72). The vicegerents of Novgorod and Pskov were the only officials outside Moscow authorized to issue slave manumissions (article 77).

due to a legislative oversight. On the other hand, it may have resulted from Moscow's recognition of the vicegerent's position as a reward for past services. His position, indeed, was officially referred to as *kormlenie* ("feeding"),[5] and Ivan had shown little sympathy in 1547 to a group of seventy Pskov burghers who had come to petition him for redress against their vicegerent's oppressive malfeasance: the tsar ordered them disrobed, poured wine on them and set fire to their beards![6] A vicegerent could, however, be fined for improperly issuing certain legal documents pertaining to slaves (article 66) or for falsifying court records (article 69), and if he or his agent illegally released, sold or punished a thief or bandit, the punishment included both a fine and imprisonment "until further decree of the sovereign [Moscow judge?]" (article 71). Where two vicegerents had sat jointly as judges and were discovered to have taken multiple fees, instead of splitting the single fee as prescribed, they were ordered to pay the injured party three times the amount of the fees (article 74).

The old evils of judicial and administrative corruption had undoubtedly proliferated in the chaotic years which preceded Ivan's accession to the throne. Taken together, the clauses in his new *Sudebnik* which we have just summarized clearly envisaged major reform in this area.

II

Judicial and administrative corruption presented only one type of problem faced by Russian lawmakers in the mid-sixteenth century. One might regard it as an internal problem—one arising within the legal system and relating particularly to the conduct

[5] See D. Golochvastov, "Istoricheskoe znachenie slova 'kormlenie'," *Russkii archiv*, IV (1889), 650, against this interpretation, and V. O. Klyuchevsky's letter in rebuttal of Golochvastov, *Russkii archiv*, V (1889), 138–45. Good discussions of *kormlenie* may be found in S. B. Veselovsky, *Feodal'noe zemlevladenie v Severo-vostochnoi Rusi* (Moscow and Leningrad, 1947), Vol. I, pp. 263–80, G. W. Lantzeff, *Siberia in the Seventeenth Century* (Berkeley, 1943), pp. 19–24.

[6] This notorious incident is quoted as evidence of Ivan's "inventive" sadism in N. N. Evreinov, *Istoryia telesnykh nakazanii v Rossii* (St. Petersburg, n. d.), Vol. I, p. 46.

of officials charged with administering that system. Another set of problems, pertaining to public order and safety, was more "external" in character. This period of Russian history was a time of fires, famine and plague. Lawlessness and disorder flourished. Sources from the decade preceding the *Sudebnik* tell of bandits terrorizing the rural districts, plundering villages and hamlets and setting fire to them, and murdering the inhabitants in large numbers.[7] The vicegerents seemed unable or unwilling to cope with the problem and the central government was placing more and more reliance on representatives of the local populace known as "district elders" (*gubnye starosty*) in the struggle against brigandage.[8] Elected from the petty gentry and the peasantry, but directly responsible to Moscow, the district elders were charged with tracking down thieves and bandits and bringing them to justice. A most important step was the *Sudebnik's* requirement that "if any person is charged with brigandage and if testimony is brought in court that the person is a notorious evildoer [and] bandit, the vicegerents shall turn over such persons to the district elders" (article 60). Since district elders were directly accountable to Moscow, this provision placed cases of banditry—the major problem in public safety—under the jurisdiction of the central government.

Custody and security procedures which the 1497 code had decreed for thieves were now extended to brigands (article 53). Scholars have been puzzled over the apparent contradiction between article 60, which authorized the vicegerents to execute thieves, murderers and other criminals except bandits, and article 71, which enjoins vicegerents from executing, selling or liberating such criminals without "reference up" (*bez dokladu*) to Moscow. It has been suggested that article 60 sets the punishment (execution), whereas article 71 defines the procedural stages in trial.[9]

---

[7] A. I. Yakovlev, *Namestnichie, gubnye i zemskie gramoty moskovskogo gosudarstva* (Moscow, 1909), pp. 51–3.

[8] It has even been suggested that the growth of crime was in some respects profitable for the vicegerents: N. E. Nosov, *Ocherki po istorii mestnogo upravleniya Russkogo gosudarstva pervoi poloviny XVI veka* (Moscow and Leningrad, 1957), p. 229.

[9] A. A. Zimin, *Reformy Ivana Groznogo* (Moscow, 1960), pp. 359–60.

Were some of the men whom Ivan's code branded as "notorious evildoers and bandits" really Muscovite counterparts of Spartacus or Robin Hood, their "evil deeds" amounting to defiance of the authority of the dominant classes which had usurped the state power? Some historians have declared that banditry in fifteenth- and sixteenth-century Russia was frequently a form of social protest. According to this interpretation the "bandits" and other "notorious evildoers" with whom the *Sudebnik* dealt so harshly were often peasants (or members of the lower classes in the cities) who had risen in "protest" against their feudal exploiters. In the class struggle which (according to Marxist-Leninist historians) was raging in medieval Russia, social discontent frequently took the form of armed uprisings. These disorders called for strong repressive measures by the state, which represented the interests of the dominant class in general and the rising *dvoryanstvo* (gentry in state service) in particular. The charters which were issued to district elders called for the punishment, not only of brigands, but of persons who had sheltered them or had collaborated with them by receiving and storing their booty. Soviet scholars see in such passages evidence that part of the population was supporting the "brigands" because they were leaders or participants in "peasant or slave movements" rather than criminals in the ordinary sense.[10]

Former slaves may well have accounted for some of the crimes and disorders which the *Sudebnik* was seeking to combat. The position of freed slaves was a peculiar one. In becoming free they were cut off from old ties and no longer belonged to any recognized social group or organization. Yakovlev has described the armed gangs of former slaves from Tver, Yaroslavl and elsewhere who roamed the streets of Moscow in the *Sudebnik* era. The influx of freed slaves and slaves who had come with their masters to Moscow created social and political problems of the first magnitude. Restless and unaccustomed to Muscovite ways of life, and having few points of contact with the local population,

[10] Some sources of this interpretation are presented by Nosov, *op. cit.*, Ch. VI.

they presented a constant source of disorder and conflict within the city.[11]

Other evidence, however, cautions against unduly extending the interpretation of bandit activities in the *Sudebnik* era as "social protest." The "exploited" elements of society were far from being the only ones to engage in banditry. Russian history furnishes accounts of brigandage by members of the petty gentry (*deti boyarskie*), despite the fact that this group theoretically stood to gain the most from the development of a strong central state government and was supposedly a bulwark of the state apparatus.[12] It has been suggested that the *Sudebnik's* vaguely worded seventy-fifth article deals with vicegerents accused of banditry![13] In Russian folk literature the bandit or brigand (*razboynik*) was traditionally a villain rather than a Robin Hood-type hero. Pre-revolutionary scholars took the anti-brigandage clauses at their face value: brigands were simply dangerous outlaws who made a career of banditry and whose plundering activities presented a threat to society at large. Some of these scholars pointed out the law-makers' concern with the defendant's reputation (was he a "notorious" bandit or evildoer?) and discerned in it an effort to establish whether he made a practice or trade (*promysl*) of his illegal activities. The humbly born "notorious criminal" was apparently regarded as a threat by members of his own social stratum, and it was the testimony of character witnesses more than any other type of evidence which determined his fate.[14]

The 1550 *Sudebnik* was a harsher code than its 1497 predecessor.

[11] A. Yakovlev, *Kholopstvo i Kholopy v moskovskom gosudarstve 17 v* (Moscow and Leningrad, 1943), Vol. I, pp. 26–7.

[12] See Nosov, *op. cit.*, 209, n. 5. The author attempts to explain this phenomenon by referring to such brigands as "declassed" elements and concedes that there were many of them.

[13] I. I. Smirnov, "Sudebnik 1550 goda," *Istoricheskie zapiski*, XXIV (1947), 267–352; here pp. 281–2.

[14] Article 58. See comments in V. Sergeevich, *Lektsii i issledovaniya po drevnei istorii russkago prava* (3rd edn., St. Petersburg, 1903), p. 426: I. D. Belyaev, *Lektsii po istorii russkago zakonodatelstva* (2nd edn., Moscow, 1888), p. 416; F. M. Dmitriev, *Istoriya sudebnykh istantsii i grazhdanskogo appelyacionnogo sudoproizvodstva* (Moscow, 1859), p. 188.

We have already noted the penalties meted out for malfeasance in office. The categories of crimes made punishable by death (brigandage, murder, treason, arson, temple robbing, repeated theft and "other such evil deeds") remained the same as those enumerated in the 1497 code (although thieves' accomplices were now to be executed (article 57), whereas the 1497 code had not been specific on this point in its fourteenth article). But flogging, imprisonment and other forms of punishment were now decreed for a considerably larger number of offenses. A whole cluster of articles dealt with litigants found to have made false accusations against officials, and with witnesses guilty of perjury. False accusation was generally punished by flogging and imprisonment (articles 6–11, 33–34 and 42); the 1497 code had contained no such provisions. A witness found guilty of perjury was now to be flogged, in addition to paying all the plaintiff's monetary damages (article 99). Convicted swindlers were to be flogged and imprisoned (article 58). Provincial litigants who had falsified the value of their property on tax rolls were to be arrested and taken to Moscow (article 72). Persons who were discovered illegally branding horses were compelled to pay monetary fines and were to be "further punished as the sovereign shall decree" (article 96).

III

The *Sudebnik* goes beyond problems of judicial and administrative reform and public safety. It has a good deal to say, as did the 1497 code, on the status of various groups or classes in Muscovite society. Many of its clauses deal with monetary payments (fees, dwelling costs, recompense for injuries) arising from transactions and relationships within specific social groups or between them. Where older sources were incorporated into the new code, the sources almost invariably underwent revision. Sometimes the changes involved a simple alteration in the amount of monetary payments and did not embody any sort of reform. Other revised provisions, along with some of the new ones, amounted to important innovations in substantive law. Still other passages may have been intended to introduce reforms of a sweeping character: some scholars have gone so far as to claim that the dreaded *oprichnina*, which Ivan set up in the following decade, was a logical outcome of the political program contained in the *Sudebnik*.[15] Let us consider some examples of each type of provision.

Various Muscovite social groups are mentioned in the *Sudebnik's* twenty-sixth article, which establishes a scale of monetary payments for "injured honor" (*beschestie*). Here we learn that a wealthy merchant's honor, when "injured," was worth ten times that of an ordinary trader, city resident or other "middle person." A woman's injured honor was valued at twice her husband's. The honor of a peasant—even a prosperous one—was reckoned at only one ruble, as was that of "common" city dwellers, but peasants were entitled to additional monetary damages for any physical injury which had accompanied the blow to their honor. Although the code has much to say about slaves in other contexts, it mentions no payment for the injured honor of slaves as such. If a slave happened to be a deputy, bailiff or other agent in a boyar's service, he presumably received compensation for injured honor equivalent to his yearly pay, as did freemen in those categories. Clergymen are not mentioned in the article. We note a particular solicitude for the injured honor of persons whose services were most needed by the tsar and his government. The principle of monetary damages corresponding to income or salary extended to petty boyars in local administration, but secretaries in central government offices and courts received "whatever compensation the tsar shall decree." If an official enjoyed the tsar's special favor, this compensation came very high indeed: the humbly born *dyak* (secretary) Vasily Shchelkalov was given an ancestral estate of two villages and ten hamlets, together with forests and grazing lands, which had belonged to Ivan Michailov, because Michailov had

---

[15] *Sudebniki XV–XVI vekov*, pp. 193–4. Another scholar who sees the *oprichnina* foreshadowed in 1550 is V. Leontovich (Leontovitsch), *Die Rechtsumwälzung unter Iwan dem Schrecklichen und die Ideologie der russischen Selbstherrschaft* (Stuttgart, 1949), pp. 102–3.

been unable to pay Shchelkalov two hundred rubles for injuring his honor.[16]

This twenty-sixth article, with its attempt to assign precise monetary values to the injured honor of various social groups in sixteenth-century society, has no counterpart in the 1497 code, but similar provisions may be found in the ancient Kievan *Russkaya Pravda*.

Equally conservative in spirit is the *Sudebnik's* ninetieth article. The *Russkaya Pravda* and the 1497 code had both recognized the plight of the travelling merchant who, entrusted with the goods and/or money of others, lost them through no fault of his own. Circumstances absolving him from personal blame included fire, shipwreck and seizure by bandits or enemy troops. In such cases the 1497 code had provided that the grand prince could issue the unfortunate merchant a special document known as a *poletnaya gramota*, which authorized him to pay back his creditors without interest—thus saving him from bankruptcy proceedings and slavery. The 1550 *Sudebnik* changed this provision only to the extent of specifying that the *poletnaya gramota* would lose its effect if the lost goods were recovered or the bandits apprehended.

Articles of this nature, while dealing with various groups and classes within Muscovite society, could hardly be considered measures of reform. Can projected reforms be found among the numerous clauses which regulate the status of the Muscovite masses—the peasants, slaves and hired laborers?

The *Sudebnik's* extreme conservatism with reference to peasants is best illustrated by its eighty-eighth article. The source of this article was the fifty-seventh article in the 1497 code, which had declared that peasants could move from their rural area (*volost'*), going from one village to live in another, only once a year: during the week before St. George's Day in the autumn (November 26) and the week after it. Before leaving, the peasants were obliged to pay their landlords for the use of living quarters. If a peasant

<hr />

[16] Russia, Archeograficheskaya Komissiya, *Akty istoricheskie* (St. Petersburg, 1841–1842), Vol. 1, pp. 431–4. The document unfortunately does not make clear how Michailov had offended Shchelkalov.

had stayed with a given lord only one year, he paid only one-fourth of the total value of these living quarters; if he stayed two years, he paid half their value; for three years he paid three-fourths and for four years he paid the total value, which was set by the 1497 code at one ruble (unless the peasant had occupied quarters in or near a forest, in which case the value was reduced by one-half, presumably because of the accessibility of building materials). The 1550 *Sudebnik* contained four innovations. First, two *altyns* (six-hundredths of a ruble) were added to the amount the peasant was to pay for his living quarters, and two more *altyns* were charged him as a "transport fee." Second, the peasant was required to pay certain sums to his lord (and to the state) in place of grain or rye which he had left in the fields. A third innovation was the curious proviso that a village priest should not be obliged to pay for living quarters before moving, and that he was free to leave at any time he pleased.[17] Fourth and last, no living quarters fees were to be collected from peasants who had sold themselves into slavery "from the fields." By thus leaving the time and conditions of peasant transfer basically unchanged from the 1497 code, the 1550 *Sudebnik* was making only superficial changes in the status of the mass of Russian peasantry.

Thirteen *Sudebnik* articles deal directly with slaves or the institution of slavery.[18] Involuntary servitude had existed in Russia from the time of its earliest recorded history and was flourishing in the reign of Ivan the Terrible. The slave's legal status was quite simple. Except for those articles of regulatory nature which we find in the *Sudebnik*, he was not under the jurisdiction of freemen's courts, but was entirely under the control of his master. A slave could pass, like inanimate property, by will or dowry. He could be sold. The *Sudebnik* recognized no recompense for the "injured honor" of slaves as such, and Eck quotes the last will and testament of a landlord who begged forgiveness for having "in moments of bad

[17] See comment on this proviso in B. A. Romanov, *O polnom kholope i selskom pope v Sudebnike Ivana Groznogo* (Akademiku Borisu Dmitrievichu Grekovu ko dnyu semidesyatiletiya. Sbornik statei, Moscow, 1952), pp. 140–5.

[18] Articles 35, 40, 63, 65–7, 76–81 and 88.

humor" beaten his male slaves, raped his virgin female slaves and even put slaves to death, for which he now prayed that his "sinful soul may be delivered in this life and in the future life."[19] Other slaveowners made more constructive use of their slaves. A slave who was intelligent and capable, and whose master recognized these qualities, might come to occupy a responsible administrative post and receive an estate for his services. Some of the city super-intendents (*gorodskie prikazchiki*) who eventually crowded the higher-born vicegerents out of local administration and attained positions of considerable power, had been slaves.[20] The deputies and agents of the vicegerents themselves were frequently slaves.

But situations had apparently arisen which earlier laws had not foreseen and which gave rise to dispute and litigation. What happened, for example, if two masters claimed the same slave and each presented a "full slave document" (*polnaya gramota*) to prove he owned the slave? Ivan's code now resolved such disputes in favor of the person holding the older document (article 79). The 1497 code provided that if enemy troops captured a slave and he escaped from capture, he became a free man. The 1550 *Sudebnik* allows him, after certain formalities, to return to his master in his former capacity (article 80) (!).

Provincial vicegerents holding "limited jurisdictional grants" were barred from issuing any documents affecting the status of slaves. If they had tried cases involving slaves and issued such papers, the *Sudebnik* pronounced them void, calling for retrial of the case and fines against the offending vicegerents or their agents (articles 63, 66 and 67). Even manumissions issued by vicegerents holding "full jurisdictional grants" in Moscow, Pskov or Novgorod were valid only after they had been signed by a secretary of the central government (article 77).

These last-cited articles make one thing clear: that Moscow was centralizing the judicial administration of questions pertaining to slaves. Why was such centralization desirable? The clauses may

---

[19] A. Eck, *Le Moyen Âge Russe* (Paris, 1933), p. 382.
[20] Nosov, *op. cit.*, p. 39.

have been aimed at abuses committed by the vicegerents themselves. Jakovlev describes how some vicegerents sent agents through
the countryside to seize free peasants. The peasants were "driven
under the yoke of slavery by the fists and clubs" of the vicegerents'
men, who would then hastily draw up a suitable document as
evidence of their slave status.[21] Another scholar has suggested that
the slave-law provisions in the 1497 code (which were carried
over into the 1550 *Sudebnik*) were designed to protect slaveowners
against forged documents drawn up under such circumstances,
rather than to safeguard the interests of the peasants.[22]

It would be difficult to determine whether the 1550 *Sudebnik*
increased the legal categories of slaves or decreased them. On the
one hand, the code forbade petty boyars and their children from
becoming slaves while the petty boyars were in the state service
(article 81). Possibly the code's intent here was not to protect
members of the petty gentry from a state of involuntary
servitude, but rather to prevent them from evading their governmental duties and responsibilities by fleeing into slavery.[23] Ivan's
law also prohibited slaves from selling their children into slavery
if these children had been born before their father became a slave.
Parents who were monks or nuns had no right to sell their children
into slavery—or to seek their freedom from slavery (article 76).
On the other hand, a whole new category of slaves not mentioned
in the 1497 code made their appearance in the 1550 *Sudebnik*: the
so-called *kabalnye lyudi* or "indentured slaves"—freemen who had
sold themselves into slavery in return for a loan (not exceeding
fifteen rubles) or in order to extinguish a debt.[24]

---

[21] Yakovlev, *Kholopstvo . . .*, p. 42.

[22] L. V. Cherepnin, *Russkie feodalnye archivy XIV–XV vekov* (Moscow, 1951),
Vol. II, p. 342.

[23] M. F. Vladimirsky-Budanov, *Obzor istorii russkago prava* (3rd edn., St.
Petersburg, 1900), pp. 136–7.

[24] Article 78. A good treatment of the indentured slaves may be found in
J. Blum, *Lord and Peasant in Russia from the Ninth to the Nineteenth Century*
(Princeton, 1961), pp. 243–5. Fifteen rubles was a very high figure and a Soviet
scholar sees this high limit as working simultaneously in the interests of the
service gentry and the great feudal aristocracy: Zimin, *op. cit.*, p. 356.

Despite the appearance of this new category of slaves, some historians have claimed that slavery was on the decline in Russia. The late B. D. Grekov wrote that this period of Russian history witnessed a gradual yielding of slavery to more "progressive" forms of labor, especially that of the hired laborer (*naymit*).[25] The hired laborer appears in the eighty-third article of the 1550 *Sudebnik*, which states that if a hired laborer leaves his employer before serving the full term agreed upon, he shall be deprived of his wages. On the other hand, the employer who refuses to pay the hired laborer his rightful wages will be compelled to pay the laborer twice the sum of the wages.[26]

Merchants, village priests, peasants, "middle" and "common" city dwellers, hired laborers and slaves—all these groups were affected by the provisions which we have just summarized. In each case the *Sudebnik* purported to regulate their status in some way. Can one speak of "reforms" here? Perhaps not in individual instances. The alteration in peasant dwelling payments, for example, may simply have reflected an overall rise in prices. But, taken together, the articles which we have enumerated certainly constituted a reform in the direction of order and legality. After decades of turmoil and lawlessness, Russia now had a code which was carefully regulating the status of various social groups, granting legal protection of the "injured honor" of individual members in different classes, and introducing new procedures for combatting crime.

The disorder which the young tsar and his legislators found at every turn was nowhere more evident than in land tenure. Russia had not yet acquired effective methods of surveying and registering its many types of landholdings: private ancestral estates of the nobility (*votchiny*); the "black" lands administered by peasant communes; the *pomestie* life estates granted to members of the

[25] *Sudebniki XV–XVI vekov*, p. 89. See also V. V. Mavrodin, *Obrazovanie edinogo russkogo gosudarstva* (Moscow, 1957), p. 177.

[26] For a comparison of the hired laborer's actual position with that of the indentured slave, see L. V. Danilova and V. T. Pashuto, "Tovarnoe proizvodstvo na Rusi (do XVII v.)," *Voprosy istorii*, XXIX (1954), 134.

petty gentry while they gave military or administrative service
to the tsar; the different types of ecclesiastical domains. Some
court reports of this era show the problems which confronted a
judge in land litigation where the issue was simply one of
boundaries.[27] Even when the boundaries of the various landholdings were acknowledged, their administration and taxation
had been complicated by the issuance of immunity charters which
removed the lands of certain lords from the jurisdiction of
Moscow's local representatives in most matters and exempted the
landholders from certain taxes and state obligations. Still other
problems arose in connection with land tenure. The tsar, for
example, needed lands for distribution as *pomestie* estates to the
"service class" members (*slushilye lyudi*) upon whom he depended
to run his armed forces and civil administration. For this reason he
and his service nobility would cast envious glances at the enormous
holdings of the church, and Ivan made sporadic attempts to
keep the church from adding still more lands to its domains.

The preoccupation of the tsar and his advisers with problems
of land tenure found clear expression in an interesting manuscript
known as the "Tsar's Questions,"[28] which called, inter alia, for
a thorough investigation of the status of all hereditary ancestral
estates, *pomestie* estates, monasterial landholdings and other forms
of land tenure. Who owned which lands, for how long and under
what conditions? The land boundaries were to be redefined if necessary and all land transactions (particularly those involving hereditary
ancestral estates) were to be carefully registered in special books.

The *Sudebnik's* provisions were less sweeping than the measures
proposed in the "Tsar's Questions" but the code did deal with
basic problems of land tenure. Some articles were merely re-

[27] See the case reported in N. P. Lichachev (ed. and comp.), *Sbornik aktov,
sobrannykh v archivakh i bibliotekakh* (St. Petersburg, 1895), Vol. II, pp. 144–71.

[28] These questions were thought at first to have been drawn up for the
ecclesiastical assembly (*stoglavny sobor*) of 1551, but Zimin believes they may
antedate the *Sudebnik: op. cit.*, pp. 336–7. For a summary of the questions on
land tenure and a modern Soviet commentary, see I. I. Smirnov, *Ocherki
politicheskoi istorii russkogo gosudarstva 30–50–kh godov XVI veka* (Moscow and
Leningrad, 1958), pp. 301–8.

enactments of clauses in the 1497 code (e.g. the statute of limitations on land suits in article 84), but new penalties were decreed for damaging enclosures and boundary markers (articles 86 and 87). Two new articles (43 and 85), relating to immunity charters and ancestral estates, are of considerable interest.

The last sentence of article 43 states that no "permanent-immunity charters" (*tarchannye gramoty*) shall be issued in the future, and old permanent-immunity charters are to be taken from all who hold them. Such charters entitled the grantee to unlimited exemption from certain taxes and obligations to the central government. Their abolition would indeed have "struck a blow at the privileged landholders" and brought new revenue to the state.[29] Since the issuance of such charters to secular landholders had ceased early in the century, ecclesiastical landholders would appear to have been the target of this article. As a practical matter, however, article 43 does not seem to have been well enforced, which has led some historians to conclude that it was a mere "declaration of principle." Old charters were collected from their holders, but only for review and reissuance.[30] Article 85 has been called a "whole code" in itself.[31] It seeks to regulate the alienation of ancestral estates (*votchiny*) by setting forth the conditions under which the estate owner's heirs (direct or collateral) may repurchase or redeem an alienated estate and by specifying certain types of transactions as void. . . .

The *Sudebnik* articles to which scholars have attributed the greatest political significance are those dealing with the reform of provincial administration by vicegerents. There can be no doubt that the *Sudebnik* deprived the vicegerents of certain functions which they had performed in the past. We have described the limitations placed on vicegerents with "limited jurisdictional grants" in issuing documents pertaining to slaves. We have also mentioned the removal of cases involving "notorious" brigands from the courts of provincial vicegerents, such cases being trans-

[29] Smirnov, "Sudebnik . . .," *loc. cit.*, p. 322.
[30] Zimin, *op. cit.*, p. 352; *Sudebniki XV–XVI vekov*, pp. 224–9.
[31] *Sudebniki XV–XVI vekov*, p. 297.

ferred to the district elders who were directly accountable to
Moscow. Another important innovation was the removal of
members of the petty gentry (*deti boyarskie*) from the jurisdiction
of the vicegerents except in cases of murder and brigandage; such,
in any case, is the interpretation scholars have given article 64.[32]
In other cases the *deti boyarskie* were to be tried in central government tribunals.

Great significance has been attached to these passages in the
Sudebnik. The claim has even been made that, by these provisions,
Moscow was preparing to abolish the whole system of administration by vicegerents,[33] which in fact did take place five years later.
In our mind, the extent of political reform planned by the
Sudebnik's compilers in 1550 was much more modest. For reasons
discussed in the next section, we do not believe that Ivan's lawmakers in 1550 thought of their code as a stepping stone to the
abolition of administration by vicegerents in the near future.

A change in Muscovite governmental structure which some
scholars think was reflected in the *Sudebnik* relates to the activity
of the *prikazy*—those sixteenth-century forerunners of centra
government departments and ministries. Some scholars believe
that a few *prikazy* were already in operation by 1550, and that
the code was referring to them.[34] Other historians question
whether the *Sudebnik* is really referring to the *prikazy* as governmental departments, and are not sure that any *prikazy* even existed
at the time the *Sudebnik* appeared.[35] At best, the code's references
to *prikazy* would seem to be indirect and incidental.

IV

The *Sudebnik's* creators clearly intended it as an instrument of
reform in the areas of judicial administration and maintenance of
public safety. It is possible, as we have seen, to give a broader
interpretation of the code's "reform" aims, extending them to
include political and economic relationships between certain

[32] *Ibid.*, pp. 260–1.   [33] See, for example, Smirnov, *Ocherki*..., p. 355.
[34] *Ibid.*, pp. 320–1.   [35] Zimin, *op. cit.*, pp. 361–4.

classes or groups in Muscovite society. But soon after its promulgation a series of developments took place which made the *Sudebnik*
largely inapplicable. In speaking of the *"Sudebnik"* we mean not
only the ninety-nine or one hundred articles in the original code,
which could easily undergo modification or extension by the
amendment procedures outlined in the ninety-eighth article
(providing for new matters to be settled by joint decree of the tsar
and the boyars, then added to the code). We are also referring to
the body of principles and objectives embodied in the document
as it appeared in 1550.

The first major development concerned provincial administration. In 1555 or 1556 Ivan's government began "energetically" to
abolish the system of administration by vicegerents, or *kormlenie*,[36]
thereby depriving the *Sudebnik's* articles on this subject of most
of their meaning. Ivan, in abolishing *kormlenie*, based this step on
alleged abuses and misrule by vicegerents. But was this the real
motive for the reform, or was Ivan simply capitalizing on the
unpopularity of certain vicegerents in order to achieve other
ends? We have already mentioned his lack of sympathy for the
Pskov citizens who had petitioned him because of their vicegerent's abuses. Why, now, was administration by vicegerents
suddenly being abolished, so soon after the publication of *Sudebnik*
provisions aimed at correcting the situation and putting provincial
government on a more solid basis? If Ivan and his lawmakers had
contemplated the imminent abolition of rule by vicegerents, why
had they devoted so much of their code to redefining the vicegerents' jurisdiction, entrusting them with important new tasks?
It seems certain to us that the *Sudebnik* had been intended to be
the new law of the land for a long time; this is clear from the
great care with which old sources had been revised and brought
up to date before incorporation into the code, and Ivan himself is

[36] Until recently scholars had assumed that a single decree, issued in 1555 or
1556, brought provincial rule by vicegerents to an end. Now it seems more
likely that this major reform came about over a number of years (1555–6 being
simply the "most energetic" period) through a succession of decrees in various
regions. A. A. Zimin, " 'Prigovor' 1555–56 g. i likvidatsiya sistemy kormlenii v
russkom gosudarstve," *Istoriya SSSR*, I (1958), 178–82.

quoted as having demanded (in 1551) that the new code retain its effect *vo veki* (literally "for centuries" or "forever").[37] We cannot believe that the *Sudebnik's* articles on vicegerent administration were intended as halfway measures or stopgap legislation; to our mind there was no plan in 1550 for replacing the vicegerents within such a short period of time. It seems more likely to us that the reform of 1555/56 came about as a result of developments which had not been foreseen (or taken into consideration) when the code was drawn up. One of these developments was the bankruptcy of the Moscow treasury resulting from the military campaigns against the Tartar khanates of Kazan and Astrakhan. The first measures abolishing *kormlenie* followed the successful but costly final conquest of Kazan and coincided with preparations to subjugate Astrakhan. In view of the burden which such campaigns put on the treasury it can hardly be doubted that a principal motive for reforming provincial administration was to acquire a larger share of income from all areas of the state than had been possible under the *kormlenie* system. Ivan may have also been more disposed, after the mistrust which had arisen between him and his closest advisers in 1553, to heed proponents of more drastic reforms—men like Ivan Peresvetov, who seems to have hated the vicegerents and all they stood for,[38] but we consider the need for revenue to have been the prime factor in abolishing *kormlenie*.

[37] Quoted in Smirnov, *Ocherki*, p. 310.

[38] A. A. Zimin, D. S. Lichachev (eds.), *Sochineniya I. Peresvetova* (Moscow and Leningrad, 1956), p. 18. Peresvetov supposedly gave Ivan some documents, in which he suggested certain governmental reforms, in 1549, but Peresvetov's proposals were so drastic, emotional—and superficial—that it seems hard to believe that they had any real influence on the compilers of the *Sudebnik*. To take a typical example: Peresvetov opposed judicial duels and suggested in their place the following procedure: litigants should be left, unarmed and naked, in a dungeon where a single razor was hidden; he who found the razor won the "duel" and had the right to butcher his opponent on the spot. The *Sudebnik's* compilers, however, not only retained the judicial duel, but widened the area of disputes which could be decided by it, liberalized the rules for litigants' participation in it and introduced new regulations intended to match combatants more evenly and to maintain order among spectators at judicial duels. See articles 9–17, 19, 51 and 89.

The large number of *Sudebnik* articles which were addressed to judges and officials in the central government system (as opposed to vicegerents in provincial administration) also lost most of their effect after a short time. It is impossible to judge the efficacy of the *Sudebnik's* anti-corruption and public safety clauses in the first years following the code's promulgation. By 1560, however, there is evidence that the reform of judicial administration had failed, and that the penalties against judges, administrators and other central government officials convicted of bribe-taking or otherwise using their position for motives of personal gain or revenge were rarely applied. At that time, according to eyewitness Heinrich von Staden,[39] there was only one fair and impartial judge in all Moscow. This was the boyar Ivan Petrovich Chelyadnin, Moscow's first judge in the absence of the tsar. Chelyadnin had won great favor among "the common people" by his conscientious dispensation of justice, but Staden makes it clear that cases not coming to Chelyadnin's attention were handled quite differently. Thus, brigands and murderers who had been apprehended and brought to a special government department (the *razboyny prikaz*)[40] for prosecution could buy their freedom by falsely implicating some wealthy peasant or trader. The accused peasant or trader was promptly seized and saw his riches confiscated by the officials of the *razboyny prikaz*. Staden further reports that many a "wrongful deed could be made right and, conversely, a rightful deed made wrong" before the person committing the deed ever reached the courts. If officials had "taken a disliking" to some merchant or trader, they would send a vagabond with wine to the merchant's home, "as if in friendship." A group of officials and "witnesses" would then burst in, practically on the heels of the wine-bearing vagabond. In the presence of the

[39] References in this paper come from Genrich Shtaden [Heinrich von Staden], *O Moskve Ivana Groznogo*, trans. I. I. Polosin (Leningrad, 1925), pp. 81–7. [Definitive edition of the German original: *Aufzeichnungen über den Moskauer Staat*, ed. F. T. Epstein (2nd edn., Hamburg, 1964). English translation: *The Land and Government of Muscovy*, ed. T. Esper (Stanford, 1967).]

[40] This *prikaz*, so far as we know, did not come into existence with the *Sudebnik*, but by later decrees: Vladimirsky-Budanov, *op. cit.*, p. 239.

"witnesses" the officials would arrest the vagabond, his "host and hostess," and all of the latter's household servants on charges of illegally maintaining a drinking establishment. The host was then obliged to shake out his money-pouch "if he wished to save his skin."

What redress was there for victims of such outrageous practices? Could the merchant and his wife, for example, invoke the *Sudebnik's* twenty-sixth article (on "injured honor") in addition to pressing charges of malfeasance and corruption against the officials? How would the merchant and his wife prove their allegations? How could they even be assured of a hearing? According to Staden,

> he who would bring a complaint to the
> grand prince was carefully watched, and
> cast into prison. If he had money he
> might get out again, but if he had none
> he remained there until his hair had grown
> from his head to his navel. All these princes,
> great boyar-administrators, secretaries, scribes,
> officials and bailiffs were connected with
> one another like links of a single chain.[41]

If one accepts this bleak account, one must conclude that the *Sudebnik* had failed as an instrument of reform in the area of judicial administration. Why?

Surely the code's anti-corruption clauses were not intended as mere "declarations of principle." It is a pity that we know so little about the background of the *Sudebnik* and the identity of its proponents and compilers. Some Muscovite lawmakers must have cherished a genuine conviction that every freeman was entitled to his day in court,[42] and must have wished to make sure that all litigants, once in court, would receive a fair trial. How,

[41] Articles 6–11 of the *Sudebnik*, as we have noted, decreed severe penalties (fines, flogging, incarceration) against persons making "false accusations" against officials in the central government court system. Under the circumstances these provisions must have discouraged some victims of official corruption from even attempting to obtain justice.

[42] This principle, set forth in article 2 of the 1497 code, was reaffirmed in article 7 of the 1550 *Sudebnik*.

then, is one to account for the dismal account of Muscovite judicial administration presented by eyewitnesses?

It is possible, of course, that the reforms had not failed to the extent depicted by Staden. There must have been competent and honest judges in Moscow besides Chelyadnin, and it seems incredible that officials made a regular practice of such abuses as Staden describes. Unhappily, other primary sources from this period (the accounts of Fletcher, Chancellor, and Schlichtling, for example) fully support Staden's discouraging account of the evils which riddled Muscovite justice after the *Sudebnik's* publication. The prevalence of such corrupt practices may well account for the sardonic tone of Old Russian proverbs dealing with judicial administration, particularly the one which says: "Fear not the law, fear the judge."

There may have been a short period of time after the *Sudebnik's* publication when Ivan and his lawmakers presented a solid front against corruption, but we suspect that this unity of purpose, if it ever existed, was broken some time after Ivan's illness (and disagreement with his close advisers) in 1553, and those who placed their hope in the *Sudebnik* as an instrument of judicial reform saw their influence quickly wane as the areas of disagreement between Ivan and his counselors of the *Sudebnik* era steadily widened (for example, over the issue of the Livonian wars which Ivan started in 1558). As Ivan became more and more the true autocrat, his personal attitude toward law and administration became an increasingly critical factor in the successful application of the *Sudebnik's* anti-corruption norms. We know that Ivan himself had sat as a judge in lawsuits even before 1550,[43] and Ivan himself

[43] See, for example, the case reported in Russia, Archeograficheskaya komissiya, *Akty, otnosyashchiesya do juridicheskogo byta drevnei Rossii* (St. Petersburg, 1857), Vol. II, pp. 192–213. Chancellor, writing of things seen and heard in 1553–1555, claimed that Ivan settled controversies "with the utmost fairness and impartiality," acting thus "from a sacred sense of duty." But "wicked magistrates, nevertheless, in the strangest way pervert his decisions. If, however, they are found guilty of such an offence, they are most severely punished by the Prince." J. M'Crindle and W. Goldsmid (trans. and eds.), *Chancellor's Voyage to Muscovy* (Edinburgh, 1886), p. 74.

had supposedly called for the legal reforms which resulted in the *Sudebnik's* compilation. But there is evidence that he was not a free agent in this earlier period, and the real initiative for drafting the *Sudebnik* may not have come from Ivan at all. He later complained to Kurbsky that his advisers had not reckoned with his wishes in ruling the country at that time (the *Sudebnik* era). His two letters to Kurbsky[44] reveal an immense distrust of judges and administrators. The letters make no reference to the *Sudebnik*; one suspects that if Ivan had felt some personal pride in its creation he would have accused his "enemies" of violating the spirit of his code, or made some such reference to the *Sudebnik* in the charges he was hurling at those who had fallen from his favor. The letters do mention a lawsuit—a case of land litigation which the court had decided (indirectly, to be sure) against Ivan's interests, and Ivan seems to cite this case as an example of the judges' lack of trustworthiness. Ivan rarely showed any understanding of the legal process or any patience with legal niceties. Even his punishment of the corrupt official (a "goose readie dressed") was a flamboyant act, more in the spirit of Peresvetov's Magmet Saltan [the Turkish sultan] than of the *Sudebnik*.

The widespread abuses committed by judges and other officials were, to be sure, acts of lawlessness which violated the spirit of the *Sudebnik*. But Ivan the Terrible, ostensibly the *Sudebnik's* creator and Muscovite Russia's supreme legislator, presently showed a contempt for law and order which surpassed that of his most corrupt underlings.

The spirit of carefully regulated legality which permeated the *Sudebnik* was completely at odds with the policies of the tsar by 1560, when Ivan held a "trial" of his two erstwhile advisers, Silvester and Adashev. Neither of the accused was allowed to defend himself, or to be present at his "trial," and both died soon afterwards. A period of terror followed. After Prince Kurbsky's defection in 1564, Ivan set up the *oprichnina*, his own state within

---

[44] The English translations of the Ivan–Kurbsky correspondence appear in J. I. Fennell (ed. and trans.), *The Correspondence between Prince A. M. Kurbsky and Tsar Ivan IV of Russia, 1564–1579* (Cambridge, 1955).

the state. The system of law embodied in the *Sudebnik* had little applicability within the *oprichnina*. Ivan issued a decree to the *zemshchina* (that part of Russia not included in the *oprichnina*) prohibiting *zemshchina* courts from convicting any *oprichnik* [member of the *oprichnina*] of any crime. "At that time," reports the *oprichnik* von Staden, "because of this decree, did the spirits of the *zemshchina* residents fall." The *oprichniki* pillaged and plundered the *zemshchina* at will. "Even the judicial duel had no effect here," gloats von Staden. "All the hired fighters who represented *zemshchina* residents would acknowledge themselves defeated . . . or they were simply not admitted [to the dueling field]." In 1567 the boyar Chelyadnin, whom Staden and others had described as a conscientious and impartial judge and who had continued to serve as a military commander in the *zemshchina*, was summoned by Ivan to Moscow and executed. His mutilated body was thrown on a dung heap. Ivan and his *oprichniki* rode out and set fire to the estates which had belonged to Chelyadnin. They burned villages and churches, and found time along the way to amuse themselves (in a manner which the *Sudebnik's* compilers had surely never envisaged in the article on "injured honor") by stripping women and girls naked and "compelling them to catch chickens in the field."[45]

There is no need in this paper to dwell further on Ivan's excesses during the *oprichnina* period, beyond pointing out the havoc which they played with a couple of other reform measures which the *Sudebnik* contained, and which we have described earlier. How ironically article 85 must have read, with its solicitude for rights of ancestral estate owners, their heirs and prospective purchasers of ancestral estates, while Ivan was executing thousands of *votchina*-holders among the boyars and confiscating their estates! On the other end of the social scale, thousands and thousands of peasants and slaves were driven to ignore the *Sudebnik's* attempt at regulating their status. They ran away. Many became Cossacks, in areas beyond the reach of Ivan, whose *oprichnina* has been called the "greatest calamity," the chief cause of the economic and social

---

[45] Staden, *op. cit.*, pp. 86–7.

upheavals which finally culminated in the Time of Troubles.[46] Less than two decades after its promulgation, the 1550 *Sudebnik* must have seemed a forgotten body of law. . . .

The *Sudebnik* lived on in the minds of some Russians as a model legal document. A few of its norms (along with norms of the 1497 code) were incorporated into the 1649 law code and, because of this, the 1550 *Sudebnik* allegedly belongs in the mainstream of Russian juridical history.[47] No one can deny the reforming purpose of the *Sudebnik's* articles on judicial administration and maintenance of public safety, and its general attempt to put Russian society on a more carefully regulated, orderly basis. We think that the scope of socio-political reforms envisaged by the code has been exaggerated by some scholars and we certainly cannot agree with those who hold that Ivan's *oprichnina* was a logical outcome of the political program outlined in the *Sudebnik*. To us it would appear that the 1550 *Sudebnik* soon lost most of its meaning as an instrument of reform in its own time.

[46] Blum, *op. cit.*, p. 159.
[47] S. V. Yushkov, *Istoriya gosudarstva i prava SSSR* (Moscow, 1950), Vol. I, pp. 255–6.

Suggestions for Further Reading

* Contains full bibliography

GENERAL WORKS

The articles reprinted in this volume should be read in conjunction with G. R. Elton, "Constitutional Development and Political Thought in Western Europe," in *The New Cambridge Modern History*, Vol. II, *The Reformation, 1520–59* (Cambridge, 1958), a masterpiece of summary and selection. Equally stimulating is H. G. Koenigsberger and G. L. Mosse, *Europe in the Sixteenth Century* (London, 1968), Ch. x: "The Monarchies." Similar surveys from a French point of view are *H. Lapeyre, *Les Monarchies européennes du XVIᵉ siècle* (Paris, 1967), Ch. XIII: "Le pouvoir royal," and Ch. XIV: "L'administration," and R. Mousnier, *Les XVIᵉ et XVIIᵉ siècles* (5th edn., Paris, 1967), Bk. I, Ch. IV: "Les nouvelles structures de l'état." "The Origins of the Modern State" may be seen through the eyes of a German historian, G. Ritter, in *The Development of the Modern State*, ed. H. Lubasz (New York, 1964). A challenging article in the same volume by F. Chabod, "Was there a Renaissance State?," deals with the period immediately prior to the Reformation, as do W. K. Ferguson, "Towards the Modern State," in *The Renaissance*, ed. W. K. Ferguson (New York, 1953), and, for individual countries, J. A. Maravall, "The Origins of the Modern State," *Journal of World History*, VI (1961), 789–808 (on Spain), and L. Tschérépnine, "La réorganisation de l'appareil d'État durant la période de la centralisation politique de la Russie. Fin du XVᵉ et début du XVIᵉ siècles," *Annali della Fondazione italiana per la storia amministrativa*, I (1964), 242–67.

GOVERNMENT AND THE REFORMATION

Apart from several chapters in *The New Cambridge Modern History*, Vol. II, there is an excellent introduction in *A. G. Dickens, *Reformation and Society in Sixteenth-Century Europe* (London, 1966). Model histories of the Reformation in a single country, with good accounts of church–state relationships, are A. G. Dickens, *The English Reformation* (2nd edn., London, 1967) and *M. Roberts, *The Early Vasas: A History of Sweden, 1523–1611* (Cambridge, 1968). There are no detailed works in English on the introduction of the Reformation in the German principalities, but much may be gleaned from H. Holborn, *A History of Modern Germany*, Vol. I, *The Reformation* (New York, 1961); J. Lortz, *The Reformation in Germany*, 2 vols. (London, 1968); A. O. Hancock, "Philip of Hesse's view of the Relationship of Prince and Church," *Church History*, xxxv (1966), 157–69; and, for a Catholic principality, G. Strauss, "The Religious Policy of Dukes Wilhelm and Ludwig of Bavaria in the First Decade of the Protestant Era," *ibid.*, xxviii (1959), 350–73. An excellent analysis of the motives of both Protestant and Catholic princes in the negotiations leading to the Peace of Augsburg is in L. W. Spitz, "Particularism and Peace: Augsburg—1555," *ibid.*, xxv (1956), 110–26.

INDIVIDUAL COUNTRIES

England is easily the best served country for monographs and works of synthesis on constitutional and administrative history. An admirable collection of documents, with introductory sections that deserve to be read and reread, can be found in *G. R. Elton (ed.), *The Tudor Constitution* (Cambridge, 1960). This work in part brings up to date the same author's *The Tudor Revolution in Government* (Cambridge, 1953), which still however remains the fundamental work on the changes of the 1530's. W. C. Richardson, *Tudor Chamber Administration, 1485–1547* (Baton Rouge, 1952) and W. C. Richardson, *History of the Court of Augmentations, 1536–1554* (Baton Rouge, 1961) are scholarly studies shedding much light on administrative institutions and the bureaucracy. The discussion provoked by Professor Elton's ideas should be followed in G. L. Harriss and P. Williams, "A Revolution in Tudor History?," *Past and Present*, xxv (1963), 3–58; *ibid.*, xxxi (1965), 87–96; G. R. Elton, "The Tudor Revolution: A Reply," *ibid.*, xxix (1964), 26–49; J. Hurstfield, "Was there a Tudor Despotism after all?," *Transactions of the Royal Historical Society*, 5th Series, xvii (1967), 83–108.

R. Doucet, *Les Institutions de la France au XVIᵉ siècle,* 2 vols. (Paris, 1948) is a mine of useful information on French government; for a good shorter account, see G. Zeller, *Les Institutions de la France au XVIᵉ siècle* (Paris, 1948). Thought-provoking is B. Guenée, "Espace et État dans la France du Bas Moyen Âge," *Annales. Économies. Sociétés. Civilisations*, xxiii (1968), 744–58. Two French institutions are fully treated in highly readable English works: J. H. Shennan, *The Parlement of Paris* (London, 1968), and N. M. Sutherland, *The French Secretaries of State in the Age of Catherine de Medici* (London, 1962). Of considerable importance are the pamphlet by R. J. Knecht, *Francis I and Absolute Monarchy* (London, 1969), and the collection of documents, with introduction, by J. H. Shennan (ed.), *Government and Society in France, 1461–1661* (London and New York, 1969).

For Spain it is only necessary to consult the excellent *Spain under the Habsburgs*, by J. Lynch (Vol. 1, Oxford, 1964), and J. H. Elliott, *Imperial Spain, 1469–1716* (London, 1963). For comparison, see V. M. Godinho, "Les Finances publiques et la structure de l'état portugais au XVIᵉᵐᵉ siècle," *Revista de Economia* (Lisbon), xiv (1962), 105–15. Among the Italian states only Sicily has been the subject of searching modern English-language publications: H. G. Koenigsberger, *The Government of Sicily under Philip II* (London, 1951), reissued as *The Practice of Empire* (New York, 1970), and D. Mack Smith, *A History of Sicily*, Vol. 1, *Medieval Sicily, 800–1713* (London, 1968). J. Delumeau, "Les progrès de la centralisation dans l'État pontificale au XVIᵉ siècle," *Revue Historique*, ccxxvi (1961), 399–410, summarizes developments mainly in the later sixteenth century.

For those with German, the works on the Reformation and on German parliaments listed elsewhere in this bibliography should be supplemented with *F. Hartung, *Deutsche Verfassungsgeschichte vom 15. Jahrhundert bis zur Gegenwart* (8th edn., Stuttgart, 1964). On Russia, J. D. Clarkson, *A History of Russia from the Ninth Century* (London, 1962) gives the best summary; see also I. Grey, *Ivan the Terrible* (London, 1962); V. O. Kluchevsky, *A History of Russia*, Vol. II (New York, 1960); G. Vernadsky, *The Tsardom of Moscow, 1547–1682*, Vol. I (New Haven and London, 1969).

REPRESENTATIVE INSTITUTIONS

From a vast and growing literature of high quality on this subject, the following are selected as outstanding for relating parliamentary history to the general problems of government: *A. J. Slavin (ed.), *The "New Monarchies" and Representative Assemblies. Medieval Constitutionalism or Modern Absolutism?* (Boston, 1964); *G. Griffiths, *Representative Government in Western Europe in the Sixteenth Century* (Oxford, 1968); J. Russell Major, *Representative Institutions in Renaissance France, 1421–1559* (Madison, 1960); *F. L. Carsten, *Princes and Parliaments in Germany from the Fifteenth to the Eighteenth Centuries* (Oxford, 1959); F. L. Carsten, *The Origins of Prussia* (Oxford, 1954), Ch. XII: "The Rule of the Estates"; J. S. Roskell, "Perspectives in English Parliamentary History," *Bulletin of the John Rylands Library*, XLVI (1964), 448–75, in conjunction with the section on parliament in Elton, *Tudor Constitution*; S. O. Schmidt, "Les premiers Zemski Sobory de l'État Russe," *Annali della Fondazione italiana per la storia amministrativa*, II (1965), 248–82.

OTHER TOPICS

On the complex of issues connected with the personnel of government, salaries, profits, patronage and corruption, see especially Koenigsberger and Mosse, *Europe in the Sixteenth Century*, pp. 233–7; K. W. Swart, *Sale of Offices in the Seventeenth*

314   SUGGESTED FURTHER READING

Century (The Hague, 1949); J. Hurstfield, "Political Corruption in Modern England: The Historian's Problem," *History*, LII (1967), 16–34.

*P. Ramsey, *Tudor Economic Problems* (London, 1963), Ch. v: "The Role of Government," provides a good summary of the English experience of an activity common to all Europe. For the ruler as entrepreneur, see Roberts, *The Early Vasas* (as also on parliament and every aspect of government), the article on Portugal by Godinho cited above, and F. Redlich, "Der deutsche fürstliche Unternehmer, eine typische Erscheinung des 16. Jahrhunderts," *Tradition: Zeitschrift für Firmengeschichte und Unternehmerbiographie*, III (1958), 17–32, 98–112. A few among the many titles on the question of poor relief are: G. R. Elton, "An early Tudor Poor Law," *Economic History Review*, 2nd Series, VI (1953), 55–67; F. R. Salter, *Some Early Tudor Tracts on Poor Relief* (London, 1926); P. Bonenfant, *Hôpitaux et bienfaisance publique dans les anciens Pays-Bas des origines à la fin du XVIIIᵉ siècle* (Annales de la Société Belge d'Histoire des Hôpitaux, III, Brussels, 1965).

Index

Aarschot, Philip of Croy, duke of, 206–8, 220
Adashev, Alexei, 307
Aguesseau, Henri-François d', 276, 281
Ailly, Pierre d', 100
Aix, 241
Aize, 280
Alba, duke of, 263
Albert (duke of Bavaria), 149, 152, 155–6, 162
Albert (duke in Prussia), 169–202
Albert Alcibiades (margrave of Kulmbach-Bayreuth), 153
Alexander VI, 101, 109
Alfonso II, 101
Allemagne, Florent d', 95
Amboise, Georges, Cardinal, 96
America, 71–2, 75–6, 84–5
Amiens, 50, 233–4, 238
Angers, 231
Angevin, house of, 100
Angoulême, 95
Angoulême, count of, 51
Anjorrant, Claude, 274
Anjou, 51, 280
Annebaut, Claude (Admiral of France), 246–8
Ansbach, see Brandenburg-Ansbach
Anthony, Order of Saint, 163
Antwerp, 21–3, 70, 206, 208, 220–1
Aragon, 22, 37, 67–8, 72–4, 76
Armagnac, count of, 52
Artois, 212–13, 280
Astrakhan, 303
Audley, Thomas, 143
Augsburg, cardinal of, 146, 148–50, 162
Augsburg, city of, 145–6, 159
Augsburg, Confession of, 151, 155, 157, 162, 180
Augsburg, Diets at, 145–6, 194
Augsburg, Interim of, 146–7
Augsburg, Peace of, 36, 145–65
Austria, 25, 33, 155, 163. See also Ferdinand I
Auvergne, 280
Aydie, Arnauld-Guillaume d', 97

Baillet, Thibault, 268

Balga, 172, 186
Baltic, 188
Bamberg, 32, 192
Barme, Roget, 268
Bartenstein, 183, 187, 194, 199. See also Plauen zu Bartenstein
Basle, Council of, 93
Bavaria, 10, 14–16, 18, 29, 32, 149, 152, 155–6, 162, 182
Bayonne, 134–5
Bellay, Jean du, 134–5
Bellay, Joachim du, 270
Berry, 268
Besenrade, Hans von, 177, 197–8
Besserer (patrician of Ulm), 163
Béziers, 243
Blackfriars, 114, 136
Blanc, Laurant le, 273
Blarer, Gerwig, 163
Blois, 234
Bohemia, 182
Boleyn, Anne, 114, 130, 138, 140
Bologna, Concordat of, 91–112
Borcke, Joachim von, 113
Bordeaux, 46, 241, 248–50, 253
Boulenais, 280
Bourbon, Charles, duke of, 19, 245
Bourdeilles, Hélie de, 94
Bourges, 96, 231
Bourges, Pragmatic Sanction of, 92–4, 98–103, 105–6, 110–12
Brabant, 212–13, 216, 220
Brandenburg, 182, 186, 190, 194, 200
Brandenburg, elector of, 151–2, 199
Brandenburg, house of, 169, 196, 202
Brandenburg-Ansbach, 192. See also Albert (duke in Prussia); George (margrave of Ansbach); George Frederick (margrave of Brandenburg-Ansbach); William (archbishop of Riga)
Brandt, Asverus von, 194
Braun, Konrad, 150, 154–5
Briçonnet, Guillaume, Cardinal, 96
Briesmann, Johannes, 171
Brill, 213
Brittany, 266, 270, 278

Brixen, 13
Brussels, 146–7, 204–5, 208, 210, 217, 260
Bueil, François de, 96–7
Burgau (family), 163
Burgundy, 46, 67, 146, 257, 260
Buz, Jean de, 97

Calvin, John, 164
Cambrai, Peace of, 205
Cambridge, Trinity College, 12
Campeggio, Lorenzo, 134
Canisius, Peter, 154, 162
Canossa, Ludovico di, 109
Canterbury, archbishopric of, 13, 135, 140, 143. See also Cranmer, Thomas; Warham, William
Carne, Edward, 140
Casimir (margrave of Kulmbach-Bayreuth), 177
Castellio, Sebastian, 164
Castile, 19, 21–2, 34, 62, 67–8, 73–5
Castile, Cortes of, 19, 68
Castile, council of, 16, 26–7, 75, 86
Catalonia, 62, 74
Catherine of Aragon, 132–3, 136, 138, 140
Chabot de Brion, Philippe (Admiral of France), 246
Champagne, 95, 271
Chancellor, Richard, 306
Chapuys, Eustace, 127, 130, 135, 138, 141
Charles V (emperor), 13–14, 18–19, 21–2, 25–7, 32, 34, 68, 70, 76, 110–11, 136, 143, 145–8, 154, 192, 203–24, 257–64
Charles II (king of Spain), 81
Charles VII (king of France), 44, 46–7, 49, 99–100, 110
Charles VIII (king of France), 101, 239, 244
Charles IX (king of France), 53, 234
Charles the Bold (duke of Burgundy), 101
Chartier, Mathieu, 274
Chelyadnin, Ivan Petrovich, 304–6, 308
Chièvres, William, lord of, 206
Choppin, René, 278
Christian III (king of Denmark), 188
Christopher (duke of Württemberg), 149–50, 159
Cibo, Innocenzo, Cardinal, 109
Clement VII, 114–15, 133, 136, 138, 140, 142
Clermont, 231
Cluny, 96
Cobos, Francisco de los, 27
Colonna, Prospero, 109
Condé, Louis II, prince of, 50
Constance, Council of, 101, 105
Coquille, Guy, 277
Cossacks, 308
Courland, 182
Cracow, 169
Cracow, Treaty of, 169–70, 175–6

Cranmer, Thomas (archbishop of Canterbury), 120, 138,
Cromwell, Thomas, 16, 23–5, 27–8, 115, 123–4, 126–44
Croy, Philip of, see Aarschot
Culmic law, 173, 183, 189
Curio, Horatio, 188

Danzig, 187–8, 202
Dauphiné, 255
Delfino, Zaccaria, 148–9
Denmark, 16, 188, 192–3, 209
Der Auerochs, 188
Dijon, 233, 241, 253
Dinkelsbühl, 162
Donauwörth, 163, 165
Dorothea (duchess of Prussia), 181, 192, 200
Dourdan, 271
Drente, 212
Dumoulin, Charles, 266, 277, 280
Duprat, Antoine, 94, 97, 105–8, 110
Duprat, Thomas, 97, 231
Durham, 30

Edward VI, 13, 15, 29
Elizabeth I, 13, 24, 29, 122
Ellwangen, 162
Empire, Holy Roman, 32, 35–6, 109, 145–165, 174. See also Germany
England, 53, 67, 69, 187, 237
England, finances of, 17, 19–20, 22–3, 86, 115–17
England, institutions of, 19–20, 27–31, 35–38, 45, 85–6, 113–25
England, Reformation in, 10–15, 17, 37–8, 92, 113–44
Ermland, 171, 179, 193, 199, 202
Esslingen, 159
Étampes, 271
Eu, 270

Ferdinand (king of Aragon), 74, 109
Ferdinand I (archduke of Austria, king of Bohemia and Hungary, later emperor), 12, 26, 145–50, 153–4, 157–61, 176, 199
Fillastre, Guillaume, Cardinal, 101
Fischer, Friedrich, 192
Fischhausen, 190, 200
Fisher, John (bishop of Rochester), 119, 139
Flanders, 76, 206, 212–13, 216, 220, 257, 261–3
Fletcher, Giles, the Elder, 306
Florence, 109, 209
Foix-Navarre, house of, 52
Fontainebleau, 50
Founier de Beaune, Martin, 97
Foxe, John, 127
France, 67–9, 80, 137, 194, 209–10, 219–20, 222

France, Church in, 17, 53, 55–6, 91–112, 136
France, finances of, 17–23, 53, 55
France, institutions of, 10–11, 14, 27–31, 33–6, 43–57, 64, 73–4, 79, 225–56, 258, 265–83
Franche-Comté, 258
Francis I (king of France), 14, 17, 27, 31, 33, 51, 91–2, 96–7, 99, 102–12, 225, 245–6, 250–1
Franconia, 153, 174, 176–7
Frankfurt, 159
Frederick (duke of Liegnitz), 174
Friedland, 187
Friesland, 205, 209, 212
Fronde, the, 50, 80, 256
Fugger (family), 188, 202, 223
Fugger, Anton, 219

Gadendorf, Claus von, 193
Gardete, René, 273
Gardiner, Stephen, 115, 121, 130, 141
Garnsee, 187
Gattinara, Mercurino, 26, 28
George (margrave of Ansbach), 174
George Frederick (margrave of Brandenburg-Ansbach), 186
Gericke, Hans, 176–7
Germany, 35–6, 67, 92, 134, 136, 204–5, 223. See also Empire, Holy Roman
Germany, principalities of, 10–13, 15–17, 19–20, 22, 25, 27, 29–33, 37–8, 145–65, 181, 191, 194, 196–7, 202, 221
Gerson, Jean, 100
Ghent, 210
Giustiniano (Venetian envoy), 98
Gmünd, see Schwäbisch-Gmünd
Golden Fleece, Order of the, 208, 210, 259
Gouffier, Aymar, 96
Grammez, Hughes de, see Wingene
Granvelle, Antoine Perrenot de, Cardinal, 259, 263
Granvelle, Nicolas Perrenot de, the Elder, 27, 259
Gravelines, 221
Grenoble, 233, 241
Grignan, count of, 251
Groningen, 212, 216
Guelders, 212, 217
Guise, duke of, 54
Guise, Charles de (archbishop of Rheims), 97
Guisnes, 280
Gustavus Vasa, see Vasa, Gustavus
Gustavus Adolphus, 29
Guyenne, 95, 245–6, 248–50

Habsburg, house of, 18, 25, 33, 36, 198, 202, 260

Haillan, Bernard du, 244
Hainault, 206, 212–13, 216, 220, 224, 262–3
Hall, Edward, 118
Hanse, 187
Hass, Heinrich, 158
Heilsberg, 169
Henry II (king of France), 246, 248–9, 252, 254
Henry III (king of France), 48, 52–3, 227, 234, 236–7, 250
Henry IV (king of France), 54, 98, 237, 250
Henry VII (king of England), 129
Henry VIII (king of England), 12–14, 17, 28–9, 36–7, 91–2, 100, 112–14, 117–18, 120–3, 125–44
Hesdin, 280
Hesse, 10–12, 19
Hohenzollern, house of, see Brandenburg, house of
Holland, 85, 206, 209, 212–13, 220, 261–3
Horkheim (family), 161
Hornung, Felix, 146
Hoya, count of, 177
Huguenots, 242, 253
Hundred Years' War, 44, 73
Hungary, 188, 194
Husson, Louis de, 97

Île-de-France, 95
Indies, West, 21, 26–7, 68, 71, 75–6
Innsbruck, 219
Inquisitions, 14, 16, 73
Insterburg, 186, 188
Ireland, 38
Issoire, 231
Italy, 10–11, 14, 18, 27, 31, 38, 51, 61, 67, 73–4, 76, 100–2, 108–12, 280
Ivan III, 284–5
Ivan IV, 39, 284–6, 288, 293, 295–304, 306–9

James I, 20
Jesuits, 154, 165
Jews, 239
John II (king of Aragon), 73
John of Paris, 100
Joinville, Edict of, 251
Julius II, 101–2, 109

Kaufbeuren, 162–3
Kaymen, 174, 176
Kazan, 303
Kennedy, John F., 48
Kiev, 294
Klingenbeck, Georg, 177, 194
Königsberg, 170–1, 176–8, 180, 182–3, 186, 192, 195, 199–201
Kulmbach-Bayreuth (margrave of), 153, 177

Kunheim, Georg von, 199
Kurbsky, Prince Andrei, 307

La Balue, Jean, Cardinal, 96
Labiau, 186–7
Lamoignon, Guillaume de, 281
Lancaster, 30
Languedoc, 46, 227–8, 245, 251, 255
Languedoïl, 46
Lannoy, Charles de, 257
La Roche-Flavin, Bernard de, 244
La Rochelle, 239
La Trémoille, Louis, 103
Laubespine, Claude de, 248
Lautrec, Odet de Foix, viscount of, 245
La Vallière, 273
League, the, 45
Leo X, 105, 108–10
Leutkirch, 163
Lille, 208, 216
Limburg, 212–13
Limoges, 95, 97
Limoux, 242
Lincolnshire, 15
Lindau, 163
Lippomano, Luigi, 149
Lithuania, 187–9, 196
Livonia, 187, 194, 306
Loitz (family), 202
London, 114
Longin, Laurens, 217–18
Longueil, Pierre de, 274
Louis VIII (king of France), 99
Louis XI (king of France), 51–2, 56, 93–5,
    100–1, 106, 110, 239
Louis XII (king of France), 51, 95, 101–2,
    105, 109–10
Louis XIV (king of France), 47, 50, 56–7
Louvain, 204
Lude, count of, 249
Lübeck, 209
Luna, Alvaro de, 73
Luther, Martin, 169–71, 177, 233
Luxemburg, 212–13, 261–3
Luxemburg, Jaak of (lord of Fiennes),
    206
Lyck, 186
Lyons, 21–2, 100, 104, 233, 240

Machiavelli, Niccolò, 45
Magdeleine, Jean de, 96
Maine, 280
Mainz, archbishop of, 149, 151, 155–6
Male, 223
Malines, 211, 221
Mandat, Guillot, 273
Mansfeld, count of, 263
Mantes, 271
Mantua, 100

Marcellus II, 148
Margaret of Austria, 258–9, 261–2
Margaret of Parma, 262
Margarit (family), 62
Marggrabowa (Markgrafenstadt), 189
Marignano, 92, 108–9
Marthonie, Mondot de la, 94
Mary (queen of England), 14–15
Mary of Hungary, 204–10, 216–19, 222,
    224, 259, 262–3
Mary (Infanta of Spain), 259
Masuria, 182
Maurice (elector of Saxony), 198
Maximilian I, 108
Mazarin, Cardinal, 225
Meaux, 95, 97
Medici, house of, 109
Mediterranean, 51, 62, 70–2, 80
Memel, 182, 187
Memmingen, 163
Menochio, Giacomo, 82
Mexico, 75
Micault, Jan, 208
Michailov, Ivan, 293–4
Milan, 21–2, 45, 72, 76, 81, 87, 94, 102,
    108–9
Miltitz, Heinrich von, 177
Moissac, 242
Molina, Luis de, 82
Montaigne, Michel de, 274
Montauban, 243
Montdidier, 271
Montfort, counts of, 163
Montfort l'Amaury, 271
Montil-les-Tours, 266, 269
Montmorency, Anne de, 50, 245
Montpezat (governor of Languedoc), 245
Montreuil, 280
More, Thomas, 117, 121
Morone, Giovanni de, Cardinal, 148
Moscow, 10, 194, 285–90, 292, 296, 301,
    303–6, 308
Mühlhausen (in Prussia), 187

Namur, 208, 212–13, 219–20
Naples, 21, 23, 45, 67, 76, 100–1, 108–10,
    209, 257
Natangen, 176, 182–3
Naumburg, 154
Navarre, king of, 249. See also Foix-
    Navarre
Netherlands, 10, 13–14, 22–3, 25, 27, 29,
    32, 34–5, 37, 146, 187–8, 203–24, 257–64
Neuburg, see Pfalz-Neuburg
Neudorf on the Nehrung, 187
Nevers, duke of, 54
Nimptsch, Hans, 188
Nivernais, 277
Nogent le Rotrou, 273

Norfolk, Thomas Howard, duke of, 115, 124, 138, 141
Normandy, 95, 246–7, 250, 253, 266, 270, 274, 278, 281
Northumberland, John Dudley, duke of, 29
Nostitz, Kaspar von, 186
Notre-Dame, 232
Novgorod, 287, 296
Nuremberg, 193–4

Oberland, 182–3
Ofen, 199
Oostvoorne, 208
Orléans, 95, 98, 103, 231, 233, 272, 282
Orléans, duke of, 50–1, 259
Ösel, bishopric of, 188
Osterode, 183, 186
Öttingen, 161
Öttingen (family), 161–2
Otto Henry (count palatine of Pfalz-Neuburg), 154
Overloepe, Pieter, d', 216
Overmaas, 212–13
Overysel, 205, 212, 216
Oxford, Christ Church, 12

Palatinate, 181
Papacy, 18, 21–2, 28, 91–113, 119, 121–2, 126, 132–42, 148–9
Paris, 95, 248, 254, 268, 271, 274, 276–8, 281–2
Paris, municipality of, 22, 232, 234–9, 242
Paris, parlement of, 14, 31, 34, 37, 45–6, 93, 102–7, 109–10, 229–32, 234–6, 238–42, 244, 255–6, 267–9, 276
Paris, university of, 93, 101, 104, 110, 231, 233
Pasquier, Étienne, 254–5
Passau, 146, 152
Passau, bishop of, 150
Passau, Treaty of, 157
Patollu (pagan Prussian deity), 172
Paul II, 100
Paul IV, 148–9
Pavia, 111, 237
Pazzi (family), 101
Pein, Johann, 188, 193
Pensart, William, 211, 216
Peresvetov, Ivan, 303, 307
Perkunos (pagan Prussian deity), 172
Péronne, 271
Peter the Great, 39
Petit, Guillaume, 96
Pfalz-Neuburg, 154, 161–2
Philip II (king of Spain), 13–14, 76, 203, 223–4, 262–3
Philip the Good (duke of Burgundy), 257
Pisa, Council of, 101–2, 110

Pius II, 100–1
Plauen zu Bartenstein, Reuss von, 169
Poitiers, 46, 95, 97, 231, 239
Poitou, 46, 245, 249, 275, 280
Poland, 51, 149, 169–71, 176, 181, 188–9, 194–6, 201
Pole, Reginald, Cardinal, 127, 140
Polentz, Georg (bishop of Samland), 170–1, 174, 176–7, 181
Pollander, Johann, 177
Pomerania, 193
Pomesanien, 170–1, 180–2
Portugal, 22, 38, 67, 71, 76
Potrimpos (pagan Prussian deity), 172
Provence, 51, 246, 250–2, 255
Prussia, 10–12, 15, 29, 51, 169–202
Pskov, 287–8, 296, 302
Pufendorf, Samuel, 164
Pusch, Hans von, 188
Pyhy, Conrad, 16

Queis, Erhard (bishop of Pomesanien), 170–1, 180–1
Quintin, Jean, 98

Ranst, 223
Ravenna, 102
Rennes, 241
Rheims, 97
Richard II, 120
Richau, Nicolaus, 176
Richelieu, Cardinal, 54, 252, 255–6
Riga, archbishop of, 187–8
Robertet, Florimond, 27
Robin Hood, 290–1
Roggenzell, 163
Rome, city of, 136, 140. See also Papacy
Rouen, 95, 233, 241, 243, 246–50, 253
Roye, 271
Russia, 10, 38–9, 284–309
Ruzé, Guillaume, 273

Saalfeld, 183, 194
Saint-Eustache, 234
Saint-Germain, 238
Saint-Omer, 280
Saint-Paul, 280
Saint-Pierre-le-Moutier, 54
Saint-Séverin, Dominique de, 97
Salisbury, bishop of, 121
Salzburg, archbishop of, 149
Samland, 170, 172, 174–6, 182
Santa Fe, Capitulations of, 75
Savoy, 182, 258
Savoy, Bastard of, 103
Savoy, Louise of, 111
Saxony, 11–12, 14–16, 19, 29, 33, 151–2, 154, 157, 164, 171, 180–2
Scandinavia, 170, 194

Schaaken, 186, 190, 200
Schlichtling, Albert, 306
Schmalkaldic War, 158, 195, 198, 201
Schwäbisch-Gmünd, 162
Schwarzenberg and Hohenlandsberg, Johann Freiherr von, 32, 191–4
Schwendi, Lazarus von, 147
Seld, Georg Sigmund, 147
Sforza, Maximilian, 94
Shchelkalov, Vasily, 293–4
Sicily, 14, 16, 76
Sigismund I (king of Poland), 169, 195
Sigismund Augustus (king of Poland), 195–6
Sijsele, 223
Silesia, 174, 176, 186–7
Silvester (priest), 307
Sixtus IV, 94, 100–1
Somerset, Edward Seymour, duke of, 29
Spain, 109, 136, 194, 257—8
Spain, Church in, 10–11, 13–14, 16–17
Spain, finances of, 17, 20–3, 27, 68, 70, 75–6, 209, 223
Spain, institutions of, 10, 14, 16, 23, 26–7, 29–30, 32, 34–5, 58, 61–2, 64–87
Spartacus, 290
Speratus, Paul, 179, 181
Speyer, Diets at, 11, 194
Staden, Heinrich von, 304–6, 308
Stephani, Joachim, 155
Stercke, Hendrik, 208
Strasbourg, 151–2, 159–60
Straubing, 162
Sully, Maximilien de Béthune, duke of, 54
Swabia, 161–5
Sweden, 10, 12–20, 29, 38, 92, 176–7
Swiss Confederation, 108–9, 146, 182

Tapiau, 176, 190, 194, 200
Tartars, 284
Tende, count of, 251–2
Tenremonde, 208
Teutonic Order, 161, 169–70, 172–3, 184–186, 189–90, 197
Thérouanne, 95, 280
Thirty Years' War, 44, 50, 69, 164–5
Thou, Christophe de, 269, 274, 280
Thuringia, 174, 176
Tillet, Jean du, 245
Tilsit, 186, 189
Time of Troubles, 309
Tonnerre, Claude de, 95
Toulouse, 46, 241–3, 253, 255
Touraine, 268, 273, 280
Tournai, 205, 213
Tours, 94, 97, 101, 273
Trent, Bernard Cles, cardinal of, 26

Trent, Council of, 14, 148, 154, 165, 230
Trier, 146
Troyes, 48, 50, 96, 239
Truchsess von Waldburg, Otto (cardinal of Augsburg), 146, 148–50, 162
Truchsess von Waldburg, William, 150
Tudor, house of, 29, 36–7, 48, 50, 116
Tunstall, Cuthbert, 139
Turenne, Henri, viscount of, 50
Turks, 70–1, 188, 199, 307
Tver, 290

Ulm, 146, 159, 163
United States, 48
Unterrohr, 163
Utrecht, 13, 205, 212

Valencia, 74
Valois, house of, 18, 46
Vasa, Gustavus, 10, 12, 18, 112, 177
Vaux, de (French envoy), 135
Veneur, Gabriel le, 97
Venice, 38, 103, 108–9, 136–7, 182, 188
Verreycken, Pieter, 211, 216
Versailles, 69, 277
Villach, 147
Villers-Cotterets, 268
Villiers, Charles de, 97
Viole, Jacques, 274

Wales, 31, 34–5
Warham, William (archbishop of Canterbury), 121, 139
Wars of Religion, French, 45–6, 54, 253
Washington, D.C., 48
Weingarten, 163
Werwik, 208
Wettin, house of, 10
William of Brandenburg-Ansbach (archbishop of Riga), 187–8
Wingene, Hughes de Grammez, lord of, 206–8, 220
Wolsey, Thomas, 28, 115–18, 130–4, 136, 143
Worcester, bishop of, 121
Worms, Diets at, 94, 145
Württemberg, 149–50, 176, 181

Yaroslav, 290
Ypres, 208

Zeeland, 206, 209, 212–13, 221
Zehmen, Achatius, 185
Zomergem, 223
Zutfen, 212, 217